Grade Aid with Practice Tests

for

Kenrick, Neuberg, and Cialdini

Social Psychology
Unraveling the Mystery

Third Edition

prepared by

Amy L. Cota-McKinley
Worcester State College

PEARSON

Boston   New York   San Francisco
Mexico City   Montreal   Toronto   London   Madrid   Munich   Paris
Hong Kong   Singapore   Tokyo   Cape Town   Sydney

ISBN 0-205-42107-5

Printed in the United States of America

10 9 8 7 6 5 4 3 2   09 08 07 06

TABLE OF CONTENTS

USING YOUR STUDY GUIDE

This study guide is designed to help you reinforce your knowledge of the material presented in the textbook *Social Psychology Unraveling the Mystery 3rd Edition* by Douglas Kenrick, Steven Neuberg, and Robert Cialdini. The authors of your book have done an excellent job of making social psychology interesting, accessible, up-to date, and sometimes even humorous. But there is a lot of information presented in each chapter, and you will need to study effectively to understand the material. This study guide will help. The philosophy that guided the development of this study guide is that new material is best remembered when it is learned actively, processed deeply, and presented in multiple ways.

Notice that most of the chapters of the book have a similar structure. Research on learning suggests that you can learn and remember more when you use a structure to organize information, so it will be immensely helpful for you to recognize and use the simplifying structure that the book provides. Each chapter begins with a mystery (for instance, why did members of the Manson Family participate in a senseless killing spree?) and is followed by definitions of terms and concepts. Next the chapters cover several goals of the behavior in question (in the aggression chapter, for example: coping with feelings of annoyance, gaining material and social rewards, gaining or maintaining status, and protecting oneself or others). For each goal, the authors then ask what factors in the person, in the situation, and in the interaction of the person and the situation are relevant to that goal. At the end of each chapter, the authors revisit the mystery to summarize what social psychological research tells us about that topic. Throughout the chapters, there are additional structural learning aids: marginal definitions and interim summaries of the main points, as well as an overall chapter summary at the end.

Each Grade Aid chapter corresponds to a chapter in the textbook and is organized into four distinct sections. The "Before You Read" section contains a brief chapter summary, learning objectives, and key terms. Think of this section as an overview of the chapter content that should be reviewed prior to your text reading to familiarize yourself with what you will be learning. If you take notes while you read you can use this section to organize your notes for later study. If, after reading the textbook chapter, you can answer all of the questions in the learning objectives, you will be prepared to do the exercises in the Grade Aid chapter. If you can't answer some of the questions, go back and look through the chapter to find the answer. In order to enhance your recall ability for key terms, you may find it useful to make flashcards for quizzing yourself or those in your study group. The flashcards would include a term on one side, and a definition on the other (with perhaps a brief example that makes sense to you).This will help you remember the information for the test.

The "As You Read" section is comprised of a collection of activities and exercises to keep you actively engaged with the material while you read. Here you will find the mysteries that were

The "As You Read" section is comprised of a collection of activities and exercises to keep you actively engaged with the material while you read. Here you will find the mysteries that were introduced in each chapter. For example: why a man would falsely confess to murdering his mother? Your job is to resolve the mystery using the general principles of human behavior discussed in the text. You will also discover in this section: (1) a series of exercises that will help clarify the concepts and research studies presented in the text, (2) chart completion exercises based upon the goals underlying the behavior covered in the text chapter, (3) matching exercises where you can test your skills at matching the correct term, experimental method, or psychological finding to its description, and (4) thought questions that are intended to give you the opportunity to integrate the knowledge you have acquired from the chapter by applying it to other areas, or by coming up with your own ideas for further research. There are generally no right or wrong answers to these questions, as they are asking for your original thoughts, ideas, and opinions about various areas of social psychology.

Next, you will have the opportunity to test your mastery of the material. In the "After You Read...Practice Tests" section you will find four exams. The first three exams contain ten multiple choice questions. The fourth exam is a comprehensive practice test that consists of fifteen multiple choice questions, eight true/false questions, and two essay questions. Multiple choice questions are by far the most common format for testing students' knowledge of the information presented in class and in the text. Answering the multiple choice questions at the end of the chapter will accomplish two goals. First, it will make you more familiar with the multiple choice format for exams. As you read the answers, first eliminate those that are obviously wrong. Among those that are left, read each carefully. They may be very similar, but one will always be "more right" than the others. The second goal is obviously to further reinforce your knowledge of the material in the chapter. Before you complete this section, quiz yourself with your flash cards, or at least go back over each of the learning objectives and key terms and make sure you know them. If you can answer all the questions in the multiple choice section correctly, you can have substantial confidence in your ability to answer the questions on the real test. Again, professors often include a section on exams where you must determine whether a statement is true or false. You need to read these statements very carefully, as just one word can change a true statement into a false one. If you believe a statement is false, think about why it is false. How would the statement have to change for it to be true? This, too, will help you process the information more deeply. In order to broaden your understanding of the chapter material, two essay questions are asked on the comprehensive test to deepen your level of thought. The answers to all of the multiple choice and true/false questions can be found in the appendix at the end of this study guide.

After you finish testing your mastery of the material, the "When You Have Finished" section contains web links and a comprehensive crossword puzzle. Here will find five to ten web links and relevant site descriptions related to the chapter. You will also find a fun comprehensive crossword puzzle that uses the key terms from the text. The answers to the crossword puzzles can be found in the appendix.

I hope you will find this study guide to be useful. Good luck and have fun.

Amy L. Cota-McKinley, Ph.D.
Assistant Professor of Psychology
Worcester State College

INTRODUCTION TO SOCIAL PSYCHOLOGY

Before You Read...

In this chapter you will be introduced to the field of social psychology, which is the scientific study of how people's thoughts, feelings, and behaviors are influenced by others. You will be given a thorough overview of the four major theoretical perspectives in social psychology which include: the sociocultural perspective, the evolutionary perspective, the social learning perspective, and the social cognitive perspective. Despite the differences between the theoretical perspectives you will learn that they all share two key assumptions. Next, you will be exposed to the detective tools psychologists use to collect data and study social behavior: descriptive methods and experimental methods. You will also discover how data from descriptive methods can reveal relationships between two or more variables known as correlation. After reviewing scientific methodology, you will explore the ethical risks involved in social psychological research, the general rule psychologists use to decide if research is ethical, and the ethical safeguards taken in social psychological research. Finally, you will investigate how social psychology is closely connected to other subdisciplines of psychology and how it is connected to other domains of knowledge.

Chapter Learning Objectives

After reading this chapter, you should be able to:

- Define social psychology

- Explain why description and explanation are important to scientific social psychology

- Give three reasons why theories are useful

- Describe the four major theoretical perspectives of social psychology

- List the two key assumptions shared by the major perspectives in social psychology

- Discuss the five fundamental motives behind goal oriented social behavior

- Explain what is meant by "the person" and "the situation" and how they become interwoven through "person-situation interactions"

- Describe the two general types of methods used by social psychologists to study behavior

- Define the five major types of descriptive methods - naturalistic observation, case studies, archives, surveys, and psychological tests

- Explain what a representative sample is and why it is important

- Discuss the difference between reliability and validity in psychological tests

- Define correlation and explain what is meant by the statement "correlation does not imply causation"

- Explain the experimental method, including several key concepts associated with experimentation

- Discuss why combining different methods of inquiry leads social psychologists to reach more confident conclusions about a social phenomenon

- Describe the ethical risks involved in social psychological research

- State the general rule psychologists use to decide if research is ethical

- Discuss the ethical safeguards taken in social psychological research

- Describe how social psychology is closely connected to other subdisciplines of psychology and how it is connected to other domains of knowledge

As You Read...

> **KEY TERMS!**
> Listed below are the key terms from the chapter that are essential for your understanding of the material. Refer to the definitions from your textbook; they are located at the end of this chapter, within the text in boldface, and in the margins throughout this chapter. In order to enhance your recall ability for these terms, you may want to consider making flashcards which include a term on one side, and a definition on the other (with perhaps a brief example that makes sense to you).

Adaptation	Experimental method	Reliability
Archival method	External validity	Representative sample
Case study	Field experimentation	Situation
Confound	Generalizability	Social cognitive perspective
Correlation	Hypothesis	Social desirability bias
Correlation coefficient	Independent variable	Social learning perspective
Culture	Internal validity	Social norm
Debriefing	Natural selection	Social psychology
Demand characteristic	Naturalistic observation	Sociocultural perspective
Dependent variable	Observer bias	Survey method
Descriptive method	Person	Theory
Evolutionary perspective	Psychological test	Validity
Experiment	Random assignment	

MAJOR THEORETICAL PERSPECTIVES IN SOCIAL PSYCHOLOGY

Complete the chart below to help you summarize the four major theoretical perspectives in social psychology. Define each theoretical perspective, know what drives the social behavior, and be able to provide an example of each.

Perspective	Definition	What drives social behavior?	Example
Sociocultural			
Evolutionary			
Social Learning			
Social Cognitive			

Matching! Match the four major theoretical perspectives in social psychology on the right side of the page with the concepts associated with each perspective on the left side of the page.

___ 1.   attention and memory

___ 2.   causes of behavior from larger social group

___ 3.   rewards and punishments

___ 4.   inherited tendencies

A.   Evolutionary

B.   Sociocultural

C.   Social Cognitive

D.   Social Learning

BASIC PRINCIPLES OF SOCIAL BEHAVIOR

Despite the differences among the major perspectives in social psychology, they share two key principles. List the two principles and provide examples from each perspective that illustrate these principles. (see pages 9 through 12 in your text for help with this exercise)

HOW PSYCHOLOGISTS STUDY SOCIAL BEHAVIOR

Matching! Match each definition on the left side of the page with the concept on the right side of the page. Each concept on the right should only be used once.

___ 1. Research method where the researcher sets out to systematically manipulate one source of influence while holding others constant

    A. Archival method

___ 2. Extent to which a test measures what it is designed to measure

    B. Confound

___ 3. Variable measured by the experimenter

    C. Correlation

___ 4. Procedure for measuring or recording behaviors, thoughts, and feelings in their natural state

    D. Debriefing

___ 5. Scientific explanation that connects and organizes existing observations and suggests paths for future research

    E. Dependent variable

___ 6. Discussion of procedures, hypotheses, and participant reactions at the completion of the study

    F. Descriptive method

___ 7. Researcher's prediction about what he or she will find

    G. Experiment

___ 8. Examination of systematic data originally collected for other purposes

    H. External validity

___ 9. Extent to which the results of an experiment can be generalized to other circumstances

    I. Hypothesis

___ 10. Practice of assigning participants to treatments so each person has an equal chance of being in any condition

    J. Independent variable

___ 11. Consistency of the score yielded by a psychological test

    K. Internal validity

___ 12. Variable that systematically changes along with the independent variable, potentially leading to a mistaken conclusion about the effect of the independent variable

    L. Random assignment

___ 13. Variable manipulated by the experimenter

    M. Reliability

___ 14. Extent to which two or more variables are associated with one another

    N. Theory

___ 15. Extent to which an experiment allows confident statements about cause and effect

    O. Validity

SUMMARY OF RESEARCH METHODS

The following exercise is designed to help you determine the strengths and weaknesses of the various descriptive correlational methods and experimental methods. Write the number of the strength or weakness next to each research method. Each number will only be used once and each method may have more than one strength or weakness.

Descriptive Correlational Methods	Strengths	Weaknesses
Naturalistic Observation		
Case Studies		
Archives		
Surveys		
Psychological tests		
Experimental Methods		
Laboratory Experiment		
Field Experiment		

	Strengths		Weaknesses
1.	Allows study of rare behaviors	12.	Tests may be unreliable
2.	Spontaneous behaviors	13.	Less control of extraneous factors than in a laboratory experiment
3.	Allows measurement of characteristics that are not always easily observable	14.	Some interesting behaviors are very rare
4.	Allows control of extraneous variables	15.	Researcher may selectively attend to certain events and ignore others
5.	Doesn't rely on people's ability to report on their own experiences	16.	Subjects may be biased or untruthful in responses
6.	Rich source of hypotheses	17.	Time consuming
7.	Easy access to large amounts of pre-recorded data	18.	People who respond may not be representative
8.	Allows cause-effect conclusions	19.	Manipulations may not represent relevant events as they naturally unfold
9.	Allows study of difficult-to-observe behaviors, thoughts, and feelings	20.	Impossible to reconstruct causes from complexity of past events
10.	Subjects give more natural responses	21.	Many interesting social behaviors are never recorded
11.	Allows cause-effect conclusions	22.	Tests may be reliable, but not valid
		23.	Artificial manipulations may not represent relevant events as they naturally unfold
		24.	Difficult to generalize findings
		25.	Researcher may interfere with ongoing behavior
		26.	Observer bias

PUTTING IT ALL TOGETHER: THOUGHT QUESTIONS

Kurt Lewin once said, "There is nothing so practical as a good theory." Based on what you have learned in the chapter, and what you know about the full-cycle approach to social psychology, what do you think is meant by this statement?

Milgram (1964) argued that his research was not unethical because none of his participants suffered long-lasting ill effects. He also felt that his study was important because it gave us a glimpse into the human response to authority we otherwise would not have had. Others argue that what Milgram did was unethical, and there are now ethical safeguards against such research. Do you think that the restrictions of informed consent, debriefing, and evaluating the costs and benefits of research procedures have helped or hurt social psychology? Why?

After You Read...Practice Tests

Practice Test 1

1. The scientific study of how people's thoughts, feelings, and behaviors are influenced by other people is called
    a. sociology.
    b. social science.
    c. social psychology.
    d. social studies.

2. An explanation that allows researchers to organize information and make predictions about future events is known as a _____.
    a. hypothesis
    b. theory
    c. correlation
    d. description

3. There were two books titled *Social Psychology* published in 1908. One took a _____ perspective, the other took a(n) _____ perspective.
    a. Sociocultural, Social Learning
    b. Social Cognitive, Social Learning
    c. Sociocultural, Evolutionary
    d. Social Cognitive, Evolutionary

4. What perspective adopts the view that human social behaviors are rooted in physical and psychological predispositions that helped our ancestors survive and reproduce?
    a. Sociocultural perspective
    b. Evolutionary perspective
    c. Social Learning perspective
    d. Social Cognitive perspective

5. Schaller, Park, and Mueller (2003) asked White and Asian Canadian college students to rate their reactions to photographs of Black men. They found that students who viewed the world as a dangerous place were prone to see the Black men as threatening when they rated the photos in a dark room and this effect was more prevalent for men raters than for women raters. The researchers interpreted these findings in terms of which perspective on intergroup relationships?
    a. Sociocultural
    b. Evolutionary
    c. Social Learning
    d. Social Cognitive

6. A group of boys started their own "Fight Club" where they bare-knuckle fought one another, imitating a movie they had seen staring Brad Pitt. Your text explains this event from the
    a. social learning perspective.
    b. evolutionary perspective.
    c. phenomenological perspective.
    d. social cognitive perspective.

7. Which theoretical viewpoint focuses on the mental processes involved in paying attention to, interpreting, and remembering social experiences?
    a. Sociocultural
    b. Evolutionary
    c. Social Learning
    d. Social Cognitive

8. It is predicted that people who feel bad about themselves might be more likely to act out in a sexual or violent way in an attempt to boost their self-esteem. This is an example of a/an
    a. confound
    b. experiment
    c. theory
    d. hypothesis

9. A researcher obtained a correlation of +.47 between Variable A and Variable B. What is the best interpretation of this correlation?
   a. A and B are unrelated
   b. as scores on A increase, scores on B tend to increase
   c. scores on A can be perfectly predicted from scores on B
   d. as scores on A decrease, scores on B tend to increase

10. Zimbardo (1970) asked students to deliver electric shocks to another student who was either easily identifiable (wore name tags and their own clothes) or anonymous (wore oversized white coats and hoods). He was interested in whether anonymity within a crowd causes people to act more antisocially The independent variable was _____ and the dependent variable was _____.
    a. different type of clothing worn; amount of shock delivered
    b. the experiment; amount of shock delivered
    c. the crowd; amount of shock delivered
    d. name tags; oversized white coats and hoods

Practice Test 2

1. Compared to her working-class Polish grandmother, a modern-day university professor has different attitudes about premarital sex and women's roles in the workplace. This example fits best with which theoretical perspective?
   a. Sociocultural
   b. Evolutionary
   c. Social Learning
   d. Social Cognitive

2. McDougall's 1908 text, entitled *Social Psychology,* adopted the view that human social behaviors are rooted in physical and psychological predispositions that helped our ancestors survive and reproduce. McDougall took a(n) _____ perspective.
   a. Sociocultural
   b. Evolutionary
   c. Social Learning
   d. Social Cognitive

3. Which perspective was strongly influenced by Charles Darwin's theory of natural selection?
   a. Sociocultural
   b. Evolutionary
   c. Social Learning
   d. Social Cognitive

4. Albert Bandura's classic "Bobo doll" study shows how children acquire aggressive behavior by being rewarded. This study can be explained from the _____ perspective.
   a. Sociocultural
   b. Evolutionary
   c. Social Learning
   d. Social Cognitive

5. You decide to run for class president, and a team of psychologists are trying to figure out why? A(n) _____ theorist is likely to focus on your past history of rewards from parents and teachers for acting like a leader, whereas a _____ theorist is likely to focus on your perceptions of the chances of winning, and your memories of past episodes that might come to mind.
   a. Sociocultural, Social Learning
   b. Evolutionary, Social Learning
   c. Social Cognitive, Evolutionary
   d. Social Learning, Social Cognitive

6. A _____ is a hunch or guess about how the evidence in a research experiment is
    likely to turn out.
    a. theory   b. hypothesis
    c. confound   d. correlation

7. Scientific explanations that connect and organize existing observations are called
    a. theories   b. hypotheses
    c. ideas   d. experiments

8. As described in the text, one researcher observed and recorded women's nonverbal
    flirtation behaviors directed towards men in singles' bars. What type of research method is
    this?
    a. naturalistic observation   b. case study
    c. survey   d. field experiment

9. Alfred Kinsey wanted to find out about the prevalence of various sexual behaviors in
    humans. He therefore attempted to interview a broad and representative sample of the
    population using the _____.
    a. survey method   b. archival method
    c. experimental method   d. case study method

10. A researcher found that alcohol use by college students correlated -.45 with their grades.
    What is the best interpretation of this correlation?
    a. alcohol and grades are unrelated
    b. alcohol causes grades to go up
    c. studying hard leads people to drink more
    d. increased alcohol consumption may contribute to lower grades

Practice Test 3
1. A/n _____ is a scientific explanation that connects many observations into an
    interconnected, coherent, and meaningful pattern.
    a. idea   b. research hypothesis
    c. theory   d. experiment

2. Which of the following is associated with the sociocultural perspective?
    a. Mob behavior results from people imitating those they see getting rewarded for such
        behavior.
    b. Men are more likely to be auto mechanics because society says it is unacceptable for
        women to be auto mechanics.
    c. More homicides are committed by men than by women because men are by nature
        more aggressive.
    d. all of the above

3. Modern evolutionary social psychologists believe that
    a. biology and the environment interact to result in human social behaviors.
    b. human social behaviors are "wired-in" at birth and cannot be changed by the environment.
    c. human social behaviors are determined completely by their environment.
    d. psychologists should study the effects of particular genes if they wish to understand human social behavior.

4. What perspective views social behavior as driven by each individual's past learning experiences with reward and punishment?
    a. Sociocultural   b. Evolutionary
    c. Social Learning   d. Social Cognitive

5. Which of the following would a social cognitive theorist most likely say about the finding that an interviewer gives a more favorable evaluation of an attractive applicant than an unattractive applicant, even when the applicant answers the questions exactly the same way?
    a. The interviewer was sexually attracted to the applicant.
    b. The interviewer was paying more attention to the applicant's looks than to their answers.
    c. The interviewer has been brought up to believe that attractive people are smarter.
    d. The interviewer was hoping to increase his reproductive success.

6. In a study by Roney (2003), high school students were asked to consider how important it was to make a lot of money in their future job. What did he find?
    a. being around girls led high school boys to inflate the value they placed on wealth
    b. high school boys rated the value of wealth the same regardless of who was present
    c. boys rated wealth as more important when in the presence of other boys
    d. high school girls rated wealth as extremely important when boys were present

7. Which goal underlies all the other social goals according to evolutionary theorists?
    a. to establish social ties   b. to defend ourselves and those we value
    c. to attract and retain mates   d. to gain and maintain status

8. Genetic, physiological, or psychological factors that are carried by an individual through different social interactions are known in social psychology as characteristics of the
    a. situation.   b. interaction of person and situation.
    c. person.   d. social context.

9. A researcher was interested in whether onlookers encourage a suicidal person to jump to their death. After examining newspaper archives, the researcher found a relationship between suicide baiting and crowd size. This is an example of _____ research.
    a. correlational   b. naturalistic observation
    c. experimental   d. survey

10. Confounding variables are variables that operate in a way such that
    a. each magnifies the effect of the other.
    b. make it difficult to know what caused the subject's behavior.
    c. each mutes the effect of the other.
    d. the effects of one variable are the same as the effects of the other.

Comprehensive Test
(Note: Items 1-15 are multiple-choice questions, items 16-23 are true-false questions, and 24-25 are essay questions.)

1. Psychological theories:
    a. organize scientific observations
    b. explain observed facts
    c. generate hypotheses
    d. do all the above

2. In 1908 the first two major textbooks titled *Social Psychology* were written by Edward Alsworth Ross and William McDougall. Each textbook emphasized a different theoretical perspective. Which two perspectives did these texts emphasize?
    a. Sociocultural, Social Learning
    b. Social Cognitive, Social Learning
    c. Sociocultural, Evolutionary
    d. Social Cognitive, Evolutionary

3. _____ is the view that a person's prejudices, preferences, and political persuasions are affected by group-level factors such as nationality, social class, and current historical trends.
    a. Sociocultural perspective
    b. Evolutionary perspective
    c. Social Learning perspective
    d. Social Cognitive perspective

4. Which of the following is an example that can be explained by the Sociocultural perspective?
    a. Dutch tulip craze of 1634
    b. Irish immigrant factory workers in 1905 compared to modern-day business women
    c. Asian and North American differences on what is appropriate behavior around others
    d. These are all examples that can be explained by the Sociocultural perspective

5. Most experts on evolution and behavior now understand that biological influences on humans and animals are usually _____ and _____ to the environment.
    a. unchanging; nonresponsive
    b. flexible; responsive
    c. instinctive; not influenced
    d. rigid; have adverse consequences

6. Three of the four perspectives emphasize the objective environment; they assume that our social behaviors are influenced by real events in the world. Which perspective is more likely to consider a person's subjective interpretation as well?
    a. Sociocultural
    b. Evolutionary
    c. Social Learning
    d. Social Cognitive

7. In the 1930's and 1940's, _____ argued that social behavior is driven by each person's subjective interpretations of events in the social world and their goals at the time.
    a. Edward Alsworth Ross
    b. Kurt Lewin
    c. Martin Daly
    d. William McDougall

8. Which of the following is a broad principle shared by all four of the perspectives discussed in your text?
   a. Social behavior is the result of our learned experiences in childhood.
   b. Social behavior is determined by our subjective view of the world.
   c. Social behavior is the result of the way in which we process information.
   d. Social behavior is goal-oriented.

9. According to your text, we have several fundamental motives. Which of the following is not listed as such a motive?
   a. to establish social ties
   b. to gain and maintain status
   c. to attract and retain mates
   d. to avoid cognitive inconsistency

10. Naturalistic observation, case studies, and surveys are examples of
   a. experimental methods
   b. descriptive correlational methods
   c. quasi-experimental methods
   d. field experiments

11. Wilson and Daly (1985) examined police reports of 512 homicides committed in Detroit during 1972. They found that victims tended to be males in their twenties who died due to conflict over social dominance. This study used the _____ method.
   a. survey
   b. archival
   c. experimental
   d. case study

12. On surveys, men report that they have had ten to twelve sexual partners in their lives while women report just over three (Einon, 1994). This illustrates the
   a. social desirability bias
   b. observer bias
   c. false consensus effect
   d. cognitive dissonance

13. IQ tests like the Wechsler Adult Intelligence Scale (WAIS) yield consistent scores over time. This is an example of
   a. construct validity
   b. reliability
   c. validity
   d. test bias

14. If we systematically vary the temperature of the room to determine its effect on aggression, we are using the _____ method; if we simply observe the relationship between outdoor temperature and a person's aggression level, we are using the _____ method.
   a. correlational; experimental
   b. role playing; correlational
   c. experimental; correlational
   d. experimental; role playing

15. A researcher finds a correlation of -.80 between hours of television watched per week and grades on math tests among fourth graders. What can the researcher conclude?
   a. Watching television causes kids to get bad grades on math tests.
   b. Smart kids don't watch television.
   c. As hours of television watched per week increases it causes grades on math tests decrease.
   d. none of the above, correlations do not allow confident causal conclusions

TRUE-FALSE

Indicate whether each statement is true or false by circling T or F. If you decide it is false, explain why. Correct answers appear at the end of the study guide in the ANSWERS section for Chapter 1.

T   F   16.   The idea that a person's social behavior is determined by nationality, social class, and current trends is associated with the evolutionary perspective.

T   F   17.   Characteristics that are well designed for particular environments are called adaptations.

T   F   18.   The social cognitive perspective examines the processes whereby people choose which social events to pay attention to, how they interpret social events, and how they remember those events.

T   F   19.   Social behavior is goal oriented and represents a continual interaction between the person and the situation.

T   F   20.   Gossiping is connected most closely to the fundamental motive to gain and maintain status.

T   F   21.   Theories are hunches or guesses about how the findings in a particular experiment will turn out.

T   F   22.   Reliability refers to consistency of a test's results and validity is the extent to which the test measures what it is supposed to measure.

T   F   23.   If we found that taller people tend to be more intelligent, that would mean that height causes intelligence.

ESSAY

24.   Define and distinguish between the following descriptive methods – naturalistic observations, case studies, and surveys. Provide an example that illustrates each descriptive method. In addition, provide one strength and one weakness for each approach.

25.   Define the following important terms relevant to experimental methodology - independent variable, dependent variable, and random assignment. Outline an actual or hypothetical experiment by defining each of these terms as it relates to the experiment and illustrate why each is important to the experiment's success.

When You Have Finished...

Now that you have had a chance to read this chapter and complete the activities associated with it, you may be interested in finding additional materials on this topic. The World Wide Web is a great and convenient resource for gathering additional information in a variety of areas. Listed below are web links and website descriptions that are relevant to this chapter.

Web Links and Website Descriptions
Be sure to visit Chapter 1 at the companion website: www.ablongman.com/knc3e
http://www.scirus.com/ Scirus is a comprehensive science-specific search engine on the Internet. Scirus searches over 150 million science-specific web pages, enabling you to quickly pinpoint scientific data, peer-reviewed articles and journals, and locate university sites and scientists' home pages.
http://www.spsp.org/ Society for Personality and Social Psychology website generates and disseminates research in personality and social psychology.
http://www.apa.org/students/ American Psychological Association's student website will help you with careers in psychology, undergraduate resources, getting into graduate school, post-doctoral information funding opportunities, and best-selling books.
http://www.psycline.org/journals/psycline.html *PSYCLINE* started in 1995 under its former name *Links to Psychological Journals* and has a high reputation as a comprehensive and up-to-date index of psychology and social science journals on the web.
http://www.hbes.com/intro_to_field.htm This is a website maintained by the Human Behavior and Evolution Society, a group of psychologists, anthropologists, biologists, and researchers from various other fields who apply the evolutionary perspective to behavior. It contains links to more detailed explanations of the perspective and the controversies surrounding it.

Comprehensive Crossword Puzzle

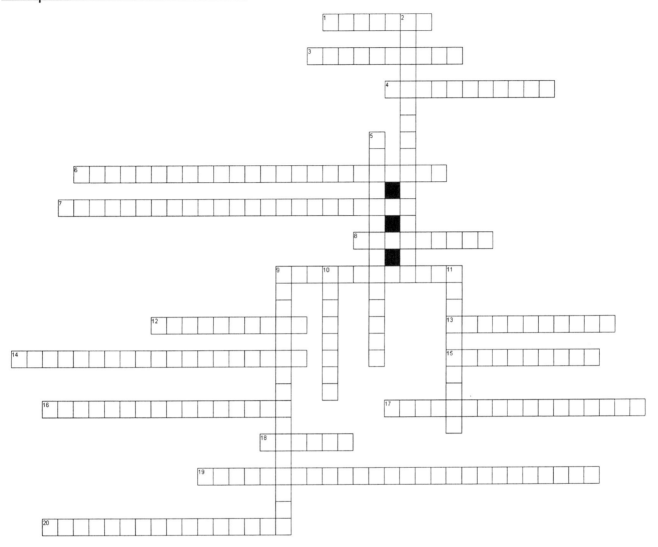

Across

1. beliefs/customs
3. rule or expectation for appropriate behavior
4. extent to which two or more variables are related
6. viewpoint that searches for the causes of social behavior from larger social groups
7. recording behaviors in natural settings
8. intensive examination of an individual
9. technique in which researcher asks people to report on their beliefs, feelings, or behaviors
12. prediction
13. consistency
14. variable manipulated
15. researcher manipulates variable of interest and holds others constant
16. results generalized
17. variable measured
18. scientific explanation that connects and organizes existing observations
19. viewpoint focused on mental processes

Across Continued

20. experiment allows confident statements about cause and effect

Down

2.   participant has equal chance of being in any condition
5.   examination of systematic data
9.   scientific study of people's thoughts feelings and behaviors are influenced by other people
10. extent to which a test measures what it is designed to measure
11. discussion at end of study

Puzzle created with Puzzlemaker at DiscoverySchool.com

THE PERSON AND THE SITUATION

Before You Read...

This chapter begins by examining social behavior from the perspective of the individual. You will first discover that each individual is a combination of motivations, knowledge, and feelings that work together to produce a wide range of social thought and behavior. You will notice that we spend a lot of time thinking about ourselves. We think about what kind of person we are, how we feel about ourselves, how we will obtain our goals, and how others view us - a process known as self-reflection. After the individual perspective is reviewed, you will learn about social behavior in the context of the situation. As a person, we also create situations for one another which can affect our thoughts, feelings, and behavior. People and situations provide us with different opportunities and threats; we assess them in an effective, proficient way. You will learn how situations also create influence through descriptive norms that help us make the right choices, while injunctive norms describe what is commonly approved or disapproved in a situation. Your text also discusses how collectivistic and individualistic cultures afford us different opportunities, and how culture governs by socially accepted scripts in everyday situations. This chapter concludes by discussing the six ways in which the person and situation can interact to shape social life.

Chapter Learning Objectives

After reading this chapter, you should be able to:

- Explain how the story of Martin Luther King, Jr. illustrates that features of neither the person nor the situation alone determine social behavior.

- Offer a definition of motivation and explain the difference between goals and motives.

- Explain how attention helps us to achieve our social goals.

- State the difference between conscious and automatic goal pursuit.

- Describe the benefits and costs of automaticity.

- Explain willpower and its relationship to goal achievement.

- Explain why suppressing thoughts that are incompatible with difficult to reach goals is ineffective ("white bears" example).

- Describe how knowledge is organized in memory with regard to exemplars and schemas.

- How does primed, accessible knowledge influence how we interpret the social world?

- Distinguish between the three general types of feelings (i.e., attitudes, emotions, and moods) and how feelings are assessed.

- Explain the genetic and cultural foundations for the origination of feelings, along with the physiological and cognitive explanations.

- What are the three reasons why feelings are important?

- What is the difference between self-concept and self-esteem?

- Describe how we use the self-regulation process to adjust our strategies to reach our goals and how we use the self-presentation process to control the impressions people form of us.

- What are the three ways in which people are situations for one another?

- Explain how pluralistic ignorance is associated with binge drinking on college campuses.

- What is the difference between injunctive norms and descriptive norms?

- Describe the difference between strong versus weak situations.

- Define collectivistic and individualistic cultures. What does culture afford for us and how might culture influence the use of social scripts in everyday situations?

- What are the six ways in which the person and situation can interact? Provide an example of each.

As You Read...

> **KEY TERMS!**
> Listed below are the key terms from the chapter that are essential for your understanding of the material. Refer to the definitions from your textbook; they are located at the end of this chapter, within the text in boldface, and in the margins throughout this chapter. In order to enhance your recall ability for these terms, you may want to consider making flashcards which include a term on one side, and a definition on the other (with perhaps a brief example that makes sense to you).

Affordance	Goal	Schema
Attention	Individualistic culture	Scripted situation
Attitude	Injunctive norm	Self-concept
Automaticity	Mood	Self-esteem
Chronic accessibility	Motivation	Self-perception process
Collectivistic culture	Motive	Self-presentation
Counterfactual thinking	Person-situation fit	Self-regulation
Descriptive norm	Pluralistic ignorance	Social comparison
Emotion	Priming	Socialization
Exemplar	Reflected appraisal process	Willpower

THE ENIGMA OF AN ORDINARY AND EXTRAORDINARY MAN

In the beginning of this chapter your authors discussed the enigmatic story of Martin Luther King, Jr.'s, rise from ordinary man to extraordinary leader of the Civil Rights movement. Please describe King's story and how his behavior can be explained by the complex interplay between features of the person and features of the situation.

INTRODUCING THE SELF

We spend a lot of time thinking about ourselves. We think about what kind of person we are, how we feel about ourselves, how we will obtain our goals, and how others view us - a process known as self-reflection. Define the following terms in relation to self and provide an example that distinguishes each item from the other.

"Who am I? How do I feel about myself?"
Self-concept -

Self-esteem -

"What do I want, and how do I get it?"
Self-regulation –

"How do I want others to view me?"
Self-presentation –

THE PERSON AND THE SITUATION INTERACT

According to Kurt Lewin (1951), the person and the situation work together to influence the way we think, feel, and behave. Your textbook examines six ways in which the person and situation influence one another and interact to shape social life. The six ways are:

(1) different persons respond differently to the same situation
(2) situations choose the person
(3) persons choose their situations
(4) different situations prime different parts of the person
(5) persons change the situation
(6) situations change the person.

Below, indicate which one of the six person/situation interactions is operating in each of the following examples.

Person/Situation Interaction	Examples
1. _____	After being rejected by two of her three top choice colleges, Marie goes to college at her third choice school.
2. _____	Tricia is a depressed college student who doesn't intentionally try to depress her roommates. Unfortunately, her depression has adversely affected her roommates and they are avoiding her.
3. _____	Kurt always considered himself to be an intelligent and independent person. After he married Diane, Kurt became dependent upon Diane and asked her opinion when making any decisions.
4. _____	Amy decided to spend this weekend going to see the latest sci-fi movie – *Matrix Revolutions*.
5. _____	After Adrian and Steve were admitted into college, Adrian felt the college was too small and that it did not offer enough opportunities for his career goals. Steve, however, loved the small college atmosphere and felt it was the perfect environment for him to accomplish his career goals.
6. _____	Maia was born with a calm disposition. After spending a year with her irresponsible parents, Maia became an anxious toddler.
7. _____	Fung-Ming, a Chinese-American student, feels a different sense of self depending upon the language he is speaking.
8. _____	After rushing all the popular fraternities, Joe wasn't selected to join any of them.
9. _____	At the company picnic, Brad is invited to play a relaxed game of "touch" football. However, Brad is a competitive person and soon turns "touch" football into "tackle" football.
10. _____	Laura decides to go to the library and study for her upcoming microbiology exam.

WORD SCRAMBLE

Word scramble! Unscramble the following words below. If you are having trouble, use the hints to assist you. When you have finished unscrambling the words, the letters within the [brackets] will reveal the "bonus" word. Ready? Go!

1. EMTELSESFE   __ __ __ __ __ [_] __ __ __ __

2. ZNOICATIASIOL   __ __ [_] __ __ __ __ __ __ __ __ __

3. XMELEARP   [_] __ __ __ __ __ __ __

4. NMPIRIG   __ __ __ [_] __ __ __

5. UATDETTI   [_] __ __ __ __ __ __ __

    BONUS WORD   __ __ H __ __ __

Hints:
1. Our attitude toward ourselves
2. Process whereby a culture teaches its members about its beliefs, customs, habits, and language
3. Mental representation of a specific episode, event, or individual
4. Process of activating knowledge or goals, of making them ready for use
5. Favorable or unfavorable evaluation of a particular person, object, event, or idea

BONUS: Mental representation capturing the general characteristics of a particular class of episodes, events, or individuals

MATCHING: KEY TERMS

Matching! Match each definition on the left side of the page with the concept on the right side of the page. Each concept on the right should only be used once.

__	1.	State of being easily activated, or primed, for use	A. Affordance
__	2.	Mental representation of a specific episode, event, or individual	B. Automaticity
__	3.	Norm that describes what is commonly approved or disapproved in a situation	C. Chronic accessibility
__	4.	Desired outcome; something one wishes to achieve or accomplish	D. Counterfactual thinking
__	5.	Opportunity or threat provided by a situation	E. Descriptive norm
__	6.	Relatively long-lasting feeling that is diffuse and not directed toward a particular, single target	F. Emotion
__	7.	Phenomenon in which people in a group misperceive the beliefs of others because everyone acts inconsistently with their beliefs	G. Exemplar
__	8.	Process through which people come to know themselves by comparing their abilities, attitudes, and beliefs with those of others	H. Goal
__	9.	Process of imagining alternative, "might have been" versions of actual events	I. Injunctive norm
__	10.	Mental representation capturing the general characteristics of a particular class of episodes, events, or individuals	J. Mood
__	11.	Self-control and strength used to overcome counterproductive impulses to achieve difficult goals	K. Motivation
__	12.	Relatively intense feelings characterized by physiological arousal and complex cognitions	L. Pluralistic ignorance
__	13.	Ability of a behavior or cognitive process to operate without conscious guidance once it's put into motion	M. Schema
__	14.	Force that moves people toward desired outcomes	N. Social comparison
__	15.	Norm that defines what is commonly done in a situation	O. Willpower

PUTTING IT ALL TOGETHER: THOUGHT QUESTIONS

You learned in the chapter that socialization and collectivistic versus individualistic orientations cause cross-cultural differences in people's goals. Though specific goals may differ, do you think that people from other cultures also have different fundamental motivations for the things they do? Why or why not? Support your answer based on what you've learned in the first two chapters.

In the first chapter, you learned about the four major perspectives in social psychology. In this chapter, you learned about many possible origins of our attitudes, feelings, emotions, and moods. Try to match each of the perspectives with the origin of affect that it would favor. Which perspective comes closest to explaining how you believe attitudes and beliefs are formed? Is just one perspective enough to explain all the origins of affect? Why or why not?

After You Read...Practice Tests

Practice Test 1

1. _____ is/are the driving force that moves people toward their desired outcomes.
   - a. Motivation
   - b. Willpower
   - c. Schemas
   - d. Goals

2. According to Langer, Blank, and Chanowitz (1978), you are more likely to let a stranger jump ahead of you to use the copy machine when they ask in which way?
   - a. "May I use the Xerox machine, because I'm in a rush"
   - b. "May I please use the Xerox machine"
   - c. "May I jump ahead of you"
   - d. "I don't mean to be rude, but can I make copies first?"

3. The strength needed to overcome powerful counterproductive impulses is called _____.
   - a. automaticity
   - b. willpower
   - c. counterfactual thinking
   - d. chronic accessibility

4. The chapter talks about particular individuals (Martin Luther King, Jr., George Washington, Mahatma Gandhi) who may represent the category "great leader" for you. These individuals would be of that category.
   - a. exemplars
   - b. schemas
   - c. scripts
   - d. visual images

5. Celeste watched a few scary movies at a friend's house on Halloween. When she came home, Celeste was convinced that someone was lurking in the bushes outside and that someone was indeed inside the house waiting to attack her. This is an example of
   - a. exemplars
   - b. offensive motivation
   - c. priming
   - d. visual images

6. People have feelings about themselves. Social psychologists call this type of affect
   - a. self-esteem
   - b. reflected appraisal
   - c. self-concept
   - d. social comparison

7. Your book described the classic pen-holding experiment by Strack, Martin, and Stepper (1988). What did the results of this experiment suggest?
   - a. Physically impaired people can write with their mouths.
   - b. Writing with a pen in your mouth can make you happy.
   - c. The movement of facial muscles can influence emotion.
   - d. Writing with a pen in your mouth can make you angry.

8. Which of the following is NOT a way in which we gather information for our self-concept?
   - a. counterfactual thinking
   - b. reflected appraisal
   - c. self-perception
   - d. social comparison

9. When you go check on your exam grade for your Social psychology class, you look to see how your classmates performed to gauge how well you are doing in the course. This example illustrates
    a. reflected appraisal process.
    b. social comparison.
    c. self-perception process.
    d. critical appraisal process.

10. Your friend says, "You're an idiot if you drink and drive. That's a really irresponsible thing to do." Your friend is conveying a/an _____ to you about drinking and driving.
    a. descriptive norm
    b. injunctive norm
    c. pluralistic ignorance
    d. situational norm

Practice Test 2

1. Martin Luther King, Jr.'s, mysterious rise from ordinary man to an extraordinary leader in the Civil Rights movement can best be explained by _____ according to your text.
    a. his personality
    b. the situation
    c. interactions of the person and the situation
    d. interactions between the situation and environmental circumstances

2. Goals can be defined as
    a. fundamental to social survival
    b. a desired outcome
    c. a wish list
    d. process through which people come to know themselves

3. Researchers ask participants to resist eating candy or to eat as much candy as they want. Later both groups are asked to spend time working on difficult math problems. Participants who had to use willpower to resist eating candy will probably
    a. be able to work longer to solve the math problems.
    b. be better able to solve the math problems correctly.
    c. be unable to figure out how to solve the math problems.
    d. be unable to make themselves spend as much time on the math problems.

4. A representation that captures general knowledge about a category, like believing that great leaders are wise, charismatic, and can influence others, is know as
    a. a cultural norm
    b. a schema
    c. a script
    d. an exemplar

5. For a person interested in recent American presidential politics, images of George W. Bush and Bill Clinton easily come to mind. This best illustrates which of the following concepts?
    a. chronic accessibility
    b. representativeness heuristic
    b. social desirability bias
    d. social comparison

6. Social psychologists consider three general types of feelings. Which of the following is not one of the general types of feelings mentioned in your text?
    a. moods
    b. emotions
    c. attitudes
    d. all of the above are general types of feelings

7. Medvec, Madey, and Gilovich (1995) demonstrated how counterfactual thinking may influence our reactions to actual events. Who is happier following their Olympic performance?
   a. silver medal winners are happier than gold medal winners
   b. bronze medal winners are happier than gold medal winners
   c. bronze medal winners are happier than silver medal winners
   d. all Olympic medal winners are equally happy

8. Reflected appraisal allows you to develop your self-concept by
   a. observing the way you act with others
   b. observing how you react in various situations
   c. observing how others view you.
   d. concentrating very hard on yourself in the mirror.

9. Shortly after you arrive at your friend's party, you notice an attractive student (Cary) from one of your college classes that you haven't had the opportunity to meet. You are very excited and busy trying to figure out your strategy to approach Cary. This is an example of
   a. self-presentation and social comparison.
   b. social comparison and self-perception.
   c. self-perception process and self-serving bias.
   d. self-regulation and self-presentation.

10. _____ is the degree to which an individual's beliefs, abilities, and personality are consistent with the situation in which they are placed.
   a. The situational constraint   b. The person-situation interaction
   c. The person-situation fit   d. The effect of the person on the situation

Practice Test 3

1. Which of the following is true regarding goals?
   a. Many of our goals are subgoals, steps toward a larger goal.
   b. Motives are goals with a broad scope, such as the desire to gain status.
   c. Achieving our goals sometimes requires considerable attention.
   d. All of the above are true.

2. You are waiting in line for the drinking fountain. A person runs up and says, "May I get a drink, because I'm thirsty." You let the person go ahead of you. Why?
   a. You were in a good mood.
   b. Your attention was focused on what the person was saying.
   c. As soon as the person said "because" you reacted mindlessly because "because" suggests there's a reason.
   d. You were following a descriptive norm.

3. Which of the following is an example of a subgoal?
   a. saving money to buy a home   b. borrowing class notes to earn a good grade
   c. looking attractive for a date   d. all of the above

4. During Steven's first year in medical school, he spent a great deal of time reading about brain abnormalities. One day Steven started having bad headaches and believed he had a brain tumor. This is an example of
    a. an exemplar
    b. a schema
    c. a script
    d. priming

5. In a study by Harold Kelley (1950), college students learned that their class would be taught by a substitute instructor for the day. He found that student evaluations of the substitute instructor were
    a. more favorable when students were led to believe that the substitute would be warm and friendly
    b. less favorable when students were led to believe that the substitute would be warm and friendly
    c. more favorable when students were led to believe that the substitute would be cold and distant
    d. based solely on the students impressions of the substitute instructor and were not influenced by priming.

6. A/an _____ is a relatively intense feeling characterized by physiological arousal and complex cognitions; whereas, _____ are relatively long-last feelings that are diffuse and not directed toward a particular, single target.
    a. mood; emotions
    b. attitude; emotions
    b. emotion; moods
    d. emotion; attitudes

7. Feelings are important because
    a. emotions alert us when something isn't normal.
    b. positive emotions in both the short- and long-term, help us deal better with negative events and crises that confront us.
    c. attitudes allow us to make quick approach/avoidance judgments without thinking too much about them.
    d. all of the above

8. Where do our self-concept and self-esteem come from?
    a. reflected appraisal process
    b. social comparison
    c. self-perception process
    d. all of these answers

9. _____ are the threats and opportunities that other people provide to you, and are an element of the situation.
    a. Attunements
    b. Affordances
    c. Social comparisons
    d. Expectations

10. Jake comes from Australia, which is an individualistic culture. Which of the following is not a cultural affordance that is likely to be provided to Jake?
    a. the knowledge that he can grow up to be whatever he wants to be
    b. a wide range of choice about what type of bread he can buy
    c. the ability to relate well to others and take their perspective
    d. the opportunity to exert control over others

Comprehensive Test
(Note: Items 1-15 are multiple-choice questions, items 16-23 are true-false questions, and 24-25 are essay questions.)

1. As a leader of the Civil Rights movement, Martin Luther King, Jr., overcame many obstacles and accomplished extraordinary deeds for blacks including: equal opportunities in education, employment, voting rights, and housing. According to your text, King's career must have been a result of
   a. his personality.
   b. the events occurring during the 1950's/1960's and the place he lived.
   c. Rosa Parks
   d. A and B

2. _____ is the force that moves people toward the _____.
   a. Motivation; subgoals
   b. Willpower; motive
   c. Motivation; goal
   d. Automaticity; goal

3. Recent findings reveal that thought suppression (e.g. dieters trying not to think of tasty desserts) can
   a. contribute to mental health difficulties.
   b. weaken the immune system.
   c. rebound those thoughts back into consciousness.
   d. all of the above

4. _____ is a mental representation of a *specific* episode, event, or individual whereas _____ is a mental representation capturing the *general* characteristics of a particular class of episodes, events, or individuals.
   a. Schema; exemplar
   b. Exemplar; schema
   c. Self-concept; chronic accessibility
   d. Heuristic; schema

5. What makes some knowledge more accessible than other knowledge?
   a. Knowledge can be primed by the situations we're in.
   b. Knowledge can be primed by related knowledge.
   c. Some thoughts come more readily to mind than others.
   d. all of the above

6. Jason doesn't like lawyers, likes dogs better than cats, and feels favorably toward drug legalization. These are examples of Jason's
   a. moods
   b. emotions
   c. attitudes
   d. affect

7. Which of the following does NOT provide converging evidence to assess what a person is feeling?
   a. self-report measures
   b. behavioral indicators
   c. physiological measures
   d. all of these allow researchers to be more confident in the assessment of feelings

8.   The finding that people from many different cultures agree about which facial expressions reflect happiness, sadness, fear, disgust, and anger suggests that
     a.   emotions are learned through socialization.
     b.   there may be a genetic basis to our emotions.
     c.   emotions are related to whether a society is collectivistic or individualistic.
     d.   none of the above

9.   Which of the following is an example of the way in which the self-perception process helps us to form our self-concept?
     a.   Joe helps his girlfriend with her homework, and comes to believe he is a helpful person.
     b.   Kristie gets into a horrible fight with her sister, and Kristie begins to think that she is a belligerent person.
     c.   Diane thinks she is very smart, but then she fails her chemistry final and decides that she is stupid.
     d.   all of the above

10.   The process through which people observe their own behavior to infer their own internal characteristics is called _____.
     a.   reflected appraisal process   b.   social comparison
     c.   self-perception process   d.   critical appraisal process

11.   Now that you finally met Cary at your friend's party, you begin to present yourself as competent, likeable, and fun to make a favorable impression. This process is known as

     _____.
     a.   self-presentation   b.   social comparison
     c.   self-perception   d.   self-regulation

12.   A/an_____ is a norm that defines what is commonly done in a situation and a/an_____ describes what is commonly approved or disapproved in a situation.
     a.   situational norm; descriptive norm   b.   injunctive norm; descriptive norm
     c.   injunctive norm; situational norm   d.   descriptive norm; injunctive norm

13.   Your text describes a young man, Scott Krueger, whose promising future ended weeks into his freshman year. Scott consumed enough beer and rum to raise his blood alcohol level to a toxic 0.41 percent during a mandatory hazing fraternity event. Scott Krueger's death may be a troubling demonstration of _____ according to the text.
     a.   diffusion of responsibility   b.   injunctive norm
     c.   pluralistic ignorance   d.   situational norm

14.   A weak situation is one which
     a.   allows many options for appropriate behavior.
     b.   is highly scripted.
     c.   has very obvious injunctive norms.
     d.   has clear descriptive norms.

15. Carlos is a Mexican American boy who feels like both of his cultures "take turns" influencing his actions. When Carlos is at home, he speaks Spanish and is actively involved in his Mexican heritage. At school though, Carlos speaks English and feels like an American boy. This example illustrates that
    a. different persons respond differently to the same situation
    b. situations choose the person
    c. persons choose their situations
    d. different situations prime different parts of the person

TRUE-FALSE
Indicate whether each statement is true or false by circling T or F. If you decide it is false, explain why. Correct answers appear at the end of the study guide in the ANSWERS section for Chapter 2.

T   F   16.   An example of a subgoal is the desire to get good grades.

T   F   17.   Socialization is our biological instinct to know our society's beliefs, customs, habits, and language.

T   F   18.   When we use willpower in one situation, we will have less of it available to achieve later goals.

T   F   19.   There are three general types of feelings – attitudes, emotions, and moods.

T   F   20.   Something one wishes to achieve or accomplish is known as counterfactual thinking.

T   F   21.   A little girl's parents tell her that they think she is very funny, and she comes to believe that she has a good sense of humor. This is an example of social comparison.

T   F   22.   An affordance helps us to know how to act in a particular situation by observing the behavior of others.

T   F   23.   Features of a situation, such as language, can prime different identities in someone who is bicultural.

ESSAY

24. Describe and distinguish between the three general types of feelings – attitudes, emotions, and moods. What are the three ways to assess feelings and why are feelings important?

25. According to Kurt Lewin (1951), the person and the situation work together to influence the way we think, feel, and behave. Your textbook examines six ways in which the person and situation influence one another and interact to shape social life. Discuss three of the six ways in which persons and situations interact and provide an example of each.

When You Have Finished...

Now that you have had a chance to read this chapter and complete the activities associated with it, you may be interested in finding additional materials on this topic. The World Wide Web is a great and convenient resource for gathering additional information in a variety of areas. Listed below are web links and website descriptions that are relevant to this chapter.

Web Links and Website Descriptions
Be sure to visit Chapter 2 at the companion website: www.ablongman.com/knc3e
http://www.sfu.ca/counterfactual/ This site is a resource for those who have an interest in counterfactual thinking and related research conducted by social psychologists. This website contains listings of in press and recently published articles, a bibliography of counterfactual publications in social psychology, and web links to the home pages of psychologists active in this area.
http://changingminds.org/explanations/theories/Theories.htm On the Changing Minds website you will be able to get in-depth descriptions of key terms from this chapter including: attitudes, counterfactual thinking, pluralistic ignorance, schemas, etc.
http://education.indiana.edu/~p540/webcourse/schema.html#notes This is a website for a learning and cognition course taught at Indiana University. You will find relevant information regarding schemas on this website.
http://www.lucs.lu.se/People/Christian.Balkenius/Thesis/Chapter06.html This website is from Lund University Cognitive Science in Sweden. This site examines the role of motivation in determining behavior and learning.
http://nobelprizes.com/nobel/peace/1964a.html Look at this site to learn more about the life of Martin Luther King, Jr.

Comprehensive Crossword Puzzle

Across

2. long lasting feeling that is diffuse
4. ability of a behavior or cognitive process to operate without conscious guidance once it's put into motion
5. culture that socializes its members to think of themselves as individuals
6. process through which people come to know themselves by comparing their abilities, attitudes, and beliefs with those of others
7. opportunity or threat provided by a situation
8. what might have been
9. desired outcome
10. our attitude toward ourselves
11. intense feeling characterized by physiological arousal and complex cognitions
12. force that moves people toward desired outcomes
13. mental representation capturing the general characteristics of a particular class of episodes events or individuals
14. self-control/strength used to overcome counterproductive impulses to achieve difficult goals
15. process of consciously focusing on aspects of our environment

Down

1. mental representation of a specific episode, event, or individual
3. a norm that defines what is commonly done in a situation
8. culture that socializes its members to think of themselves as members of the larger group

Puzzle created with Puzzlemaker at DiscoverySchool.com

SOCIAL COGNITION: UNDERSTANDING OURSELVES AND OTHERS

Before You Read...

This chapter discusses the important role social cognition plays in determining behavior and the four fundamental processes needed to accomplish the task of thinking about the world around you. You will learn how people are motivated tacticians, that we adopt different styles of thought depending upon our goals at the time. You will be given a thorough overview of the three main goals that influence social thought which include: conserving mental effort, managing self-image, and seeking accuracy. You will learn that we conserve our mental effort due to our limited attentional capacity and complex social environment. Because of this complexity, we employ a variety of cognitive strategies to help us make "good enough" judgments while expending minimal mental effort. However, these strategies sometimes lead to inaccurate judgments regarding situations (i.e., self-fulfilling prophecy) or inaccuracies with regard to people (i.e., fundamental attribution error and actor observer difference). You will then discover how we manage our self-image and how positive self-regard equips us with the confidence and energy we need to accomplish our goals. Specifically, you will examine how we utilize cognitive strategies to enhance and protect our self-image (i.e., downward and upward social comparison, self-serving bias, exaggerating our strengths and diminishing our weaknesses, and believing we have control) and when these strategies are employed due to situations that threaten our self-esteem. After exploring these simplification and self-serving strategies, you will see that people also have a desire to seek accuracy in their social environment. Our accuracy can be enhanced through an unbiased gathering of information and by considering alternative possibilities. Finally, you will learn that in order to increase accuracy, people may use attributional logic to better understand the causes of others' actions and under what circumstances an individual will employ these accuracy motivated strategies.

Chapter Learning Objectives

After reading this chapter, you should be able to:

- Define social cognition and describe the four core processes of social cognition

- Explain why we need cognitive strategies that lead to effective decision making

- Explain how our expectations help us evaluate people and situations

- Define the self-fulfilling prophecy. When are self-fulfilling prophecies likely to occur?

- Define dispositional inference. When are we most likely to make a dispositional inference?

- Explain the difference between correspondence bias and actor-observer difference

- Describe the fundamental attribution error and its relevance to individualistic versus collectivistic cultures

- Describe the various cognitive shortcuts and provide examples of each - including the representativeness heuristic, the availability heuristic, and the anchoring and adjustment heuristic

- Explain how arousal, circadian rhythms, and need for structure affect our use of cognitive shortcuts

- Describe why complex situations and time pressure increases the likelihood of relying on cognitive shortcuts

- Outline the reasons why we desire positive self-regard

- Describe how you can use social comparison to enhance your self-image

- Explain the self-serving bias

- Explain the role perception of control plays in our self-image and how control affects our health

- Describe the relationship between self-esteem and self-enhancing strategies

- Provide examples of situational threats to self-esteem. What cognitive processes do people use to repair damaged self-esteem?

- Discuss the strategies people use to reach a more accurate understanding of their social world

- Compare and contrast the key elements of Jones and Davis' correspondent inference theory and Kelley's Covariation model

- Describe the discounting and augmenting principles

- Explain how our mood and need for cognition affects our use of cognitive shortcuts

- Outline the two situational circumstances that make us think in more complex ways

- Explain how insufficient cognitive resources affect accuracy and our tendency to simplify

As You Read...

> **KEY TERMS!**
> Listed below are the key terms from the chapter that are essential for your understanding of the material. Refer to the definitions from your textbook; they are located at the end of this chapter, within the text in boldface, and in the margins throughout this chapter. In order to enhance your recall ability for these terms, you may want to consider making flashcards which include a term on one side, and a definition on the other (with perhaps a brief example that makes sense to you).

Actor-observer difference	Correspondence bias (fundamental attribution error)	False consensus effect
Anchoring and adjustment heuristic	Correspondent inference theory	Representativeness heuristic
Attribution theories	Covariation model	Self-fulfilling prophecy
Augmenting principle	Discounting principle	Self-serving bias
Availability heuristic	Dispositional inference	Social cognition
Cognitive heuristic	Downward social comparison	Upward social comparison

PORTRAITS OF HILLARY RODHAM CLINTON

In the beginning of this chapter your authors discussed the diverging views held about Hillary Rodham Clinton. Throughout this chapter, research was presented to help you understand how your expectations and perspectives influence your interpretation of the world. Please explain then, how observers of Senator Clinton could view her so differently by using the terms presented in the text.

ERRORS IN SOCIAL COGNITION

This chapter discusses how people are motivated tacticians; as our goals change we adopt different styles of thought. Sometimes we simplify our thoughts, make poor judgments, attribute behavior to the wrong causes, and have inaccurate expectations about people and the social world in which we live. Listed below are five terms that students sometimes have trouble distinguishing between. Your task is to figure out which one of the terms is operating in each of the following examples.

(1) Actor-observer difference
(2) Correspondence bias (fundamental attribution error)
(3) False consensus effect
(4) Self-fulfilling prophecy
(5) Self-serving bias

Term	Examples
1. _____	After he was defeated in a competition for a prestigious academic award, Dr. Gang Lu went on a rampage killing six people including himself. Journalists described Lu as "darkly disturbed" and had a "psychological problem with being challenged."
2. _____	After winning his first set in the tennis tournament, Jeff comments about how his hard work and skill are paying off. Upon losing his second set, Jeff starts screaming at the judges for unfair calls.
3. _____	Jessica slips on an icy patch and comments "Wow, that's slick!" Jessica's friend Steve slips on the same icy patch and she chuckles "Steve, you sure are clumsy!"
4. _____	Kim and Gary, strict vegetarians, are hosting Thanksgiving dinner and proudly present their masterpiece tofu-turkey to their guests. Gary's mom looks at Kim in disbelief and remarks sharply "You roasted a real turkey too, correct?"
5. _____	Television news programs present "exaggerated" information regarding the country's "mildly" troubled economy. As a result, many people panic upon hearing the news broadcasts and stop buying goods and services. This results in severe economic decline.
6. _____	Bill is an hour late for his important business meeting due to a plane delay. When he arrives in the boardroom, he trips over the audio-visual equipment cords and drops his meeting notes, breaks his glasses, and coffee is spilt everywhere. Bill then hears people commenting at the meeting under their breath, "moron – klutz – idiot."
7. _____	House Republicans insist that they finally will be able to impeach President Bill Clinton on perjury charges. They feel that the rest of the country is also behind this decision and impeach Clinton in the House of Representatives. In the senate, he is not impeached and Clinton finishes out his presidency.

KELLY'S COVARIATION MODEL

Your text discusses Kelly's Covariation model which proposes that people determine the cause of an actor's behavior by assessing whether other people act in similar ways (consensus), the actor behaves similarly in similar situations (distinctiveness), and the actor behaves similarly in the same situation (consistency). For this exercise determine whether consensus, distinctiveness, and consistency is high or low for this particular situation; Jack has asked Jill to marry him. You try to determine whether Jack's behavior reflects something about Jack, something special about Jill, or a combination between Jack and Jill.

Let's say that you find out that Jill has not been dating anyone over the past few years because other men did not find Jill to be very interesting. You also know that Jack has a history of asking every girl he dates to marry him and he has been asking Jill to marry him for the past four weekends.

Let's say that you find out that Jill is very attractive, fun, and outgoing. Every man that she has dated over the past few years has proposed to her. You also find out that Jack for the first time feels like he has found "the right person" for him. So, Jack proposes to Jill every chance he gets hoping someday she will say yes.

Let's say that you find out that Jill has not been dating anyone over the past few years either because she is highly selective or no one has shown interest. You know that Jack has been smitten with Jill since they started dating. Jack feels that he has finally found *the* woman of his dreams. Now, he eagerly waits for Jill to accept his marriage proposal by asking her to marry him every day.

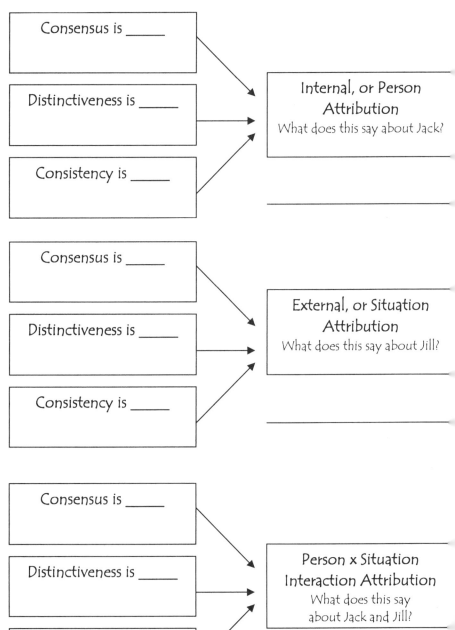

Consensus is _____

Distinctiveness is _____

Consistency is _____

Internal, or Person Attribution
What does this say about Jack?

Consensus is _____

Distinctiveness is _____

Consistency is _____

External, or Situation Attribution
What does this say about Jill?

Consensus is _____

Distinctiveness is _____

Consistency is _____

Person x Situation Interaction Attribution
What does this say about Jack and Jill?

SUMMARY OF THE GOALS INFLUENCING SOCIAL COGNITION

Complete the chart below to help you summarize the three goals that influence social cognition and the factors related to them. If you need assistance, see page 110 in your text (but be sure to use your own words in this exercise, rather than just copying).

The Goal	The Person	The Situation	Interactions
To Conserve Mental Effort	• • •	• •	•
To Manage Self-image	•	•	•
To Be Accurate	• • •	• •	•

MATCHING: KEY TERMS

Matching! Match each definition on the left side of the page with the concept on the right side of the page. Each concept on the right should only be used once.

__	1.	Mental shortcut where one estimates the likelihood of an event by the ease with which instances of that event come to mind
__	2.	Tendency to overestimate extent to which others agree with us
__	3.	Judgment that a person's behavior has been caused by an aspect of that person's personality
__	4.	Mental shortcut used to make a judgment
__	5.	Process of comparing ourselves with those who are less well off
__	6.	Tendency to take personal credit for our successes and to blame external factors for our failures
__	7.	Tendency for individuals to judge their own behaviors as caused by situational forces but the behavior of others as caused by aspects of their personalities
__	8.	Mental shortcut through which people classify something as belonging to a certain category to the extent that it is similar to a typical case from that category
__	9.	Judgmental rule that states that as the number of possible causes for an event increases, our confidence that any particular cause is the true one should decrease
__	10.	Theories designed to explain how people determine the causes of behavior
__	11.	When an initially inaccurate expectation leads to actions that cause the expectation to come true
__	12.	Tendency for observers to overestimate the causal influence of personality factors on behavior and to underestimate the causal role of situational influences
__	13.	Process of thinking about oneself and others
__	14.	Process of comparing ourselves with those who are better off than ourselves
__	15.	Judgmental rule that states that if an event occurs despite the presence of strong opposing forces, we should give more weight to those possible causes that lead toward the event

A. Actor-observer difference

B. Attribution theories

C. Augmenting principle

D. Availability heuristic

E. Cognitive heuristic

F. Correspondence bias

G. Discounting principle

H. Dispositional inference

I. Downward social comparison

J. False consensus effect

K. Representativeness heuristic

L. Self-fulfilling prophecy

M. Self-serving bias

N. Social cognition

O. Upward social comparison

PUTTING IT ALL TOGETHER: THOUGHT QUESTIONS

The chapter discussed perceptions of control and how people with health problems often react differently depending upon whether they are internals or externals. Do you think it would be helpful to doctors to know whether their patients had an external or internal locus of control? Do you think it would change they way they talk to their patients about their illnesses and about how best to treat the illness?

The book described a number of experiments where participants were given false feedback about their performance or had their self-image threatened in some other way. Knowing that having your self-image threatened is unpleasant, do you think this practice is ethical? What types of informed consent and debriefing would be required in these experiments? How would you inform participants what will be happening to them without actually telling them that the threat to their self-image is not real?

After You Read...Practice Tests

Practice Test 1

1. Attention, interpretation, judgment, and memory are the core processes of
   a. social expectations
   b. cognitive heuristics
   c. social cognition
   d. expectation confirmation

2. We live in a complex social world where we encounter a huge amount of information at any given moment. Because of this, we need cognitive strategies that
   a. allow us to understand all of this complex information.
   b. are simple and help us make "good enough" judgments.
   c. are unbiased and help us reach logical conclusions
   d. help us take the "path of least resistance" at all times

3. Your neighbor, Linda, owns a Harley Davidson motorcycle. You notice that she hosts many parties with her rowdy biker friends, her and biker friends are always working on their motorcycles, and when she looks tired in the morning you assume it is due to her "partying ways." In fact, whenever you think of her, you can only remember things associated with her rowdy behavior. This example illustrates how we
   a. interpret ambiguous events in ways that support our expectations.
   b. seek out information that confirms our expectations.
   c. have a tendency to recall events and characteristics consistent with our expectations.
   d. all of the above

4. In a demonstration of the fundamental attribution error, participants in the "Castro" experiment were asked to guess the true beliefs of someone who wrote an essay. What did this experiment show?
   a. When participants were told that the author had no choice about which essay to write, they made dispositional inferences anyway.
   b. When participants were told that the author had no choice about which essay to write, they did not make dispositional inferences.
   c. When participants were told that the author chose which essay to write, they did not make dispositional inferences.
   d. all of the above

5. After ranking the causes of death in the United States, you find out that you underestimated the risks for diabetes, pneumonia, and prostate cancer and overestimated the risks from homicide, AIDS and firearm accidents. This illustrates the _____.
   a. representativeness heuristic.
   b. availability heuristic
   c. anchoring-and-adjustment heuristic
   d. false consensus effect

6. Your book describes a finding by Bodenhausen (1990) about the relationship between circadian rhythms and the use of heuristics. What did Bodenhausen find?
   a. Morning people are more likely to use heuristics in the morning.
   b. Morning people are more likely to use heuristics in the evening.
   c. Most people use heuristics more in the morning.
   d. Evening people are more likely to use heuristics in the evening.

7. Festinger (1954) argued that people have a fundamental drive to evaluate their abilities and opinions and often do so by engaging in _____.
   a. social cognition
   b. dispositional inference
   c. social comparison
   d. attribution

8. Brandi received an A on her first social psychology exam where she attributes her success to her understanding of the material and her studying effort. On the second social psychology exam she earned a D and attributed this to her teacher writing unfair questions. This is an example of the
   a. actor-observer difference.
   b. fundamental attribution error.
   c. availability heuristic.
   d. self-serving bias.

9. Studies of post-operative hospital patients show that patients who control their own dosage of pain medication
   a. recover slower because they give themselves less pain medication.
   b. recover faster because they give themselves more pain medication.
   c. recover faster because they have a sense of control over their situation.
   d. recover slower because they feel as though they are being ignored.

10. Which theory proposes that people determine the cause of an actor's behavior by assessing consensus, distinctiveness, and consistency?
    a. Covariation model
    b. Correspondent inference theory
    c. Elaboration likelihood model
    d. Balance theory

Practice Test 2

1. Social cognition is defined as
   a. the process of thinking about oneself and others
   b. the process of thinking collectively
   c. a mental shortcut for the way we think about the world around us
   d. the process of comparing ourselves with others

2. Hillary Rodham Clinton elicits vast differences in public opinion; by many she is adored and by so many others reviled. These wildly divergent opinions of Hillary Clinton can be understood through certain fundamental cognitive processes of
   a. attention, interpretation, judgment, and memory.
   b. actor-observer difference.
   c. self-fulfilling prophecy.
   d. upward social comparison and downward social comparison.

3. Under which of the following circumstances are self-fulfilling prophecies most likely to occur?
   a. when the person holding the inaccurate expectation is in control of the social encounter
   b. when the target of the expectations believes that he or she is in control of the social encounter
   c. when the person holding the inaccurate expectation has a low cognitive load
   d. when the target of expectations knows that others hold inaccurate expectations of them

4.   Greg is late for work and tells his boss that it was due to heavy traffic. Five minutes after Greg arrives to work, Jill comes in late too. Greg says under his breath, "Late, typical woman." This is an example of
a.   disposition inference.
b.   fundamental attribution error.
c.   actor-observer difference.
d.   availability heuristic.

5.   Hillary Clinton decides that she wants to run for president in 2008 because she believes other democrats and registered independents view her favorably and would vote for her. This is an example of _____.
a.   false consensus effect
b.   magical thinking
c.   expectation fallacy
d.   vividness effect

6.   Which stable personality trait influences whether we use simple or more complex cognitive strategies?
a.   extraversion
b.   need for structure
c.   neuroticism
d.   positive affect

7.   Americans desire positive self-regard and because of this most report
a.   having high self-esteem.
b.   view their future prospects optimistically
c.   more favorable characteristics and abilities about themselves than the average person
d.   all of the above

8.   In a study described in your book, experimenters asked Christian students to write about what would happen when they die. Later, those students evaluated a Christian person more favorably than an otherwise identical Jewish person. These results suggest that mortality salience
a.   distracts people from their worries.
b.   makes people more giving to others.
c.   threatens one's self-image
d.   activates beliefs of fairness.

9.   You want to discourage your roommate from using oversimplified cognitive heuristics in deciding what classes to take next semester. Which of the following would not help him/her to make an accurate decision?
a.   making a conscious effort to be accurate
b.   playing devil's advocate with themselves/considering the alternatives
c.   concentrating on information that confirms their expectations
d.   paying attention to information that disconfirms their expectations

10. According to the attribution theory proposed by Jones and Davis, we are most likely to conclude that others' behavior reflects stable traits when that behavior is _____, _____, _____, and _____.
a.   intentional; consequences foreseeable; freely chosen; occur despite countervailing forces
b.   intentional; consequences unforeseeable; not freely chosen; occur despite countervailing forces
c.   unintentional; consequences unforeseeable; freely chosen; occur despite countervailing forces
d.   unintentional; consequences unforeseeable; not freely chosen; do not occur because of countervailing forces

Practice Test 3

1. _____ is selecting information while _____ gives the information meaning.
   - a. Attention; judgment
   - b. Attention; interpretation
   - c. Interpretation; judgment
   - d. Interpretation; Memory

2. Which statement is true with regard to our expectations?
   - a. We think in ways that will preserve our expectations.
   - b. We interpret ambiguous events and behaviors in ways that support our expectations.
   - c. We tend to remember people and events that are consistent with our expectations.
   - d. All of these statements are true with regard to our expectations.

3. U.S. banks went out of business by the thousands in the 1930s. Rumors of impending bank failures made many depositors jittery and fearful that this could happen to them so they would withdraw their savings too. This example can be explained by the _____.
   - a. discounting principle
   - b. augmenting principle
   - c. self-serving bias
   - d. self-fulfilling prophecy

4. Duane lives on your dorm floor and spends most of his time in the library, doesn't date much, and gets very high grades. You assume that Duane is probably a member of the honor society. You are using the
   - a. representativeness heuristic.
   - b. availability heuristic.
   - c. anchoring-and-adjustment heuristic.
   - d. false consensus effect.

5. You're in charge of inviting people from your dorm floor to a party. You don't invite Duane (from question 4) because you assume everyone else will also think that he's boring. You are using the
   - a. representativeness heuristic.
   - b. availability heuristic.
   - c. anchoring-and-adjustment heuristic.
   - d. self-fulfilling prophecy.

6. If a person is highly disorganized, loves spontaneity, and can't stand it when things are too predictable in his/her life, we can assume he or she is low in
   - a. need for structure.
   - b. self-esteem.
   - c. need for cognition.
   - d. covariation.

7. John, the star quarterback, sprained his ankle and won't be able to play in the homecoming game. According to your book, how can he use downward social comparison to make himself feel better?
   - a. He can enhance his view of his teams' chance to win the game.
   - b. He can compare himself to the guy who broke his shoulder and is out for the whole season.
   - c. He can cut himself off from his team and concentrate on other things.
   - d. He can compare himself to the replacement quarterback.

8. Lau and Russell (1980) collected newspaper articles to see how players, coaches, and sports commentators explained home-team victories and defeats. Their analysis discovered evidence for the _____.
   a. actor-observer difference.
   b. fundamental attribution error.
   c. self-serving bias.
   d. availability heuristic.

9. Which theory proposes that people determine whether a behavior corresponds to an actor's internal disposition by asking whether the behavior was intended, the behavior's consequences were foreseeable, the behavior was freely chosen, and the behavior occurred despite countervailing forces?
   a. Covariation model
   b. Correspondent inference theory
   c. Elaboration likelihood model
   d. Balance theory

10. The President of the United States nominates a woman for a seat on the US Supreme Court. Why did he do this? You learn that the president will loose his chance for reelection by nominating a woman. Now that you know this, will you be more certain about her qualifications? This is an example of the _____.
                    25.
    a. the discounting principle.
    b. correspondent inference.
    c. the augmenting principle.
    d. upward social comparison.

Comprehensive Test
(Note: Items 1-15 are multiple-choice questions, items 16-23 are true-false questions, and 24-25 are essay questions.)

1. Which of the following is NOT a core process of social cognition?
   a. attention
   b. interpretation
   c. judgment
   d. accuracy

2. You learn that your classmate belongs to a fraternity. You would probably be better at remembering when this fraternity member boasted about drinking 5 consecutive beers in a row than his volunteer work with his church. This is an example of
   a. interpreting ambiguous events in ways that support our expectations.
   b. seeking out information that confirms our expectations.
   c. a self-fulfilling prophecy.
   d. our tendency to recall events and characteristics consistent with our expectations.

3. _____ are more likely than _____ to create self-fulfilling prophecies.
   a. Men; women
   b. Women; men
   c. Job applicants; interviewers
   d. Students; teachers

4. Your book describes cross-cultural differences in the fundamental attribution error. Which of the following is true?
   a. Collectivist societies are more likely to make the fundamental attribution error.
   b. The error is truly "fundamental;" both collectivist and individualistic societies were equally likely to make it.
   c. Individualistic societies were more likely to make the fundamental attribution error.
   d. Individualistic societies tend to place more emphasis on the situation than on the person.

5. Lori is a liberal Democrat who strongly believes that Hillary Clinton should run for president in 2008. Lori is convinced that the rest of the nation will vote for Hillary Clinton. This example illustrates the _____.
   a. false consensus effect
   b. magical thinking
   c. expectation fallacy
   d. vividness effect

6. The research of Bodenhausen (1990) indicates that individuals lose attentional resources during certain periods of _____.
   a. sexual arousal
   b. their circadian cycles
   c. their biorhythmic cycles
   d. the lunar cycle

7. People are more likely to rely on cognitive shortcuts when
   a. situations are complex.
   b. time is short.
   c. highly aroused.
   d. all of these answers

8. In an attempt to create positive self-regard, you decide to compare yourself to the exceptionally sharp student in your statistics class to motivate yourself toward self-improvement in statistics. This is an example of
   a. upward social comparison
   b. dispositional inference
   c. downward social comparison
   d. self-fulfilling prophecy

9. For the upcoming Powerball lottery, Jill decides to pick her own numbers because she believes it will improve her chance of winning. By picking her own numbers, Jill is creating
   a. the perception of control.
   b. a better chance of winning.
   c. a self-fulfilling prophecy.
   d. an external locus of control.

10. Research contrasting Japanese with North Americans suggests that
   a. Americans are less likely to self-enhance than are Japanese
   b. collectivistic cultures self-enhance just as much as those from individualistic cultures, but do so in different ways
   c. Japanese are more likely to self-enhance when they describe themselves as being unique and self-reliant
   d. Americans are more likely to self-enhance when they describe themselves as being cooperative and loyal.

11. Self-esteem, self-esteem instability, and threat interact with one another. In a study described in your book, which students were most likely to generate self-image boosting excuses to explain their poor performance on an exam?
    a. students with low and stable self-esteem
    b. students with high and stable self-esteem
    c. students with low and unstable self-esteem
    d. students with high and unstable self-esteem

12. According to the correspondent inference theory, we infer that an event was caused by factors within the person when
    a. the behavior was not intended.
    b. the consequences of the behavior were foreseeable.
    c. the actor had no free choice.
    d. there were no countervailing forces.

13. Your best friend doesn't show up to go out with you. You know he has an unreliable car, a huge final tomorrow, a new girlfriend, and was feeling ill earlier in the day. There are so many possibilities for why he didn't show you can't place much stock in any one cause. This is an example of
    a. the discounting principle.   b. correspondent inference.
    c. the augmenting principle.   d. upward social comparison.

14. According to Kelly's Covariation Model, we are more likely to infer that a behavior is due to an actor's situation if
    a. many other people would have acted the same way in that situation.
    b. the actor doesn't act this way in other situations.
    c. the actor has acted the same way in the same situation before.
    d. all of the above

15. We sometimes encounter situations that challenge our sense of control and lead us to desire accuracy. Which of the following situational factors would NOT increase our desire for accuracy?
    a. people who are high in the need for cognition
    b. having many other things on our mind (i.e., we have a heavy cognitive load)
    c. people experiencing mild-to-moderate sadness
    d. being interdependent with other people

TRUE-FALSE

Indicate whether each statement is true or false by circling T or F. If you decide it is false, explain why. Correct answers appear at the end of the study guide in the ANSWERS section for Chapter 3.

T   F   16. A self-fulfilling prophecy occurs when an expectation someone has about you leads you to behave in a way consistent with his or her expectations.

T   F   17. When you judge that a person's behavior is caused by his or her personality, and not by the situation, you are making a dispositional inference.

T   F   18. Plane crashes are much more salient in your mind than pneumonia, and so you assume that more people die in plane crashes that from pneumonia. This is an example of the representativeness heuristic.

T   F   19. Under heavy cognitive load, we are more likely to engage in correspondence bias.

T   F   20. When situations don't fit our expectations, we are even more likely to rely on cognitive shortcuts.

T   F   21. Collectivistic cultures self-enhance just as much as those from individualistic cultures, but they do so in different ways when describing themselves.

T   F   22. Kelly's Covariation model proposes that people determine whether a behavior corresponds to an actor's internal disposition by asking whether the behavior was intended, consequences were foreseeable, freely chosen, and occurred despite countervailing forces.

T   F   23. Accuracy-motivated strategies are used more frequently by people who are mildly sad.

ESSAY

24.   Describe how the four core social-cognitive processes of attention, interpretation, judgment, and memory contribute to the divergent opinions of Hillary Rodham Clinton.

25. Some features of the person and situation increase the likelihood that people use cognitive heuristics, whereas other features of the person and situation decreases the likelihood that people use cognitive heuristics. Imagine that you are the director of personnel at a large company and want to ensure that all job applicants are interviewed fairly and assigned to the jobs for which they are most qualified. In light of what you've learned from this chapter, what would you do to accomplish this?

When You Have Finished…

Now that you have had a chance to read this chapter and complete the activities associated with it, you may be interested in finding additional materials on this topic. The World Wide Web is a great and convenient resource for gathering additional information in a variety of areas. Listed below are web links and website descriptions that are relevant to this chapter.

Web Links and Website Descriptions
Be sure to visit Chapter 3 at the companion website: www.ablongman.com/knc3e
http://hsc.usf.edu/~kmbrown/Attribution_Theory_Overview.htm This website provides useful information on attribution theories including: the originators, purpose of the theory, year of origin, circumstances that led to model development, and key terms.
http://changingminds.org/explanations/theories/Theories.htm On the Changing Minds website you will be able to get in-depth descriptions of key terms from this chapter including: the actor-observer difference, anchoring and adjustment heuristic, augmenting principle, availability heuristic, etc.
http://www.indiana.edu/~soccog/scarch.html This website is for the social cognition paper archive. There are several types of information available including: preprints or abstracts of papers or presentations and links to information about active researchers in the area.

Comprehensive Crossword Puzzle

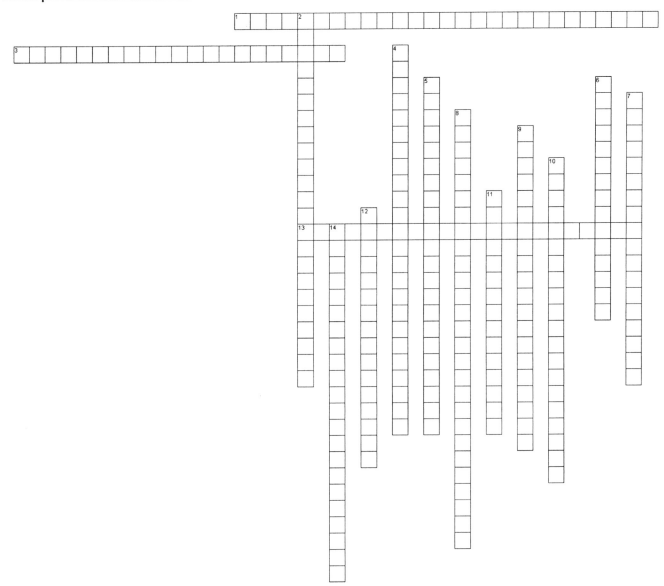

Across

1. tendency for observers to overestimate the causal influence of personality factors on behavior and to underestimate the causal role of situational influences
3. mental shortcut through which one estimates the likelihood of an event by the ease with which instances of that event come to mind
13. judgment that a persons behavior has been caused by an aspect of that person's personality

Down

2. tendency for individuals to judge their own behaviors as caused by situational forces but the behavior of others as caused by aspects of their personalities
4. process of comparing ourselves with those who are less well off
5. process of comparing ourselves with those who are better off than ourselves
6. process of thinking about oneself and others

Down Continued

7. mental shortcut used to make a judgment
8. mental shortcut through which people classify something as belonging to a certain category
9. judgmental rule that states that as the number of possible causes for an event increases our confidence that any particular cause is the true one should decrease
10. tendency to overestimate the extent to which others agree with us
11. tendency to take personal credit for our successes and to blame external factors for our failures
12. theory that proposes that people determine the cause of an actors behavior by assessing - consensus, distinctiveness, and consistency
14. when an initially inaccurate expectation leads to actions that cause the expectation to come true

Puzzle created with Puzzlemaker at DiscoverySchool.com

 PRESENTING THE SELF

Before You Read...

In this chapter you will learn about the importance of self-presentation, sometimes referred to as impression management. You will find that we self-present to obtain desirable resources, to help "construct" our self-image, and to help social encounters run more smoothly. You will also discover the circumstances in which people are more likely to self-present, the three goals served by self-presentation, the strategies people use to reach these goals, and the person and situation factors related to them.

Chapter Learning Objectives

After reading this chapter, you should be able to:

- Define self-presentation

- List the three major reasons why people self-present

- Explain public self-consciousness

- Describe when people are concerned with strategic self-presentation

- Discuss the difference between high and low self-monitors in a social situation

- Discuss social anxiety as a self-presentational failure and describe situations in which people experience it

- Describe the techniques used to detect deception and under what circumstances, if any, people are better at detecting lies

- Outline the four strategies people use to appear likable to others

- Describe how you can detect a false smile

- Explain the cultural differences found in the social acceptability of boastfulness

- Describe gender differences with regard to the goal of being liked

- Describe the circumstances in which people especially want to be seen as likable

- Give an example of a multiple audience dilemma and explain how people solve such dilemmas

- Outline the four strategies people use to appear competent to others

- Define self-handicapping. Explain how and why people self-handicap and how self-esteem influences the likelihood of self-handicapping.

- Explain competence motivation and its relationship to shyness

- Describe the settings in which people wish to appear competent

- Explain the interpersonal cycle of self-promotion

- Outline the four strategies people use to convey status and power to others

- Describe the nonverbal expressions people use to communicate images of status and power

- Describe gender differences associated with status and power and how self-presentational dilemma affects aspiring women

- Describe the circumstances in which people are especially interested in conveying status and power

- Explain how the gender of an audience influences the strategies adopted by male and female presenters

As You Read…

KEY TERMS!
Listed below are the key terms from the chapter that are essential for your understanding of the material. Refer to the definitions from your textbook; they are located at the end of this chapter, within the text in boldface, and in the margins throughout this chapter. In order to enhance your recall ability for these terms, you may want to consider making flashcards which include a term on one side, and a definition on the other (with perhaps a brief example that makes sense to you).

Basking in reflected glory	Ingratiation	Self-presentation
Body language	Multiple audience dilemma	Self-promotion
Competence motivation	Public self-consciousness	Shyness
Cutting off reflected failure	Self-handicapping	Social anxiety
Dramaturgical perspective	Self-monitoring	

THE AMAZING LIVES OF FRED DEMARA

In the beginning of this chapter your authors introduced Fred Demara, a.k.a. "The Great Imposter." Demara played many roles, including that of a surgeon, a college professor, and a prison warden. Discuss three different self-presentational techniques from the chapter that Demara might have employed to effectively convince thousands of people that he was qualified for high-level jobs for which he lacked legitimate credentials.

STRATEGIES USED TO PROMOTE SELF-PRESENTATION GOALS

People employ a variety of strategies to get others to like them, appear competent, and convey status and power. For each of the three self-presentation goals, list the strategies people use to promote the goal and provide an example of each.

	Ingratiation Strategies	Example
GOAL **To Appear Likable**	▪	▪
	▪	▪
	▪	▪
	▪	▪

	Ingratiation Strategies	Example
GOAL **To Appear Competent**	▪	▪
	▪	▪
	▪	▪
	▪	▪

	Ingratiation Strategies	Example
GOAL **To Convey Status and Power**	▪	▪
	▪	▪
	▪	▪
	▪	▪

SUMMARY OF THE GOALS SERVED BY SELF-PRESENTATION

Complete the chart below to help you summarize the goals served by self-presentation and the factors related to them. If you need assistance, see page 132 in your text (but be sure to use your own words in this exercise, rather than just copying).

The Goal	The Person	The Situation	Interactions
Appearing Likable	• •	• •	•
Appearing Competent	• •	• •	• •
Conveying Status and Power	•	• •	•

MATCHING: KEY TERMS

Matching! Match each definition on the left side of the page with the concept on the right side of the page. Each concept on the right should be used only once.

___ 1. Process of distancing ourselves from unsuccessful, low-status others or events

A. Basking in reflected glory

___ 2. Tendency to have a chronic awareness of oneself as being in the public eye

B. Body language

___ 3. Situation in which a person needs to present different images to different audiences, often at the same time

C. Competence motivation

___ 4. Tendencies to be chronically concerned with one's public image and to adjust one's actions to fit the needs of the current situation

D. Cutting off reflected failure

___ 5. Process of presenting our associations with successful, high-status others or events

E. Dramaturgical perspective

___ 6. Desire to perform effectively

F. Ingratiation

___ 7. Process through which we try to control the impressions people form of us; synonymous with impression management

G. Multiple audience dilemma

___ 8. Popular term for nonverbal behaviors like facial expressions, posture, body orientation, and hand gestures

H. Public self-consciousness

___ 9. An attempt to get others to see us as competent

I. Self-handicapping

___ 10. The fear people experience while doubting that they'll be able to create a desired impression

J. Self-monitoring

___ 11. Tendency to feel tense, worried, or awkward in novel social situations and with unfamiliar people

K. Self-presentation

___ 12. An attempt to get others to like us

L. Self-promotion

___ 13. Behavior of withdrawing effort or creating obstacles to one's future successes

M. Shyness

___ 14. Perspective that much of social interaction can be thought of as a play, with actors, performances, settings, scripts, props, roles, and so forth

N. Social anxiety

PUTTING IT ALL TOGETHER: THOUGHT QUESTIONS

Your book described different characteristics of people who are high self-monitors versus low self-monitors, and generally pointed out the advantages of being a high self-monitor. Can you think of situations in which it might be detrimental to be a high self-monitor? Design an experiment to test your hypothesis.

There appear to be quite a few gender differences in self-presentation. Two tactics of self-presentation described in the book were "basking in reflected glory" and "cutting off reflected failure." These are both tools of self-presentation used to increase status and power by personal association. Do you think that there are gender differences in these two strategies? Base your answer on what you've learned so far. Can you think of a way to test your hypothesis experimentally?

After You Read...Practice Tests

Practice Test 1

1. The process through which we try to control the impression people form of us is called
   a. impression management.
   b. social perception.
   c. self-monitoring.
   d. public self-consciousness.

2. In many social encounters, Lisa considers herself an actor playing a role in a play. This is consistent with the text's discussion of
   a. public self-consciousness.
   b. self-promotion
   c. basking in reflected glory
   d. dramaturgical perspective

3. We are more likely to focus on self-presentation when
   a. observers can influence whether or not we obtain our goals.
   b. our goals are important to us.
   c. we think observers have impressions different from the ones we want to project.
   d. all of the above

4. _____ refers to the fear people experience while doubting that they'll be able to create a desired impression.
   a. Competence motivation
   b. Self-handicapping
   c. Shyness
   d. Social anxiety

5. In the Zanna and Pack (1975) experiment, women anticipated interacting with men who were either highly desirable or not and who held either traditional or untraditional views of women. The findings of this experiment demonstrate that
   a. people sometimes change their public opinions to create similarity with desirable others, in order to get desirable others to like them.
   b. people will express liking for others when compliments are given.
   c. people will make themselves look more physically attractive to gain acceptance.
   d. people will act modest around desirable individuals with different viewpoints.

6. What is one explanation why ingratiation is relatively more important for women than for men?
   a. Women have higher levels of testosterone.
   b. Being seen as having high status and power is also more important for women.
   c. Society expects women to be more likable, so it rewards them for acting that way.
   d. Men tend to be naturally better at ingratiation, so women must work harder at it.

7. _____ refers to a situation in which a person needs to present different images to different audiences, often at the same time.
   a. Public self-consciousness
   b. Multiple audience dilemma
   c. Self-monitoring
   d. Self-promotion

8. Staging performances, self-handicapping, and making excuses are all self-promotional strategies used to get others to see them as
    a. likable
    b. having power and status
    c. competent
    d. seeking social support

9. Before the baseball game begins, Jeff is already complaining of the blinding sun in the outfield and how it will interfere with his ability to catch the ball. Despite the sun, Jeff manages to catch several balls. Which self-promotion strategy is Jeff using?
    a. staging performances of competence
    b. displaying the trappings of competence
    c. claiming competence
    d. claiming obstacles to competence

10. What is one reason that the judge's bench is always placed at a higher level than all the other chairs in the courtroom?
    a. judges generally can't see too well.
    b. to convey high status and power
    c. to convey competence
    d. for the purpose of ingratiation

Practice Test 2

1. In which of the following situations is self-presentation most likely to be important for Heather?
    a. Heather is the manager of a clothing store, and must fire one of her employees.
    b. Heather has a date with her boyfriend of two years, and they are going to a new restaurant.
    c. Heather has to ask permission from a professor to take a class, but she got a "D" in the last class she took from this professor.
    d. Heather is curled up alone at home reading a novel.

2. _____ is the tendency to be chronically concerned with one's public image and to adjust one's actions to fit the needs of the current situation.
    a. Self-monitoring
    b. Basking in reflected glory
    c. Public self-consciousness
    d. Dramaturgical perspective

3. The accuracy of the polygraph decreases when
    a. the suspect doesn't believe that the test is effective.
    b. people who experience little guilt and anxiety are questioned for their crime.
    c. innocent suspects become anxious when asked about engaging in illicit activities.
    d. all of the above

4. If someone flashed a true enjoyment smile at you, what would this look like?
    a. Their lips would be pulled back toward their cheekbones.
    b. Their eyes would be narrowed.
    c. They would have "crows-feet" wrinkles at the corners of the eyes.
    d. all of the above

5. Which of the following self-presentation strategies most directly increases one's likeability?
    a. conspicuous consumption
    b. associating oneself with successful others
    c. making oneself physically attractive
    d. staging favorable performances

6.   Emily is extremely bright. When she is inducted into the National Honor Society she says she deserves it because she's so intelligent. Who will be most likely to tolerate this sort of boasting?
    a. African Americans
    b. European Americans
    c. Asian Americans
    d. Hispanic Americans

7.   A 10-year old gymnast is about to perform on the balance beam, her best event. Just before she begins, she shouts to her father who is talking with other parents, "Daddy, watch!" This is an example of which of the following self-promotion strategies?
    a. staging performances of competence
    b. displaying the trappings of competence
    c. claiming competence
    d. claiming obstacles to competence

8.   As described in your book, which of the following is an example of self-handicapping?
    a. choosing unattainable goals
    b. avoiding practice
    c. taking drugs or drinking alcohol
    d. all of the above

9.   According to the findings of Sadalla and Krull (1995), why are people reluctant to recycle?
    a. They don't want to be viewed as being of lesser status.
    b. They may be liked less if they recycle.
    c. They don't want to be viewed as incompetent.
    d. They don't want to be associated with radical political groups.

10.   Which of the following is NOT an example of a strategy people use to achieve the goal of self-promotion?
    a. A little boy is up to bat, but before he gets to the plate, he turns to the stands and yells "Hey Mom, watch me!!"
    b. The boss walks up to one of her employees, stands right beside his chair, looks him straight in the eye and says "How's that project coming along?"
    c. A student tells his professor that he is doing very well in all his classes.
    d. A businessman has his assistant call him several times during a meeting with a client so that he looks very busy.

Practice Test 3

1.   Self-presentation is synonymous with _____.
    a. impression management
    b. social perception
    c. self-monitoring
    d. public self-consciousness

2.   In an experiment by Gilovich et al. (2000), college students wore a t-shirt bearing a picture of Barry Manilow and entered a room where others were working. Most of the observers didn't notice the out-dated t-shirt. This experiment illustrates a phenomenon known as
    a. the multiple audience dilemma.
    b. basking in reflected glory.
    c. the spotlight effect.
    d. dramaturgical perspective.

3. What is the best way to detect a lie?
    a. polygraph examination
    b. thermal imaging techniques
    c. look at what people say and how they say it
    d. fMRI imaging techniques

4. Asking people for advice, smiling at them, and flattering them are all strategies of
    a. self-monitoring.   b. dominance displays.
    c. ingratiation.   d. visual dominance behavior.

5. Which of the following best describes the correlation between income and physical attractiveness?
    a. Physically unattractive people tend to work harder and make more money.
    b. Physically attractive people tend to make more money than unattractive people.
    c. Physically attractive people make more money when they are young, but less money after age forty-six.
    d. Psychologists have found no significant correlation between physical attractiveness and income.

6. Which strategy is effective when confronted with the multiple audience dilemma?
    a. segregate the audience
    b. texture the message so it means different things to different audiences
    c. present different messages on different communication channels
    d. all of these are effective

7. During a job interview, Eric openly talks about his accomplishments in advertising and brings letters of reference from highly credible sources. Which self-promotional strategy is Eric using?
    a. staging performances of competence   b. claiming competence
    c. claiming obstacles to competence   d. self-handicapping

8. Which of the following is NOT a reason that shy people tend to be underemployed and relatively unsuccessful in their careers?
    a. They are too self-preoccupied to effectively appear competent.
    b. They are more likely to self-handicap, and thus fail more often.
    c. They are less likely to boldly promote their competence.
    d. They don't take advantage of handicaps in the situation.

9. Which of the following is an effective strategy for enhancing the appearance of status and power?
    a. give things away   b. recycle
    c. ask people to buy you drinks   d. all of the above

10. Cialdini et al. (1976) found that college students were more likely to wear their school's team logos on days after the football team had won. This is an example of gaining social status by
    a. staging performances of competence.   b. self-monitoring.
    c. self-promoting.   d. basking in reflected glory.

67

Comprehensive Test

(Note: Items 1-15 are multiple-choice questions, items 16-23 are true-false questions, and 24-25 are essay questions.)

1. Why do people self-present?
    a. to acquire desirable resources
    b. to help "construct" our self-images
    c. to enable our social encounters to run more smoothly
    d. all of the above

2. Which of the following is true about people who are high self-monitors?
    a. They are more concerned with their own behavior than with the impressions others form of them.
    b. They are less likely to achieve leadership positions.
    c. They act the same way, regardless of the situation.
    d. They are better at detecting when others are being manipulative.

3. _____ tend to be especially good at detecting deception.
    a. Customs inspectors   b. U.S. Secret Service agents
    c. Psychiatrists   d. Judges

4. You have your coworker subtly mention to your boss how much you respect him. Will this form of ingratiation work to your advantage?
    a. Yes, it can be successful and is perceived as non-manipulative.
    b. No, it can backfire and appear manipulative.
    c. It depends on how your coworker is perceived by your boss which makes this strategy extremely risky.
    d. none of the above

5. Which of the following is NOT a goal of self-presentation?
    a. appearing likable   b. appearing competent
    c. getting information   d. conveying status and power

6. Which of the following is NOT true of false smiles?
    a. False smiles are less symmetrical.
    b. False smiles are jerkier, less smooth.
    c. False smiles are held longer than natural.
    d. False smiles involve the movement of two major facial muscle groups which includes the movement of the lips and eyes.

7. What are the benefits of being attractive?
    a. Attractive people are seen as more honest.
    b. Attractive people are more likely to be hired for managerial positions and elected to public office.
    c. Attractive people receive lesser fines and bail judgments in misdemeanor cases, and shorter sentences in felony cases.
    d. all of the above are benefits of being attractive

8. There is a cultural disparity between African Americans and European Americans in the social acceptability of boastfulness. African Americans tend to like _____ more than European Americans.
   a. truthful braggers
   b. untruthful braggers
   c. nonbraggers
   d. truthful braggers and nonbraggers

9. Who would be more likely to behave in an ingratiating manner?
   a. a female
   b. a person with high levels of testosterone
   c. a person with high status
   d. a low self-monitor

10. Serena owns her own business, and whenever a client enters her office she picks up the phone and pretends to talk to another client while simultaneously typing up a report on her expensive computer. Which self-promotion strategy is Serena using?
   a. staging performances of competence
   b. displaying the trappings of competence
   c. claiming competence
   d. claiming obstacles to competence

11. In the Baumeister, Hutton, and Tice (1989) experiment, when one participant promoted him/herself as strongly as possible
   a. the other participant was more modest in self-presentation.
   b. the other participant self-promoted more.
   c. the other participant requested that the self-promoter act more modestly.
   d. the other participant rated the self-promoter as more physically attractive.

12. _____ is the process of distancing ourselves from unsuccessful, low-status others or events.
   a. Basking in reflected glory
   b. Cutting off reflected failure
   c. Social anxiety
   d. Public self-consciousness

13. Which of the following is NOT true of the nonverbal behavior of those with higher status?
   a. High status individuals tend to take up more space and lay claim to greater territory.
   b. High status individuals tend to maintain a high level of eye contact when speaking but pay less attention when listening.
   c. High status individuals are more likely to interrupt others.
   d. High status individuals are less likely to touch others.

14. According to your book, men are most likely to respond aggressively when insulted in front of an audience when
   a. the audience is female.
   b. the audience is mixed (both men and women).
   c. the audience is male.
   d. there is a multiple audience dilemma.

15. Which of the following factors may have contributed to Hillary Clinton being disliked?
   a. Her success as a lawyer in a male dominated field
   b. Her direct communication style
   c. Her ambition
   d. all of the above

TRUE-FALSE

Indicate whether each statement is true or false by circling T or F. If you decide it is false, explain why. Correct answers appear at the end of the study guide in the ANSWERS section for Chapter 4.

T   F   16.   Public self-consciousness is the degree to which people believe others pay attention to them.

T   F   17.   The polygraph is not a highly accurate method of detecting lies.

T   F   18.   We can express liking for others via many nonverbal behaviors such as head nodding, eye contact, and smiling.

T   F   19.   It is easy for people under normal circumstances to detect the differences between a false smile and an enjoyment smile.

T   F   20.   Staging performances is one strategy of self-promotion that people use to demonstrate competence.

T   F   21.   Shy people are very nervous in social situations, so they tend to self-handicap more than non-shy people.

T   F   22.   Men often display dominance through their nonverbal behavior, whereas women do not.

T   F   23.   Presentations of status and power are more important to men.

ESSAY

24.   Describe the polygraph. What is the underlying assumption behind its use? How accurate is it at detecting deception? What alternative approaches are researchers examining as a means for detecting deception?

25. List and describe the four strategies people use to convince others of their high status and power. Provide an example to illustrate each strategy.

When You Have Finished...

Now that you have had a chance to read this chapter and complete the activities associated with it, you may be interested in finding additional materials on this topic. The World Wide Web is a great and convenient resource for gathering additional information in a variety of areas. Listed below are web links and website descriptions that are relevant to this chapter.

Web Links and Website Descriptions
Be sure to visit Chapter 4 at the companion website: www.ablongman.com/knc3e
http://www.anakin.com/pretender/who.html This website provides a brief biography of the two most famous impostors of the 20th century -- Frank Abagnale Jr. (as chronicled in *Catch Me If You Can*) and Ferdinand Waldo Demara (as chronicled in *The Great Impostor* and *The Rascal and the Road*).
http://nonverbal.ucsc.edu/ This web site gives you a chance to learn more about nonverbal communication and the chance to test your ability at identifying types of nonverbal communication.
http://crs.uvm.edu/gopher/nerl/personal/comm/f.html This is a site containing additional material on non-verbal expression.
http://www.shyness.com/shyness-institute.html The Shyness Institute is a non-profit research corporation dedicated to research regarding shyness, social anxiety, and related anxiety disorders. This website includes information on The Social Fitness Model, handouts and questionnaires, and selected readings.

Comprehensive Crossword Puzzle

Across

4. Tendencies to be chronically concerned with one's public image and to adjust one's actions to fit the needs of the current situation

11. Desire to perform effectively

13. An attempt to get others to see us as competent

14. Tendency to have a chronic awareness of oneself as being in the public eye

Down

1. Process of presenting our associations with successful, high-status others or events
2. Process of distancing ourselves from unsuccessful, low-status others or events
3. Process through which we try to control the impressions people form of us; synonymous with impression management
5. Behavior of withdrawing effort or creating obstacles to one's future successes
6. Situation in which a person needs to present different images to different audiences, often at the same time
7. Perspective that much of social interaction can be thought of as a play, with actors, performances, settings, scripts, props, roles, and so forth
8. Tendency to feel tense, worried, or awkward in novel social situations and with unfamiliar people
9. The fear people experience while doubting that they'll be able to create a desired impression
10. Popular term for nonverbal behaviors like facial expressions, posture, body orientation, and hand gestures
12. An attempt to get others to like us

Puzzle created with Puzzlemaker at DiscoverySchool.com

ATTITUDES AND PERSUASION

Before You Read...

In this chapter you will explore the nature of attitudes and how persuasive messages are designed to change your attitudes. Specifically, you will learn how attitudes are formed, what determines their strength, and the factors that influence attitude-behavior consistencies. Next you will discover why researchers use covert measures and after-only designs to measure persuasion. You will then be given a framework for understanding how attitude change occurs when exposed to a persuasive message via self-talk. You will learn how dual process models recognize that attitude change can occur through either central or peripheral routes of processing based upon the persuasive message's arguments. Finally, you will examine why individuals may yield to persuasive messages: in order to hold a more accurate view of the world, be consistent with themselves, or gain social approval.

Chapter Learning Objectives

After reading this chapter, you should be able to:

- Explain how attitudes are formed via classical conditioning, operant conditioning, and observational learning

- Describe attitude strength in terms of commitment and embeddedness

- Outline the factors that influence the likelihood of attitude-behavior consistency

- Describe Fishbein and Ajzen's theory of planned behavior

- Offer a definition of persuasion

- Describe when persuasion researchers prefer nonreactive measurement techniques to self-report measures

- Explain why after-only designs are preferred by scientists who study persuasion

- Describe the cognitive response model proposed by Greenwald

- Explain how inoculation and counterarguments are used to defeat persuasive messages

- Explain the elaboration likelihood model to persuasion

- Outline the factors that influence a person's motivation to process a message centrally

- List the three reasons why an individual might yield to a persuasive message

- Explain the three forms of shortcut evidence people use to judge accuracy

- Explain how a person's mood and their involvement in an issue affects persuasion

- Explain what features of the situation actually reduce the desire for accuracy

- Explain why it is important to accompany high fear messages with specific recommendations for decreasing the danger

- Describe how expertise of the communicator and complexity of the message interact

- Describe the consistency principle

- Explain Heider's balance theory and how advertisers capitalize on balance theory

- Explain Festinger's cognitive dissonance theory

- Explain the desire for cognitive consistency

- Describe the different emphasis placed on advertisements in individualistic versus collectivistic cultures

- Define impression motivation

- Explain why high or low self-monitors are more likely to be persuaded

- Explain gender differences related to persuasion

- Describe how the expectation of discussion affects one's position on an issue

- Describe how self-monitoring and the expectation of discussion affect the goal of social approval

As You Read...

> **KEY TERMS!**
>
> Listed below are the key terms from the chapter that are essential for your understanding of the material. Refer to the definitions from your textbook; they are located at the end of this chapter, within the text in boldface, and in the margins throughout this chapter. In order to enhance your recall ability for these terms, you may want to consider making flashcards which include a term on one side, and a definition on the other (with perhaps a brief example that makes sense to you).

Balance theory	Cognitive dissonance	Nonreactive measurement
Classical conditioning	Dual process model of persuasion	Observational learning
Cognitive response model	Elaboration likelihood model	Operant conditioning
Consistency principle	Impression motivation	Persuasion
Counterargument	Inoculation procedure	Postdecisional dissonance
Counterattitudinal action	Need for cognition	

THE CHANGING STORY OF PETER REILLY

In the beginning of this chapter your authors introduced Peter Reilly, a man who falsely confessed to murdering his mother. Please describe the techniques used by Reilly's interrogators to manufacture an admission of murder. Why does the initial prosecution team still believe that Reilly is guilty even after hidden evidence exonerated him?

FISHBEIN AND AJZEN'S THEORY OF PLANNED BEHAVIOR

Your text discusses Fishbein and Ajzen's theory of planned behavior which states that behavioral intentions are the best predictor of a person's behavior; intentions are influenced by one's attitude toward the specific behavior, subjective norms regarding the behavior, and perceived behavioral control. For this exercise determine whether or not Greg or Beth will engage in a particular behavior using the theory of planned behavior.

Will Greg purchase a gun?
Greg has always liked playing with toy guns. When he became a teenager, Greg was fascinated with all violent movies that had epic gun scenes. Greg's good friends, active supporters of gun control laws, are terrified by the thought of anyone owning a gun. Greg was recently in trouble with the police and knows that to own a gun requires a background check.

Will Beth get her eyebrow pierced?
Every time Beth sees a person with a body piercing she is completely captivated by how "cool" it looks. In fact, several of her friends have their body pierced and they have assured Beth that it is a quick and simple procedure with minimal pain.

Is Greg's attitude positive or negative towards owning a gun?

Is Beth's attitude positive or negative towards getting a piercing?

What do important other's think of Greg owning a gun?

What do important other's think of Beth getting her piercing?

Will purchasing the gun be difficult or easy for Greg to perform?

Will Beth's eyebrow piercing be difficult or easy to perform?

Will Greg purchase a gun?

Will Beth get her eyebrow pierced?

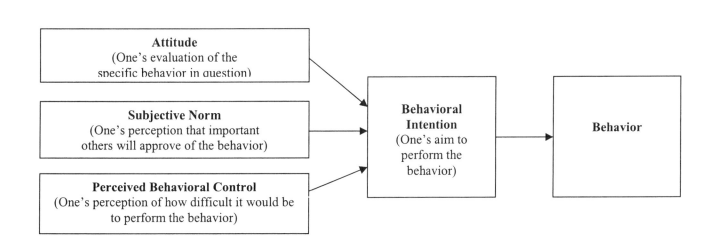

MEASURING ATTITUDE CHANGE

What is a before-after design? Provide an example to illustrate this research design. Please use the table below to help design your study. How would you design a study to eliminate pretest sensitization? See pages 146 through 148 in your text for help with this exercise.

Before-After Design				
Random Assignment to Groups	Before-Measure	Message	After-Measure	Conclusion
Experimental Group				
Control Group				

What is an after-only design? Provide an example to illustrate this research design. Please use the table below to help design your study. Why do persuasion researchers prefer to use the after-only design?

After-Only Design				
Random Assignment to Groups	Before-Measure	Message	After-Measure	Conclusion
Experimental Group				
Control Group				

FOCUS ON APPLICATION: SMOKING THE TOBACCO COMPANIES WITH COUNTERARGUMENTS

Why did the tobacco industry propose to ban all advertising of their products on radio and television? What were the prevailing forces surrounding the decision to abandon their most influential sales route to customers? How did the ban impact sales? What lesson did the tobacco companies learn from the use of counterarguments by tobacco opponents? See pages 150 through 151 in your text for help with this exercise.

DUAL ROUTES TO SUCCESSFUL PERSUASION

Describe the elaboration likelihood model by Petty and Cacioppo (1986) and complete the flow chart below. See pages 151 through 152 in your text for help with this exercise.

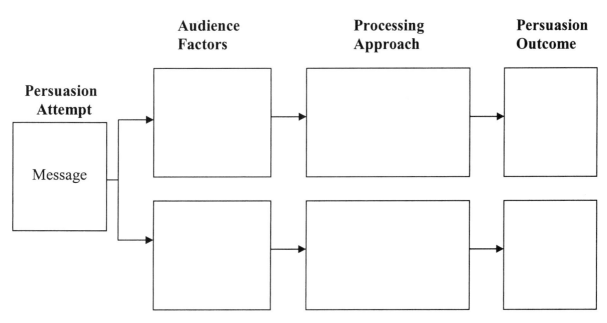

SEEKING ACCURACY: WHEN SOMETHING BAD MAKES SOMETHING GOOD

The Volkswagen advertisement in your text, for the VW Beatle, is an example of one advertising company's approach to selling cars in the United States – *"Ugly is only skin-deep."* How did this ad make VW sales in the United States so successful?

BEING CONSISTENT: BALANCE THEORY

Michael Jackson rose to fame as the lead singer of the Jackson 5 during the 1960s. Michael's debut solo album in the late 1970s earned him a Grammy and three American Music Awards. His 1982 album, *Thriller*, is one of the best-selling albums of all time and was awarded nine Grammys and eight American Music Awards which launched Jackson to pop icon status. Recently, Michael Jackson was issued a warrant for his arrest on "multiple counts" of allegedly molesting a child. It is the second time in ten years that such allegations have been made against the performer. Despite these charges, fans and friends of Jackson believe that he is "absolutely innocent" of child molestation charges and that he will be "vindicated." How do these adoring fans and friends handle these charges? How does this information fit with balance theory?

SUMMARY OF PERSUASION GOALS

Complete the chart below to help you summarize the goals served by persuasion and the factors related to them. If you need assistance, see page 172 in your text (but be sure to use your own words in this exercise, rather than just copying)

The Goal	The Person	The Situation	Interactions
Seeking Accuracy	• •	• •	• •
Being Consistent	• •	• •	•
Gaining Social Approval	• •	•	•

MATCHING: KEY TERMS

Matching! Match each definition on the left side of the page with the concept on the right side of the page. Each concept on the right should only be used once.

__	1.	Argument that challenges and opposes other arguments	A.	Balance theory
__	2.	Process through which people learn by being rewarded or punished	B.	Cognitive response model
__	3.	Motivation to achieve approval by making a good impression on others	C.	Consistency principle
__	4.	Conflict one feels about a decision that could possibly be wrong	D.	Counterargument
__	5.	Principle that people will change their attitudes, beliefs, perceptions, and actions to make them consistent with each other	E.	Counterattitudinal action
__	6.	Model of persuasive communication that holds that there are two routes to attitude change – central route and peripheral route	F.	Cognitive dissonance
__	7.	Measurement that does not change a subject's response while recording them	G.	Dual process model of persuasion
__	8.	Technique for increasing individuals' resistance to a strong argument by first giving them weak, easily defeated versions of it	H.	Elaboration likelihood model
__	9.	Unpleasant state of psychological arousal resulting from an inconsistency within one's important attitudes, beliefs, or behaviors	I.	Impression motivation
__	10.	Heider's theory that people prefer harmony and consistency in their views of the world	J.	Inoculation procedure
__	11.	Change in a private attitude or belief as a result of receiving a message	K.	Need for cognition
__	12.	Tendency to enjoy and engage in deliberative thought	L.	Nonreactive measurement
__	13.	Model that accounts for the two basic ways that attitude change occurs-with and without much thought	M.	Persuasion
__	14.	Behavior that is inconsistent with an existing attitude	N.	Operant Conditioning
__	15.	A theory that locates the most direct cause of persuasion in the self-talk of the persuasion target	O.	Postdecisional dissonance

PUTTING IT ALL TOGETHER: THOUGHT QUESTIONS

Imagine that you are a political advisor, and your candidate comes to you and says that a tax increase is going to be necessary. The candidate says that since virtually everyone is against tax increases, he or she needs a way to persuade the constituency that a tax increase is a good idea. How would you advise your candidate? What could he or she do to persuade people that the tax increase is indeed necessary? Use as many of the principles of persuasion discussed in the chapter as you need to.

In the early days of the HIV/AIDS epidemic, most of the appeals for behavior change came in the form of simple messages like "AIDS Kills." These efforts were not particularly successful by themselves. Currently, HIV/AIDS messages stress all the ways that you can prevent yourself from getting HIV, such as ceasing to engage in high-risk behavior. These messages have been more successful at inducing behavior change. Given what you learned in the chapter, why were the early efforts unsuccessful? Why are more recent efforts more successful? Think of another health behavior (e.g., seatbelt use, exercise) and design a persuasive appeal to try to change people's attitudes and behaviors with regard to the behavior.

After You Read...Practice Tests

Practice Test 1

1. Which of the following is an example of acquiring an attitude through operant conditioning?
    a. You meet Mark for the first time in a hot, sticky room; afterwards you report not liking him very much.
    b. Jeffrey, a five year old, screams from the top of his lungs "Fords are superior to Chevys!" Jeffrey's father smiles at him and gives him a "high five."
    c. Samantha witnessed her sister being bitten by a dog and now she is afraid of all dogs.
    d. Nicholas has negative views of smoking ever since his aunt died of lung cancer.

2. Attitudes toward the death penalty or censorship are much more likely to be influenced by _____ than are attitudes toward teenage drivers.
    a. classical conditioning
    b. operant conditioning
    b. observational learning
    d. heredity

3. The political campaign study by Fazio and Williams (1986) asked potential voters to express their attitudes toward presidential candidates Ronald Regan and Walter Mondale. Their findings suggest that
    a. knowledge of the candidates did not play a role in whom they voted for.
    b. the quicker potential voters indicated their preferences, the more likely they voted in line with those preferences in the voting booth several months later.
    c. the quicker potential voters indicated their preferences, the less likely they voted in line with those preferences in the voting booth several months later.
    d. attitude accessibility does not stimulate voting actions.

4. Persuasion can be defined as
    a. a change in a private attitude or belief as a result of receiving a message.
    b. a tendency to enjoy and engage in deliberate thought.
    c. a message that challenges our current thinking.
    d. a change in the way we think due to the influence of others we know and like.

5. When are covert measuring techniques preferred over self-report measures?
    a. when people have a good reason to be less than honest about their true feelings
    b. when there is no good reason for people to hide their feelings
    c. under most circumstances covert measures are preferred because they are nonreactive
    d. no preference for either technique, the researcher should do whatever is easier

6. How did anti-tobacco forces, such as the American Cancer Society, undercut tobacco ad effectiveness?
    a. increased counterarguments
    b. increased cognitive dissonance
    c. increased the anti-tobacco ad budget
    d. increased the actor-observer difference

7. Which of the following are characteristics of a credible communicator?
   a. trustworthiness and consistency
   b. expertise and consistency
   c. expertise and trustworthiness
   d. consistency and impression motivation

8. In order to reduce denial as a way to cope with fear producing messages, the message should be given
   a. by an expert.
   b. with specific recommendations for behavior that will diminish the danger.
   c. in a clear, concise manner.
   d. in a way that allows for vivid imagery of the fearful message.

9. In the Festinger and Carlsmith (1959) cognitive dissonance study, why did participants who were paid $1 to lie to the next participant change their attitudes toward the enjoyableness of the task?
   a. They were upset that they didn't get $20, so they didn't mind lying.
   b. Participants who were paid $1 got to do a more enjoyable task.
   c. They didn't feel that they had sufficient justification for lying, so they decided that they must have enjoyed the task after all.
   d. Participants who got $20 experienced cognitive dissonance, so they enjoyed the task less.

10. Many advertisers appeal to consumers by promoting a desired image associated with their product. According to your book, who is most susceptible to these appeals?
    a. low self-monitors
    b. high self-monitors
    c. men
    d. people low in preference for consistency

Practice Test 2

1. _____ is the process through which people associate new objects or events with feelings about previously experienced events.
   a. Classical conditioning
   b. Operant conditioning
   b. Observational learning
   d. Heredity

2. _____ causes us to be able to resist messages contrary to our attitude, while _____ makes it difficult for our attitudes to move in any direction.
   a. Consistency; commitment
   b. Commitment; embeddedness
   c. Dissonance; embeddedness
   d. Embeddedness; commitment

3. Jordan thinks that his family will hate the idea of him getting a tattoo. His intention to get a tattoo is weakened because of
   a. subjective norms
   b. perceived behavioral control
   c. his attitudes toward the piercing
   d. cognitive interpretation

4. How did Cialdini and Baumann (1981) predict the outcome of a presidential election?
   a. They observed voter behavior before entering the voting booth.
   b. They observed that voters at the polls were less likely to litter flyers they found on their car windshields if the flyers' message supported their favored candidate.
   c. They observed that voters at the polls were more likely to litter flyers they found on their car windshields if the flyers' message supported their favored candidate.
   d. They timed how quickly the voter responded to questions regarding particular candidates

5. What was the model of persuasion that added this important insight: The effectiveness of a persuasive message depends on the self-talk people engage in after being exposed to the message?
   a. dual process model
   b. balance theory model
   c. cognitive dissonance model
   d. cognitive response model

6. According to dual process models of persuasion, how should you present your message in order to have lasting attitude change that resists fading and counterattacks?
   a. Focus your audience on surface features of the communicator, such as attractiveness.
   b. Distract your audience with other stimuli besides your message.
   c. Present a large number of arguments.
   d. Focus your audience on the quality of your strongest arguments.

7. A single expert opinion news story in the *New York Times* is associated with a _____ percent shift in public opinion nationwide and _____ when the expert's statement is aired on national television.
   a. 10; doubles
   b. 2; doubles
   c. 1; triples
   d. 5; doubles

8. What two techniques make an idea more cognitively ready?
   a. present the idea several times and imagine the idea or event
   b. arousal and consistent messages
   c. salience and the level of self-monitoring that is occurring
   d. availability heuristics and representativeness heuristics

9. Why were jurors in the Cooper, Bennett, and Sukel (1996) study more likely to believe the testimony of the highly expert doctor only when the testimony was complex?
   a. The jurors who heard the simple testimony were told the doctor was only a moderate expert.
   b. The highly expert doctor gave more complex testimony.
   c. When the testimony was too hard to understand, the jurors had to rely on the reputation of the expert.
   d. The jurors were bored by they simple testimony and paid more attention to the complex testimony.

10. Who is more persuaded under private circumstances?
    a. women
    b. high self-monitors
    c. men
    d. none of these answers is correct

Practice Test 3

1. The process through which people learn by being rewarded and punished is called
    a. classical conditioning
    b. operant conditioning
    b. observational learning
    d. heredity

2. In a study by Krosnick et al. (1992), students viewed a series of slides of a woman engaging in daily routine activities and they were asked to form an impression of her. Before each slide, they were subliminally exposed to photos of either positive or negative objects. What did these researchers find?
    a. subliminally exposed photos had no effect on the impressions formed of the woman
    b. students exposed to subliminally negative objects resulted in positive attitudes toward the woman
    c. students exposed to subliminally positive objects formed a more favorable attitude toward the woman
    d. since the objects were subliminally exposed, no one noticed the slides and all ratings of the woman were based on whether they thought the woman was attractive

3. What factor/s influence the likelihood that a person's attitude will be consistent with his or her behavior?
    a. knowledge
    b. personal relevance
    c. attitude accessibility
    d. all of the these answers are correct

4. What is the advantage of conducting a study with an after-only design with random assignment to conditions?
    a. If you find a difference between the experimental and control groups, you can assume your message caused the effect.
    b. If you don't find a difference between the experimental and control groups, you can assume that random assignment failed.
    c. If you find a difference between the experimental and control groups, you can assume your experimental group was sensitized to your message.
    d. If you don't find a difference between the experimental and control groups, you can attribute it to pre-existing differences between the groups.

5. Which of the following is NOT an effective method of inhibiting the formation of counterarguments in your audience?
    a. Have an expert espouse your position.
    b. Give your audience lots of time to make their decision.
    c. Force your audience to make a decision quickly.
    d. Distract your audience with a burdensome task.

6. When persuasive messages are based on the quality of the message arguments and people are motivated to think about the message, they are using the _____ route to persuasion.
    a. peripheral
    b. elaborative
    c. heuristic
    d. central

7. According to your book, why are lawyers taught to point out weaknesses in their own cases before the opposing lawyer does?
   a. to enhance their credibility status as leaders
   b. to create a perception of honesty in the eyes of the jury members
   c. to enhance cognitive dissonance in the minds of the jury members
   d. to allow the jury to process the message deeply

8. Ditto and Lopez (1992) used a new saliva test to identify students who had an enzyme deficiency; this test predicted pancreatic disease in later life. Students were asked if there were any irregularities in their diet, sleep, or activity patterns over the last 48 hours that might have affected the accuracy of the test. How did the students who received the health-threatening results react?
   a. asked to receive information about services available to people who had the deficiency
   b. demanded to be retested for the enzyme deficiency
   c. ignored the warning entirely
   d. searched for ways to undercut evidence contradicting their preferred image of healthiness

9. Shana loves her cat. Shana also loves her boyfriend Greg. Greg hates Shana's cat. According to Heider's balance theory, what will Shana probably do?
   a. She will decide she doesn't like her cat so much after all.
   b. She will decide she doesn't like Greg so much after all.
   c. She will begin to dislike both her cat and Greg.
   d. either a or b

10. The Canadian racetrack study by Knox and Inkster (1968) is a great illustration of postdecisional dissonance. How did the bettors demonstrate this concept?
    a. Before placing a bet, people thought that their horse had a 50/50 chance of winning.
    b. Before placing a bet, people had more confidence in their horse winning.
    c. After placing a bet, people had more confidence in their horse winning.
    d. After placing a bet, people had less confidence in their horse winning.

Comprehensive Test
(Note: Items 1-15 are multiple-choice questions, items 16-23 are true-false questions, and 24-25 are essay questions.)

1. How are attitudes formed?
   a. classical conditioning
   b. operant conditioning
   c. observational learning
   d. all of these are sources for attitude formation

2. Your book describes an experiment by Krosnick et al. (1992) where participants were shown subliminal images of either positive or negative objects that were paired with a series of slides of a woman going about her daily routine. Later, they expressed more favorable emotions toward a woman in the slides if they had seen the positive image. This is an example of how _____ can shape our attitudes.
   a. classical conditioning
   b. operant conditioning
   b. observational learning
   d. instrumental conditioning

3. According to the theory of planned behavior, what are the best predictors of attitudes?
   a. subjective norms
   b. perceived behavioral control
   c. attitudes
   d. behavioral intentions

4. Which of the following is an example of persuasion?
   a. Jeff hears his boss say that he's a big football fan, so Jeff tells the boss that he is a fan as well.
   b. Jeff is hounded by a campaign worker to sign a petition endorsing her candidate. Jeff signs it just to get her to leave him alone.
   c. Jeff sees a television program about the destruction of the rainforest, and decides that he should be more concerned about the issue.
   d. Jeff's girlfriend asks if he likes her new dress, and he says he does to avoid a fight.

5. Why are before-after designs NOT the best way to assess whether a persuasive message was effective?
   a. does not use random assignment
   b. pretest sensitization
   c. lack of a control group
   d. methodological pluralism

6. If you are trying to enhance positive cognitive responses to your persuasive message, you should _____ positive self-talk and _____ counterarguments.
   a. increase; increase
   b. decrease; increase
   c. increase; decrease
   d. decrease; decrease

7. Petty and Cacioppo (1984) conducted a study testing the effect of personal relevance on attitude change favoring comprehensive exams. What did they find?
   a. Students who read 9 arguments favored comprehensive exams more than students who read 3 arguments.
   b. When students thought the comprehensive exams would take effect in 10 years, they focused on message quality, not quantity.
   c. When students thought the comprehensive exams would take effect immediately, they processed the message deeply.
   d. When an expert said that the comprehensive exams would take effect immediately, the students focused on the expertise of the communicator.

8. Your text discusses three major persuasion goals; individuals may yield to a persuasive message in order to do all of the following except _____.
   a. hold a more accurate view of the world
   b. be consistent within themselves
   c. gain social approval and acceptance
   d. to conserve mental effort

9. In the Kassin and Kiechel (1996) experiment, college students performed a computer task and were accused by the researcher of pressing a specific key that they had been warned to avoid, which erased all of the data. Under what condition/s did the students admit their guilt 100 percent of the time?
    a. students who were cognitively overloaded while performing the computer task
    b. students who were falsely accused by a witness
    c. students who were both overloaded by the situation and falsely accused by a witness
    d. students who were falsely accused by a witness and worked at a slow pace

10. _____ proposes that people prefer harmony and consistency in their views of the world.
    a. Elaboration likelihood model   b. Cognitive response model
    c. Balance Theory   d. Heuristic-systematic model

11. What was the major contribution of dissonance theory to persuasion research?
    a. It showed that changing a behavior can lead to changes in related attitudes.
    b. It introduced the idea of consistency as an important factor in attitude change.
    c. It disproved balance theory.
    d. It showed that people are motivated to reduce dissonance by changing their attitudes about an issue, regardless of how important that issue may be to them.

12. Who is more likely to experience dissonance effects?
    a. Type A personalities
    b. those who are not aroused easily
    c. those who score high on the Preference for Consistency scale
    d. a sociopath

13. Which advertisement slogan is more likely to appeal to someone from a collectivistic culture?
    a. "The best relationships are lasting ones."
    b. "Treat yourself to a breath-freshening experience."
    c. "Toyota, I love what you do for me."
    d. "You're worth it."

14. _____ have been referred to as attitudinal chameleons since they adapt their opinions as they move from situation to situation.
    a. Low self-monitors   b. Men
    c. High self-monitors   d. Women

15. Even after receiving good evidence that Peter Reilly was innocent, why were his interrogators still convinced that he was guilty?
    a. They didn't believe the evidence.
    b. Believing that they had trapped and imprisoned an innocent man is inconsistent with their conception of themselves as fair and just.
    c. The evidence came from a source that was not credible.
    d. The interrogators were presented with multiple, high quality counterarguments against the new evidence.

TRUE-FALSE

Indicate whether each statement is true or false by circling T or F. If you decide it is false, explain why. Correct answers appear at the end of the study guide in the ANSWERS section for Chapter 5.

T   F   16.   The embeddedness of an attitude causes people to reject contrary information, and thus makes attitude change less likely.

T   F   17.   According to the cognitive response model, the best indication of how much change a communicator will produce lies in what the targets say to themselves as a result of the communication.

T   F   18.   Inoculation procedures involve sending an unconvincing message supporting your opponent's position.

T   F   19.   When a message is about a topic with personal relevance, we are more likely to process its arguments deeply.

T   F   20.   To increase trustworthiness, communicators should present a strong argument favoring their attitude, and no information about the opposing argument.

T   F   21.   By asking an audience to imagine an idea or event, communicators making the idea more cognitively ready in the minds of the audience.

T   F   22.   High fear appeals cause denial, so they should not be used in persuasive appeals to get people to change their unhealthy behavior.

T   F   23.   Low self-monitors are especially susceptible to advertising that promotes socially appealing images associated with a particular product.

ESSAY

24.   What is the cognitive response model and how is it different from early approaches to attitude change?

25. Describe the two main consistency theories, balance theory and cognitive dissonance theory, which have guided persuasion researchers.

When You Have Finished...

Now that you have had a chance to read this chapter and complete the activities associated with it, you may be interested in finding additional materials on this topic. The World Wide Web is a great and convenient resource for gathering additional information in a variety of areas. Listed below are web links and website descriptions that are relevant to this chapter.

Web Links and Website Descriptions
Be sure to visit Chapter 5 at the companion website: www.ablongman.com/knc3e
http://www.influenceatwork.com/ Influence at Work is a firm that offers services which include influence-related consulting, training, and presentations to corporations, government, and non-profit agencies.
http://www.adcouncil.org/ The Ad Council identifies a select number of significant public issues and stimulates action on those issues through communications programs.
http://www.aaf.org/ The American Advertising Federation protects and promotes the *well-being* of advertising.
http://www.sellingpower.com/homepage/index.html? The selling power website includes professional selling skills, motivation and sales management know-how in the business-to-business environment.
http://www.changingminds.org/ The Changing Minds site includes information on how we change one another's minds.

Comprehensive Crossword Puzzle

Across

1. Principle that people will change their attitudes, beliefs, perceptions, and actions to make them consistent with each other
9. Conditioning process through which people learn by being rewarded or punished
11. Learning process through which people learn by watching others get rewarded or punished
12. Tendency to enjoy and engage in deliberative thought
13. Conditioning process through which people associate new objects or events with feelings about previously experienced events
14. Change in a private attitude or belief as a result of receiving a message
15. A theory that locates the most direct cause of persuasion in the self-talk of the persuasion target

Down

2. Measurement that does not change a subject's response while recording them
3. Model that accounts for the two basic ways that attitude change occurs-with and without much thought
4. Heider's theory that people prefer harmony and consistency in their views of the world
5. Model of persuasive communication that holds that there are two routes to attitude change —central route and peripheral route
6. Conflict one feels about a decision that could possibly be wrong
7. Behavior that is inconsistent with an existing attitude
8. Argument that challenges and opposes other arguments
10. Motivation to achieve approval by making a good impression on others

Puzzle created with Puzzlemaker at DiscoverySchool.com

SOCIAL INFLUENCE: CONFORMITY, COMPLIANCE, AND OBEDIENCE

Before You Read...

In this chapter you will be introduced to an area of social psychology known as social influence. The chapter begins by examining the three major categories of social influence: conformity, compliance, and obedience. You will then be exposed to the three basic goals of social influence: choosing correctly, gaining social approval, and being consistent with commitments.

Chapter Learning Objectives

After reading this chapter, you should be able to:

- Define social influence and explain how it is distinct from persuasion

- Describe the three major categories of social influence

- Describe Asch's (1956) classic conformity experiment

- Define the foot-in-the-door technique and provide an example

- Discuss the six principles of influence that emerged from Cialdini's program of participant observation

- Describe the findings of Milgram's (1974) series of obedience experiments

- Explain each of the three goals of social influence

- Describe why uncertainty makes conformity more likely

- Describe the two factors that people rely on to choose correctly and how these factors relate to conformity

- Explain the difference between injunctive norms and descriptive norms

- Explain how businesses and fund raisers make use of the norm of reciprocity

- Explain how the door-in-the-face and that's-not-all techniques make use of the principal of reciprocal concessions

- Describe the three characteristics of the person that affect conformity to achieve the goal of gaining social approval

- Describe how others' appeal and public observability alter motivations to gain approval

- Explain how the foot-in-the-door, low-ball, bait-and-switch, and labeling techniques capitalize on people's desire to be consistent

- Describe how the existing values of a person can enhance their commitment toward a course of action

- Outline the two characteristics of the situation that enhance commitment

- Describe how gender affects public conformity

As You Read...

KEY TERMS!

Listed below are the key terms from the chapter that are essential for your understanding of the material. Refer to the definitions from your textbook; they are located at the end of this chapter, within the text in boldface, and in the margins throughout this chapter. In order to enhance your recall ability for these terms, you may want to consider making flashcards which include a term on one side, and a definition on the other (with perhaps a brief example that makes sense to you).

Bait and switch technique	Foot-in-the-door technique	Personal commitment
Compliance	Labeling technique	Reactance theory
Conformity	Low-ball technique	Social influence
Disrupt-then-reframe technique	Norm of reciprocity	Social validation
Door-in-the-face technique	Obedience	That's-not-all technique
Expert power	Participant observation	

THE EXTRAORDINARY TURNAROUND OF STEVE HASSAN

In the beginning of this chapter your authors introduced Steve Hassan, a man who was a member of the Unification Church – an organization better known as the Moonies. Describe how the principles of conformity, compliance and obedience worked in terms of the three goals of social influence on Hassan in joining the Unification Church and how they were also used in deprogramming Hassan when he left the Unification organization.

CONFORMITY: ASCH'S RESEARCH ON GROUP INFLUENCE

Please describe Solomon Asch's 1956 classic "line-judging" research that investigated the processes of conformity and independence within a group. What are the implications of this research? If you need a little assistance, see pages 180 through 181 in your text.

COMPLIANCE: FREEDMAN AND FRASER'S RESEARCH USING THE "FOOT-IN-THE-DOOR" TECHNIQUE

Please describe Jonathan Freedman and Scott Fraser's 1966 experiments that investigated how a person can be induced to do something they would rather not do. What are the implications of this research? If you need a little assistance, see page 182 in your text.

PARTICIPANT OBSERVATION: THE 6 PRINCIPLES OF INFLUENCE

Describe how Robert Cialdini used participant observation to examine the influence practices of various professions. What are the six principles of influence that emerged from this program of participant observation? Provide an example of each to illustrate these principles. If you need a little assistance, see pages 182 through 184 in your text.

OBEDIENCE: MILGRAM'S SHOCK(ING) PROCEDURE

Please describe Stanley Milgram's experiments on the obedience-inducing power of an authority figure. What are the implications of this research? If you need a little assistance, see pages 184 through 186 in your text.

COMPLIANCE TECHNIQUES

This chapter discusses a variety of compliance techniques that influence professionals utilize against us. Listed below are six of the compliance techniques discussed in your text. Your task is to figure out which one of the techniques is utilized in each of the following examples. Each term is only used once.

(1) Bait and Switch
(2) Door-in-the-Face
(3) Foot-in-the-Door
(4) Labeling
(5) Low-Ball
(6) That's-Not-All

Term	Examples
1. _____	After being allowed to take an extended overnight test drive of the new Toyota 4-Runner, Maia has agreed to purchase it for $36,000. However, just before she gets ready to sign the contract, the salesperson tells Maia that the sales manager will not approve the contract because the dealership would be losing money at that price. Maia decides to buy even though the new price is $38,500.
2. _____	A late-night infomercial advertises a new hair removal system. But before telling you the price, the announcer says that in addition to getting the 12 ounce hair removal gel, they will double the size for free and throw in some soothing lotion.
3. _____	Jessica discovers that the new CD she wants is on sale and goes to the store to purchase it. When she gets there, she finds they are out of that CD, so Jessica buys another one at full price.
4. _____	Lisa asks Tricia to baby-sit for Zach for two hours while she finishes up her Christmas shopping. Tricia agrees to this request. After two hours, Lisa calls Tricia and asks if she wouldn't mind staying for an additional hour while she goes to one last store; Tricia agrees to this request. Before long the phone rings again and Lisa says "Hey Tricia, since you are already over watching Zach, could you take him to his doctor's appointment?" Tricia agrees again to the request and wonders how she ever got talked into staying for so long.
5. _____	Mike asks his professor if she would be willing to spend one hour a week with him for the entire semester reviewing the covered lecture material. She refuses the request. Mike then asks, "how about a half hour review session before the three exams?" The professor agrees to this request.
6. _____	Brad was told by his high school teacher "You look like the kind of young man who understands how important it is to recycle." The following week, Brad helped his parents start a recycling routine at home.

SUMMARY OF THE GOALS SERVED BY SOCIAL INFLUENCE

Complete the chart below to help summarize the goals served by social influence and the factors related to them. If you need assistance, see page 209 in your text (but be sure to use your own words in this exercise, rather than just copying)

The Goal	The Person	The Situation	Interactions
Choosing Correctly	•	• •	•
Gaining Social Approval	• • •	• •	•
Being Consistent with Commitments	•	• •	•

MATCHING: KEY TERMS

Matching! Match each definition on the left side of the page with the concept on the right side of the page. Each concept on the right should be used only once.

___ 1. Capacity to influence that flows from one's presumed wisdom or knowledge

    A. Bait and switch technique

___ 2. Norm that requires that we repay others with the form of behavior they have given us

    B. Compliance

___ 3. Research approach in which the researcher infiltrates the setting to be studied and observes its workings from within

    C. Conformity

___ 4. Gaining commitment to an arrangement, then making the arrangement unavailable or unappealing and offering a more costly arrangement

    D. Disrupt-then-reframe technique

___ 5. Anything that connects an individual's identity more closely to a position or course of action

    E. Door-in-the-face technique

___ 6. Behavior change that occurs as a result of a direct request

    F. Expert power

___ 7. Technique that increases compliance by beginning with a large favor likely to be rejected and then retreating to a more moderate favor

    G. Foot-in-the-door technique

___ 8. Technique that increases compliance with a large request by first getting compliance with a smaller, related request

    H. Labeling technique

___ 9. Interpersonal way to locate and validate the correct choice

    I. Low-ball technique

___ 10. Behavior change designed to match the actions of others

    J. Norm of reciprocity

___ 11. Theory that we react against threats to our freedoms by reasserting those freedoms, often by doing the opposite of what we are being pressured to do

    K. Obedience

___ 12. Gaining a commitment to an arrangement and then raising the cost of carrying out the arrangement

    L. Participant observation

___ 13. Change in overt behavior caused by real or imagined pressure from others

    M. Personal commitment

___ 14. Technique that increases compliance by sweetening an offer with additional benefits

    N. Reactance theory

___ 15. Assigning a label to an individual and then requesting a favor that is consistent with the label

    O. Social influence

___ 16. Compliance that occurs in response to a directive from an authority figure

    P. Social validation

___ 17. Tactic that operates to increase compliance by disrupting one's initial, resistance-laden view of a request and quickly reframing the request in more favorable terms

    Q. That's-not-all technique

PUTTING IT ALL TOGETHER: THOUGHT QUESTIONS

Spend half an hour watching prime time television, but instead of getting up to go to the bathroom or to get a soda during the commercials, pay very close attention to them. Try to pick out the influence tactic being used in each commercial during the half hour. Are some more common than others? Are particular influence tactics associated with particular types of products?

Can you think of other applications of influence tactics besides getting people to buy things or join cults? How could influence tactics be used to get people to engage in health behaviors, such as exercising, going to the doctor regularly, flossing their teeth, or eating right? Can you think of any health promotion programs that use influence tactics?

After You Read...Practice Tests

Practice Test 1

1. _____ is defined as a change in overt behavior caused by real or imagined pressure from others.
   a. Persuasion
   b. Social influence
   c. Compliance
   d. Conformity

2. The salesperson at the local electronics store says to you "You should buy this big screen television today because we can't guarantee this model will be here tomorrow." If you were to follow her advice, you would be displaying
   a. reactance.
   b. conformity.
   c. compliance.
   d. obedience.

3. In Asch's (1956) classic line judging experiment, most participants gave the wrong answer about which line was longest. Why?
   a. They were uncertain which line was longer.
   b. An authority figure told them they had to agree with the group.
   c. They had to state their decision privately so they could not compare their answers with the group's answers.
   d. They felt pressure to conform to the group's opinion.

4. One of your textbook authors, Robert Cialdini, enrolled in training programs for sales, advertising, fund raising, etc. to learn the tactics of compliance professionals. This methodological approach is known as
   a. experimental observation.
   b. participant observation.
   c. contrived observation.
   d. undisguised observation.

5. The Tupperware party, where friends and acquaintances can purchase food storage containers, uses primarily which compliance principle?
   a. authority
   b. social validation
   c. liking/friendship
   d. scarcity

6. Which of the following is NOT one of the three basic goals of social influence discussed in your text?
   a. choosing correctly
   b. appearing competent
   c. gaining social approval
   d. managing self-image

7. According to your textbook, why are less educated individuals more obedient to authority figures?
   a. They are not as intelligent as more educated people.
   b. They assume that authorities know more than they do.
   c. They are seeking social validation.
   d. They are less likely to be anticonformists.

8. In a study by Baron et al. (1996) participants had to pick a criminal out of a lineup. To make accuracy especially important for one group of students, researchers promised a $20 prize if they were correct. But, for some students there was an added complication - they only got a short time (half a second each) to see the pictures in the lineup making their judgments uncertain. Other students did not encounter this uncertainty and had five seconds to view each picture on the screen. What happened?
   a. Students who were unsure of their judgments conformed to the group most when accuracy was important.
   b. Students who were sure of their judgments conformed to the group only when accuracy was important.
   c. All students for whom accuracy was important conformed to the group equally.
   d. All students who were sure of their judgments conformed to the group equally.

9. A technique that increases compliance by beginning with a large favor that is likely to be rejected and then retreating to a more moderate favor is known as the
   a. foot-in-the-door technique.   b. door-in-the-face technique.
   c. low-ball technique.   d. that's-not-all technique.

10. A late-night infomercial advertises a piece of kitchen equipment that slices everything into any imaginable shape. But before telling you the price, the announcer says that in addition to the slicer, you will also get a microwave egg cooker and an all-purpose kitchen knife. The infomercial uses the
   a. foot-in-the-door technique.   b. door-in-the-face technique.
   c. reciprocal concessions technique.   d. that's-not-all technique.

Practice Test 2

1. Which of the following is NOT one of the three major categories of social influence?
   a. conformity   b. compliance
   c. expert power   d. obedience

2. Behavior change that occurs as a result of a direct request is known as _____.
   a. public commitment   b. conformity
   c. compliance   d. obedience

3. Asch's classic 1956 experiment, where subjects judged a standard line to comparison lines, was arranged to test the limits of
   a. conformity   b. social perception
   c. coercive power   d. indoctrination

4. Which compliance technique starts with a small request and advances to larger requests?
   a. door-in-the-face   b. low-ball
   c. bait and switch   d. foot-in-the-door

5. Approximately what percentage of the subjects in Milgram's original "shocking" experiment went all the way to the 450 volt level despite the victim's repeated screams and subsequent silence?
    a. 0%
    b. .01%
    c. just under 4%
    d. 65%

6. Residents of Los Angeles received information describing the regular curbside recycling behavior of many of their neighbors. This information produced an immediate increase in the recycling behaviors of these residents. This study illustrates the _____ principle. (204 b)
    a. authority
    b. social validation
    c. liking/friendship
    d. scarcity

7. Schachter (1951) observed how groups pressure members who deviate from the consensus. He found that groups can respond with affection to those whose opinion deviates, provided
    a. the dissenters admit the error of their ways and adopt the group's view.
    b. the dissenters never discuss the different opinion again.
    c. the dissenters stick to their opinion and beliefs no matter what.
    d. the dissenters leave the group immediately.

8. Which technique increases compliance by "sweetening" an offer with additional benefits?
    a. foot-in-the-door technique
    b. door-in-the-face technique
    c. reciprocal concessions technique
    d. that's-not-all technique

9. What personal factors increase the need to be socially approved?
    a. desire for approval, collectivistic sense of self, and less resistance
    b. desire for approval, individualistic sense of self, and less resistance
    c. desire for approval, collectivistic sense of self, and resistance
    d. desire for approval, individualistic sense of self, and resistance

10. Steven has agreed to purchase a new Mustang for $24,000. However, just before he gets ready to sign the contract, the salesman tells Steven that the sales manager will not approve the amount allowed for his trade-in, and that the contract will have to be higher, probably around $25,500. The sales manager states "we'd be losing money at that price." Steven proceeds with the purchase and has just been the victim of
    a. foot in the door technique.
    b. door in the face technique.
    c. low-ball technique.
    d. reversing the tables technique.

Practice Test 3

1. Behavior change designed to match the actions of others is known as _____.
    a. public commitment
    b. conformity
    c. compliance
    d. obedience

2. During the holiday season, everyone works overtime because the boss demands it. This is an example of
    a. expert power.
    b. conformity.
    c. social validation.
    d. obedience.

3.   In a study by Freedman and Fraser (1966), housewives were asked to answer a series of eight questions about household soaps. Three days later they were contacted again and asked if a team of six men could come into their home for two hours and classify all the household products they owned. The researchers in this experiment were using which technique to gain compliance to the requests?
     a.   foot-in-the-door   b.   low-ball
     c.   bait and switch   d.   labeling

4.   Advertising copy, used by a movie theater owner, reading "Exclusive, limited engagement, ends soon" is attempting to influence consumers using the _____ principle.
     a.   reciprocation.   b.   commitment/consistency.
     c.   social validation.   d.   scarcity.

5.   Under which of the following circumstances did the majority of participants refuse to shock their partners in Milgram's shock procedure studies?
     a.   when the victim was in another room
     b.   when the victim begged for the participant to stop
     c.   when the authority figure ordered the participant to stop shocking the victim
     d.   when the victim fell deathly silent

6.   Sherif (1936) projected a dot of light on the wall of a darkened room and asked subjects to indicate how much the light had moved while they were watching it. When subjects announced their movement estimates in groups, these estimates
     a.   were strongly influenced by other group members; nearly everyone changed toward the group average.
     b.   had no impact on the subjects original estimate.
     c.   changed 50 percent of the time.
     d.   only affected older participants

7.   How did Morris and Miller (1975) demonstrate a break in group consensus using Asch's (1956) line-judging task?
     a.   They had participants give their answers in private.
     b.   They had one confederate disagree with the group.
     c.   They had participants publicly commit to their answers.
     d.   They reduced the number of confederates.

8.   According to your book, many cult-like groups engage in "lovebombing," initially showering new members with affection. What social goal is this influence tactic capitalizing on?
     a.   the goal to manage self-image   b.   the goal to choose correctly
     c.   the goal to gain social approval   d.   the goal to gain status

9.   Charlie is a door-to-door solicitor selling a packet of 8 greeting cards for $3. Instead of using the usual sales pitch of "They're $3. It's a bargain." Charlie changes the wording to "These cards sell for 300 pennies…that's $3. It's a bargain." By saying something unexpected, Charlie was able to use the
     a.   foot-in-the-door technique.   b.   door-in-the-face technique.
     c.   disrupt-then-reframe technique.   d.   reciprocal concessions technique.

10. Which of the following is true about personal commitments and their effect on the goal to manage self-image?
    a. A personal commitment is ineffective unless made to a large group of people.
    b. A personal commitment is ineffective if made to a computer, rather than an actual person.
    c. Personal commitments work because most people want to be seen as consistent.
    d. all of the above

Comprehensive Test
(Note: Items 1-15 are multiple-choice questions, items 16-23 are true-false questions, and 24-25 are essay questions.)

1. The amount of overt pressure associated with the categories of social influence escalates as one moves from _____ to _____ and, finally, to _____.
    a. conformity; compliance; obedience   b. compliance; conformity; obedience
    c. conformity; obedience; compliance   d. obedience; compliance; conformity

2. Compliance that occurs in response to a directive from an authority figure is known as
    a. social influence.   b. conformity.
    c. expert power.   d. obedience.

3. In Asch's (1956) classic line judging experiment, what did participants do when everyone else in the room gave wrong answers?
    a. all the participants ignored the wrong answers and gave only correct answers
    b. most participants convinced the other people in the room that their answer was correct
    c. most participants agreed with the incorrect answers given by the group
    d. most participants refused to give any answer

4. Free samples in supermarkets, free home inspections by exterminating companies, and free gifts through the mail from marketers are effective ways to increase compliance. This exemplifies the influence principle of
    a. reciprocation.   b. commitment/consistency.
    c. social validation.   d. scarcity.

5. Stanley Milgram's experiment in which a "teacher" was asked to give shocks to a "learner" was designed to test the limits of
    a. expert power   b. conformity
    c. obedience   d. indoctrination

6. What two social influence principles will we rely upon to make correct decisions?
    a. liking/friendship and social validation b. authority and social validation
    c. authority and liking/friendship   d. scarcity and commitment/consistency

7. In the Hofling et al. (1966) experiment, nurses were given an order to issue medication to a ward patient. What caused these nurses to obey?
    a. The authority figure was wearing a uniform.
    b. The nurses were told to do so by a "Dr."
    c. The person making the request was wearing a badge that identified himself as a hospital employee.
    d. The patient was someone they were familiar with.

8. Your book describes a study in which New Yorkers were strongly influenced to return a wallet after hearing that another New Yorker had done so, but were not at all influenced when told that a foreigner had returned a wallet. This study indicates how important _____ can be in social influence.
    a. similarity   b. authority
    c. expert power   d. reciprocation

9. Schachter (1951) observed how groups pressure members who deviate from the consensus. What social goal is this influence tactic capitalizing on?
    a. the goal to manage self-image   b. the goal to choose correctly
    c. the goal to gain social approval   d. the goal to gain status

10. Jeremy's friends think that it's wrong to drink and drive, but then on Saturday nights someone invariably ends up driving home drunk after the group has been out drinking. The groups' _____ norms are against drunk driving, but judging by their _____ norms you'd think they were all for it.
    a. social; injunctive   b. injunctive; descriptive
    c. descriptive; injunctive   d. descriptive; social

11. A Boy Scout approaches you and asks if you want to buy any $5 tickets to the circus. After you decline, the Boy Scout then asks if you would be willing to buy some $1 chocolate bars. You buy two bars. What influence technique was used here?
    a. foot-in-the-door technique   b. door-in-the-face technique
    c. reciprocal concessions technique d. that's-not-all technique

12. In order to increase the sale of baked goods, Jerry stated that cupcakes were each $1, but before customers responded, he added two cookies to the deal at no extra cost. Jerry was using the
    a. foot-in-the-door technique.   b. door-in-the-face technique.
    c. reciprocal concessions technique. d. that's-not-all technique.

13. An experiment on judging an ambiguous blue-green color by Insko and colleagues (1985) showed that observability is an important situational influence on conformity. In what condition was conformity most likely to occur?
    a. when participants had to write down their judgments
    b. when participants had to announce their judgment aloud in front of others
    c. when participants had to announce their judgment aloud in a room by themselves
    d. when participants only had to think about their judgments

14. Referring to an advertised DVD player as inferior and then offering a more expensive model is known as the _____.
    a. foot in the door technique
    b. bait and switch technique
    c. low-ball technique
    d. labeling technique

15. In a study by Cioffi and Garner (1996), people who volunteered to participate in an AIDS education program were more likely to actually show up when they filled out a form saying they'd participate than when they did not fill out a form saying they would not participate. Why?
    a. Passive commitment made the participants think the researchers weren't serious about the education program.
    b. Passive commitments tell us more about our self-image, and are thus more likely to shape our behavior.
    c. The active commitment was made in public, so it was more likely to shape behavior.
    d. Active commitments give us the information we use to shape our self-image, and are thus more likely to shape our behavior.

TRUE-FALSE

Indicate whether each statement is true or false by circling T or F. If you decide it is false, explain why. Correct answers appear at the end of the study guide in the ANSWERS section for Chapter 6.

T   F   16. When Freedman and Fraser convinced housewives to allow a 2-hour inspection after having them first agree to answer a short survey, they were using the door-in-the-face tactic.

T   F   17. Participant observation is when a researcher infiltrates the setting she is interested in and examines it from within.

T   F   18. In Sherif's autokinetic effect experiment, participants changed their estimates to the group average only because they wanted to gain social approval.

T   F   19. According to Schachter's studies, when someone initially disagrees with the group, then gradually conforms to group pressure, they are embraced fully into the group.

T   F   20. When businesses offer "free gifts" for listening to a sales pitch or "free weekends" at resorts they are using the norm of reciprocity to get people to buy products and services.

T   F   21. The norms of obligation appear to be equal across all cultures.

T   F   22. People who characterize themselves in collectivist terms, or come from collectivist cultures, are more likely to conform.

T   F   23. If you want people to act in a way that is consistent with their commitments, it's best to ask them to make their commitments active and public.

ESSAY

24. Describe each of the three major categories of social influence and provide an example of each.

25. Distinguish between the following compliance techniques: foot-in-the-door technique, low-ball technique, bait and switch technique, and labeling technique. Provide an example of each to illustrate your distinguishing points.

When You Have Finished...

Now that you have had a chance to read this chapter and complete the activities associated with it, you may be interested in finding additional materials on this topic. The World Wide Web is a great and convenient resource for gathering additional information in a variety of areas. Listed below are web links and website descriptions that are relevant to this chapter.

Web Links and Website Descriptions
Be sure to visit Chapter 6 at the companion website: www.ablongman.com/knc3e
http://www.workingpsychology.com/ This website presents an introduction to the study of influence, persuasion, compliance, propaganda, "brainwashing," and the ethics that surrounds these issues.
http://www.influenceatwork.com/ Influence at Work is a firm that offers services which include influence-related consulting, training, and presentations to corporations, government, and non-profit agencies.
http://www.freedomofmind.com/ This is the website for Steven Alan Hassan's Freedom of Mind Center. It is a resource for educating people about destructive cults, helping a friend or loved one involved in a destructive group or relationship, and in becoming an active and aware consumer. This website also offers resources for former members of destructive groups.
http://www.unification.org/ This is the homepage for The Unification Church. Use this information to supplement your text discussion of the church and Steve Hassan.
http://religiousmovements.lib.virginia.edu/lectures/influence/ This website includes PowerPoint lecture material from a professor at The University of Virginia on social influence and includes an overview of Robert Cialdini's six principles of influence.
http://religiousmovements.lib.virginia.edu/lectures/moonies.html This website includes lecture material from a professor at The University of Virginia on Reverend Moon and his movement, unification beliefs, and the future of the Unification Church

Comprehensive Crossword Puzzle

Across

1. Anything that connects an individual's identity more closely to a position or course of action
7. Norm that requires that we repay others with the form of behavior they have given us
9. Capacity to influence that flows from one's presumed wisdom or knowledge
12. Change in overt behavior caused by real or imagined pressure from others
13. Behavior change that occurs as a result of a direct request
15. Gaining commitment to an arrangement, then making the arrangement unavailable or unappealing and offering a more costly arrangement
16. Technique that increases compliance by beginning with a large favor likely to be rejected and then retreating to a more moderate favor

Down

2. Technique that increases compliance by sweetening an offer with additional benefits
3. Interpersonal way to locate and validate the correct choice
4. Research approach in which the researcher infiltrates the setting to be studied and observes its workings from within
5. Assigning a label to an individual and then requesting a favor that is consistent with the label
6. Technique that increases compliance with a large request by first getting compliance with a smaller, related request
8. Compliance that occurs in response to a directive from an authority figure
10. Behavior change designed to match the actions of others
11. Gaining a commitment to an arrangement and then raising the cost of carrying out the arrangement
14. Brehm's theory that we react against threats to our freedoms by reasserting those freedoms, often by doing the opposite of what we are being pressured to do

Puzzle created with Puzzlemaker at DiscoverySchool.com

AFFILIATION AND FRIENDSHIP

Before You Read...

The need to affiliate with others is fundamental to human interaction. In this chapter, you will discover that friendships are unique relationships that differ from those with relatives or lovers. You will learn about the research techniques that have been developed to study these relationships in an unbiased and complete way. Next you will be introduced to two theories for why we want to affiliate with others which suggests that we are either motivated by the desire to feel good or to maximize the ratio of benefits to costs. Finally, you will examine in detail the four social goals of affiliation and friendship: getting social support, getting information, gaining status, and exchanging material benefits.

Chapter Learning Objectives

After reading this chapter, you should be able to:

- Define the affiliation motive

- Describe the experience sampling method of studying friendship

- Describe the reinforcement-affect model and social exchange theory of affiliation and friendship and explain why they are called "domain-general" models

- Briefly outline the four affiliation and friendship goals

- Define social support

- Describe the circumstances in which people will seek emotional support.

- Describe the circumstances in which people push social support away

- Explain how lonely and depressed people self-perpetuate their lack of social support

- Explain how childhood attachment affects emotional support networks as children grow into adulthood

- Describe why people seek information from similar others

- Define self-disclosure.

- Discuss gender differences in self-disclose

- Describe the situational characteristics that affect our desire to make social comparisons

- Describe self-esteem maintenance theory including how this theory explains comparisons with similar others and what self-esteem maintenance theory suggests about chronically happy people

- Explain who is most likely to desire to be friends with people who are powerful and why

- Explain why both men and women place more value on their friendships with women

- Describe when people are more likely to affiliate with others to gain status. When are they less likely to do so?

- Explain the concept of equity in relationships

- Define the four forms of social exchange and provide an example of each

- Explain the difference between communal and exchange relationships

- Describe the proximity-attraction principle and how it affects social exchanges

- Describe the differences found in exchange relationships for Western and Non-Western cultures and give reasons why they may be different.

As You Read...

KEY TERMS!
Listed below are the key terms from the chapter that are essential for your understanding of the material. Refer to the definitions from your textbook; they are located at the end of this chapter, within the text in boldface, and in the margins throughout this chapter. In order to enhance your recall ability for these terms, you may want to consider making flashcards which include a term on one side, and a definition on the other (with perhaps a brief example that makes sense to you).

Affiliation motive	Equity	Proximity-attraction principle
Authority ranking	Experience sampling method	Reinforcement-affect model
Communal sharing	Friend	Self-disclosure
Domain-general model	Health psychology	Social capital
Domain-specific model	Market pricing	Social exchange
Equality matching	Mere exposure effect	Social support

THE FUGITIVE WHO BEFRIENDED THE GOD-KING

In the beginning of this chapter your authors introduced Heinrich Harrer, a man who was a penniless and starving fugitive that became friends with the Dalai Lama. Describe how the friendship between the Dalai Lama and Harrer benefited both of them in different ways according to the four goals of friendship and affiliation.

WORD SCRAMBLE

Word scramble! Unscramble the following words below. If you are having trouble, use the hints to assist you. When you have finished unscrambling the words, the letters within the [brackets] will reveal the "bonus" word. Ready? Go!

1. NAFITAIOFIL   __ [_] __ __ __ __ __ __ __ __

   VOITME   __ __ __ __ __ __

2. LEFS   __ __ __ __

   CDERLISOSU   __ __ __ __ __ __ __ __ [_] __

3. IOLSAC   __ __ __ [_] __ __

   TPURSPO   __ __ __ __ __ __ __

4. YUQETI   [_] __ __ __ __ __

5. NEEPXIERCE   __ __ __ __ __ __ __ [_] __ __

   GPMLIASN   __ __ __ __ __ __ __ __

   DTMOEH   __ __ __ __ __ [_]

   BONUS WORD   __ __ __ __ __ __

Hints:
1. Desire to be near others and to have pleasant interactions with them
2. Sharing of intimate information about oneself
3. Emotional, material, or informational assistance provided by other people
4. State of affairs in which one person's benefits and costs from a relationship are proportional to the benefits and costs incurred by his or her partner
5. Observational technique in which subjects fill out frequent descriptions of who they are with and what is going on

BONUS: Someone with whom we have an affectionate relationship

118

SOCIAL DYSFUNCTION

Describe how depression and loneliness work together to drive away social support. Then, complete the following flow chart regarding the self-perpetuating cycle of loneliness and depression. See pages 225 through 227 in your text for help with this exercise.

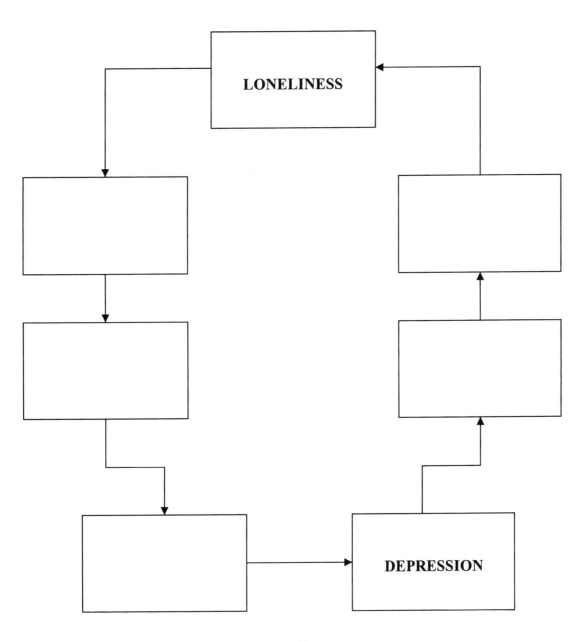

FUNDAMENTAL PATTERNS OF SOCIAL EXCHANGE

According to Alan Fiske, people all over the world categorize relationships into four fundamental categories based upon different sets of exchange rules. For each model of social exchange, provide two examples to illustrate the rule and answer the questions below.

Model of Social Relations	Rules of Exchange	Example Using the Rule
Communal Sharing		▪ ▪
Authority Ranking		▪ ▪
Equality Matching		▪ ▪
Market Pricing		▪ ▪

How do people decide which form of social exchange to use in a given situation? Make a list of five people you have interacted with in the past few days – which form of social exchange did you use with each person? Why?

	Name of Person	Form of Social Exchange	Why?
1.			
2.			
3.			
4.			
5.			

SUMMARY OF THE DIFFERENT INFLUENCES ON FRIENDSHIP AND AFFILIATION

Complete the chart below to help you summarize the goals served by friendship and affiliation and the factors related to them. If you need assistance, see page 240 in your text (but be sure to use your own words in this exercise, rather than just copying).

The Goal	The Person	The Situation	Interactions
Getting Social Support	• •	• •	• • •
Getting Information	• •	• •	• •
Gaining Status	•	• • •	• •
Exchanging Material Benefits	•	• •	•

MATCHING: KEY TERMS

Matching! Match each definition on the left side of the page with the concept on the right side of the page. Each concept on the right should be used only once.

___ 1. Form of exchange in which each person gets the same as the others

___ 2. Model that presumes that the governing principles vary from one domain of behavior to another

___ 3. Form of exchange in which everyone gets out in proportion to what they put in

___ 4. Theory that we like people with whom we associate positive feelings and dislike those with whom we associate negative feelings

___ 5. Form of exchange in which members of a group share a pool of resources, taking when in need and giving when others are in need

___ 6. Tendency to become friends with those who live or work nearby

___ 7. Study of behavioral and psychological factors that affect illness

___ 8. Model that attempts to explain a wide range of different behaviors according to a simple general rule

___ 9. Emotional, material, or informational assistance provided by other people

___ 10. Form of exchange in which goods are divided according to a person's status in the group

___ 11. Assets that can be drawn from one's network of personal relationships

___ 12. Someone with whom we have an affectionate relationship

___ 13. Observational technique in which subjects fill out frequent descriptions of who they are with and what is going on

___ 14. Tendency to feel positively toward people, places, or things we have seen frequently

___ 15. Trading of benefits within relationships

___ 16. Desire to be near others and to have pleasant interactions with them

___ 17. Sharing of intimate information about oneself

___ 18. State of affairs in which one person's benefits and costs from a relationship are proportional to the benefits and costs incurred by his or her partner

A. Affiliation motive

B. Authority ranking

C. Communal sharing

D. Domain-general model

E. Domain-specific model

F. Equality matching

G. Equity

H. Experience sampling method

I. Friend

J. Health psychology

K. Market pricing

L. Mere exposure effect

M. Proximity-attraction principle

N. Reinforcement-affect model

O. Self-disclosure

P. Social capital

Q. Social exchange

R. Social support

PUTTING IT ALL TOGETHER: THOUGHT QUESTIONS

People who are lonely or depressed tend to push social support away. One situation where this is especially likely is when people move away form home to start college. Imagine that you are in charge of programs for new freshman at your school. Using what you learned in the chapter, what kinds of things would you do to prevent students from getting into the self-perpetuating cycle of loneliness and depression?

One of the goals that influences friendship and affiliation is the exchange of material benefits. The book described how communally-oriented individuals tend to act in relationships with other individuals. Do you think communal orientation could affect people's relationships at a broader, societal level? Are people who are communally-oriented more likely to give to charities, volunteer to help the homeless, etc.? Why or why not? How would you test your hypothesis?

After You Read...Practice Tests

Practice Test 1

1. According to your book, which of the following is true about friends?
   a. Friendships are generally less voluntary than other types of relationships
   b. Our ancestors tended to live in groups where one's closest friends were not relatives.
   c. A friend is someone with whom we have an affectionate relationship.
   d. Friendships are characterized by passion.

2. An observational technique in which subjects fill out frequent descriptions of who they "are with and what is going on" is known as
   a. contrived observation
   b. participant observation
   c. experience sampling method
   d. successive independent sampling method

3. According to the reinforcement-affect model, people are motivated by one very simple goal-
   a. to maximize the ratio of benefits to costs.
   b. the desire to feel good.
   c. the need to care for others.
   d. the desire to exchange material benefits.

4. _____ is defined as emotional, material, or informational assistance provided by other people.
   a. Social support
   b. Friendship
   c. Affiliation motive
   d. Communal sharing

5. After reviewing the literature, Taylor and her colleagues found that under stress males tend to engage in the "fight or flight" response while females "tend and befriend." According to which perspective did they interpret these findings?
   a. Sociocultural
   b. Evolutionary
   c. Social Learning
   d. Social Cognitive

6. According to your book, in which of the following situations would you be LEAST likely to want social support?
   a. You have to do something embarrassing.
   b. You are in an experiment and are about to receive painful electric shock.
   c. You have just started college, don't have a car, and are living alone.
   d. all of the above

7. Self-disclosure is discussed in relation to which friendship and affiliation goal?
   a. getting social support
   b. getting information
   c. gaining status
   d. exchanging material benefits

8. Chartrand and Bargh (1999) videotaped students while they were talking with an experimental confederate who either shook his foot or rubbed his face. What did they find?
   a. Students tended to underutilize these nonverbal actions to create similarity.
   b. Students' attempts to utilize nonverbal behaviors to create similarity went unnoticed by other participants.
   c. Students tended to imitate the subtle nonverbal actions of the confederate which made the students more likeable and created a smoother interaction.
   d. Students tended to imitate the subtle nonverbal actions of the confederate which made the students more irritating and less likeable.

9. According to a study by Nakao (1987), Japanese workers like people of higher status the most, whereas American workers like people of similar status the most. According to your book, which is the most likely explanation for this difference?
   a. Japan is a more individualistic culture.   b. Japan is a more status-oriented culture.
   c. America is a more collectivist culture.   d. America is a more egalitarian culture.

10. _____ relationships are based on a mutual concern for one another's welfare, whereas _____ relationships are based on rewards and benefits traded.
    a. Market; communal
    b. Exchange; authority
    c. Exchange; communal
    d. Communal; exchange

Practice Test 2

1. _____ is the desire to be near others and to have pleasant and affectionate interactions with them.
   a. Friendship
   b. Affiliation motive
   c. Need for social contact
   d. Interaction drive

2. In which of the following methodological approaches would a participant fill out a short questionnaire after every meaningful social interaction (for example, after a conversation)?
   a. Rochester Interaction Record
   b. participant observation
   c. contrived sampling method
   d. successive independent sampling method

3. The reinforcement-affect model is _____; that is, it attempts to explain all behavior using one simple rule.
   a. domain specific
   b. domain general
   c. dependency specific
   d. situation general

4. _____ is the study of behavioral and psychological factors that affect illness.
   a. Behavioral neuroscience
   b. Abnormal psychology
   c. Health psychology
   d. Holistic pharmacology

5. Research by Allen et al. (1991) found that when women had to do stressful tasks, their anxiety was lowest when they
   a. were alone.
   b. had their dog with them.
   c. had their best friend with them.
   d. had their boyfriend with them.

6. Warren Jones and his colleagues (1985) summarized a number of factors that boost feelings of social isolation. These factors include
   a. having recently moved.
   b. starting college.
   c. having inadequate transportation.
   d. all of the above

7. According to social comparison theory, why do people want to engage in social comparison with and obtain information about themselves from similar others?
   a. so that the comparison group is relevant
   b. because similar others are uniquely situated to provide us with objective information
   c. because similar others are usually more willing to engage in friendly competition
   d. all of the above

8. Men's relationships are marked more by _____ while women's relationships focus more on _____.
   a. hierarchy and instrumentality; emotional support and intimacy
   b. emotional support and intimacy; hierarchy and instrumentality
   c. career advancement and emotional support; a blend of career advancement and intimacy
   d. status seeking; exchange of material benefits

9. John gets straight A's and constantly talks about how great he is doing in school. Despite his success, he doesn't have many good friends at school. According to your book, why might this be?
   a. John's emphasis on status makes him less desirable as a friend.
   b. People are jealous of John's success and generally prefer to affiliate with less successful people.
   c. John is probably a first born and they tend to be less desirable friends.
   d. John is smart enough not to need social support.

10. In what way are personal relationships different in Western cultures versus traditional cultures?
    a. Relationships in Western cultures tend to be more voluntary.
    b. Relationships in Western cultures tend to be more permanent and continuous.
    c. Relationships in Western cultures tend to be less individualistic.
    d. Relationships in Western cultures tend to be based more on family ties.

Practice Test 3

1. The affiliation motive can
   a. drive us to interact with complete strangers.
   b. instigate contacts with casual acquaintances.
   c. inspire close relationships with friends, relatives, and lovers.
   d. all of the above

2. What is the advantage of having people record their own interactions right after they occur?
   a. They get information about real, ongoing, behavior, without the problem of an observer interfering with the actual interaction.
   b. Recording interactions soon after they occur reduces memory biases.
   c. By waiting until the interaction naturally ends, the recording process is less likely to change the normal course of events.
   d. all of the above

3. DePaulo and Kashy (1998) found that _____ were more likely to tell self-serving lies, whereas _____ were more likely to tell lies that made the other person feel better.
   a. friends; strangers
   b. strangers; relatives
   c. strangers; friends
   d. relatives; friends

4. A domain-general model
   a. attempts to explain all behavior using some simple rule.
   b. presumes we think and feel very differently depending on the adaptive problem posed by particular kinds of relationships.
   c. seeks to optimize the ratio of costs to benefits in all our relationships.
   d. does an excellent job at explaining why some things feel good and others feel bad.

5. According to social exchange theory, affiliations and friendship are motivated by a simple and general goal –
   a. the desire to feel good.
   b. to maximize the ratio of benefits to costs.
   c. the need to care for others.
   d. the desire to exchange material benefits.

6. In a study by Wisman and Koole (2003), students were asked to ponder their own death for a few minutes and then they were sent into a room for group discussion. How did the mortality question affect student seating behaviors?
   a. Students who had been pondering their own deaths overwhelmingly chose to be sociable.
   b. Students who had been pondering their own deaths chose to sit alone.
   c. Students who had been pondering their own deaths distanced themselves from the group by approximately two feet.
   d. Students who had been pondering their own deaths became depressed and opted out of the study.

7. What two factors work hand-in-hand to drive away social support?
   a. dominance and dependency
   b. attachment and agreeableness
   c. depression and loneliness
   d. neuroticism and extraversion

8. Heinrich Harrer's friendship with the Dalai Lama resulted in an increase in Harrer's salary and he was looked upon more favorably by other Tibetans. This shows that Harrer's friendship with the Dalai Lama served which of the following goals?
   a. the goal to gain intimacy
   b. the goal to be accurate
   c. the goal to gain status
   d. the goal to gain information

9. According to social exchange theory, why are people so often drawn to friendships in which they experience equity?
   a. People are drawn to those who agree with their attitudes.
   b. In equitable relationships, people's gains greatly outweigh their costs.
   c. People are inclined to look for a good deal; if a friendship is too one-sided, the person getting a bad deal will likely end the friendship.
   d. People are genuinely good and enjoy returning favors.

10. _____ is a form of exchange in which everyone gets out in proportion to what they put in while _____ involves exchange in which no one gets more than the others.
   a. Communal sharing; authority ranking b. Equality matching; market pricing
   c. Authority ranking; communal sharing d. Market pricing; equality matching

Comprehensive Test
(Note: Items 1-15 are multiple-choice questions, items 16-23 are true-false questions, and 24-25 are essay questions.)

1. In a study by Davis and Todd (1985), students agreed on a number of features of friendship. Which of the following is NOT a characteristic of friendship?
   a. Friends help each other in times of need.
   b. Friends trust one another to act in their best interest.
   c. Friends confide in one another.
   d. Friends tend to shape one another into new people.

2. How does the Rochester Interaction Record differ from the experience sampling method?
   a. The Rochester Interaction Record has participants record their behavior after their portable beepers sound whereas the experience sampling method has participants engage in conversations with other research participants and rate the quality of the conversation.
   b. The Rochester Interaction Record has participants fill out a brief questionnaire after every significant social interaction whereas the experience sampling method has participants record their behavior after their portable beeper sound.
   c. The Rochester Interaction Record has participants engage in conversations with other research participants and rate the quality of the conversation whereas the experience sampling method has participants record their behavior after their portable beepers sound.
   d. The Rochester Interaction Record has participants record their friends behavior while interacting with other people whereas the experience sampling method has participants record their behavior after their portable beepers sound.

3. The reinforcement-affect model and social exchange theory both take a/n _____ approach.
   a. domain-specific   b. domain-general
   c. domain-sensitive   d. idiographic

4. Which of the following is NOT a social goal of affiliation and friendship described in the chapter?
   a. managing self-image
   b. getting information
   c. gaining status
   d. getting social support

5. Bolger and Eckenrode (1991) measured student's levels of extraversion, emotional instability, daily stresses, and contacts with others before they took the medical entrance exam. What did they find?
   a. Students who were extraverted were less traumatized by the exam.
   b. Students who were emotionally stable were less traumatized by the exam.
   c. Students who had fewer daily stresses were less traumatized by the exam.
   d. Students with more social contacts were less traumatized by the exam.

6. After reviewing the literature, Taylor and her colleagues found that under stress males secrete androgens (associated with aggressive behavior) while females secrete oxytocin (associated with nurturing maternal behaviors and attachment). According to which perspective did they interpret these findings?
   a. Sociocultural
   b. Evolutionary
   c. Social Learning
   d. Social Cognitive

7. When a realistic radio report of Martians invading New Jersey led to massive panic on October 30, 1938, Cantril recorded many stories of people turning to one another for
   a. social support.
   b. social exchange.
   c. communal sharing.
   d. self-disclosure.

8. Which of the following behaviors do lonely students engage in that may be counterproductive to establishing friendships?
   a. When around others, lonely students make more inappropriate self-disclosures.
   b. When around others, lonely students change the topic more frequently.
   c. When around others, lonely students ask fewer questions about their conversational partners.
   d. all of the above

9. The sharing of intimate information about oneself is known as _____.
   a. social exchange
   b. communal sharing
   c. self-disclosure
   d. catharsis

10. Michelle and her best friend Karen are both artists. Karen tells Michelle that she has just won an award for her painting. According to the self-esteem maintenance theory, how is Michelle likely to react to this news?
    a. She will focus on the fact that Karen is a painter, while she is a sculptor.
    b. She will decide that being an artist really isn't that important to her.
    c. She will feel bad that she did not win an award.
    d. any of the above are possible according to the self-esteem maintenance theory

11. According to your book, why do both men and women place more value on their friendships with women?
    a. Women are more likely to give instrumental support.
    b. Women place more emphasis on the social hierarchy.
    c. Women are more emotionally supportive of their friends.
    d. Women get more respect in their friendships.

12. The norm of reciprocity has been a key to our ancestors' survival during difficult times. Although relevant to several social goals, which friendship goal does reciprocity most neatly fit under?
    a. getting social support
    b. getting information
    c. gaining status
    d. exchanging material benefits

13. A professor and two graduate students go out for Thai food, which is served family style. Although they split the bill evenly, the graduate students let the professor take an extra spring roll and allow him to have larger portions of each main dish. What form of social exchange is this?
    a. communal sharing
    b. authority ranking
    c. equality matching
    d. market pricing

14. In a classic study of friendships, Festinger, Schachter, and Back (1950) found that residents in a housing project were most likely to pick their neighbor as the person they most liked in the complex. Which of the following is not a reason why people liked their neighbors best?
    a. People had chosen to live near their friends.
    b. People who live close are more familiar to us.
    c. Physical proximity makes it easier to engage in social exchanges.
    d. There are low costs to interacting with a neighbor.

15. Relationships in traditional cultures tend to be
    a. less voluntary than those in Western cultures
    b. permanent and continuous
    c. collectivistic
    d. all of the above

TRUE-FALSE

Indicate whether each statement is true or false by circling T or F. If you decide it is false, explain why. Correct answers appear at the end of the study guide in the ANSWERS section for Chapter 7.

T   F   16.   The affiliation motive can drive us to interact with complete strangers and instigate contacts with casual acquaintances.

T   F   17.   When people are uncertain, they are more likely to make social comparisons.

T   F   18.   Men find their friendships with men more emotionally satisfying than their friendships with women, but women find their friendships with women more emotionally satisfying than their friendships with men.

T   F   19.   People are more concerned about status in relationships when the social hierarchy is salient.

T   F   20.   Increased internet usage results in increased depression and loneliness for introverted people.

T   F   21.   Market pricing is a form of exchange in which goods are divided according to a person's status in the group.

T   F   22.   People low in communal orientation tend to keep careful track of inputs and outputs in their relationships with others.

T   F   23.   Relationships in Western cultures are voluntary, so they tend to be more permanent and continuous than relationships in traditional cultures.

ESSAY

24.   Describe the experience sampling method and the Rochester Interaction Record for studying intimate relationships. What are the advantages of using these techniques?

25.   Discuss the three relationship differences that Moghaddam, Taylor, and Wright (1993) found between Western and Non-Western cultures. What are the implications of these findings on "market-based" rules of exchange?

When You Have Finished...

Now that you have had a chance to read this chapter and complete the activities associated with it, you may be interested in finding additional materials on this topic. The World Wide Web is a great and convenient resource for gathering additional information in a variety of areas. Listed below are web links and website descriptions that are relevant to this chapter.

Web Links and Website Descriptions
Be sure to visit Chapter 7 at the companion website: www.ablongman.com/knc3e
http://wps.ablongman.com/ab_baronbyrne_socialpsych_10/0,4608,185934-,00.html This is the companion website for the Baron and Byrne Social Psychology textbook. This website contains information relevant to close relationships and includes learning objectives, multiple choice questions, true-false questions, essay questions, activities, flashcards, and additional web links.
http://www.smithsonianmag.si.edu/smithsonian/issues97/oct97/harrer.html This website provides additional information on Heinrich Harrer's life journey and friendship with the Dalai Lama.
http://www.health-psych.org/ This is the American Psychological Association's division of Health Psychology website. Here you will find additional information on the behavioral aspects of physical and mental health.
http://www.mayoclinic.com/ This website is owned by the Mayo Foundation for Medical Education and Research. The Mayo Clinic's mission is to empower people to manage their health. This website provides useful information on diseases and conditions, healthy living, prescription and over-the-counter drugs, and health tools for treating or preventing a condition.
http://www.cnn.com/HEALTH/library/MH/00041.html This website contains an article on the health benefits of social support.

Comprehensive Crossword Puzzle

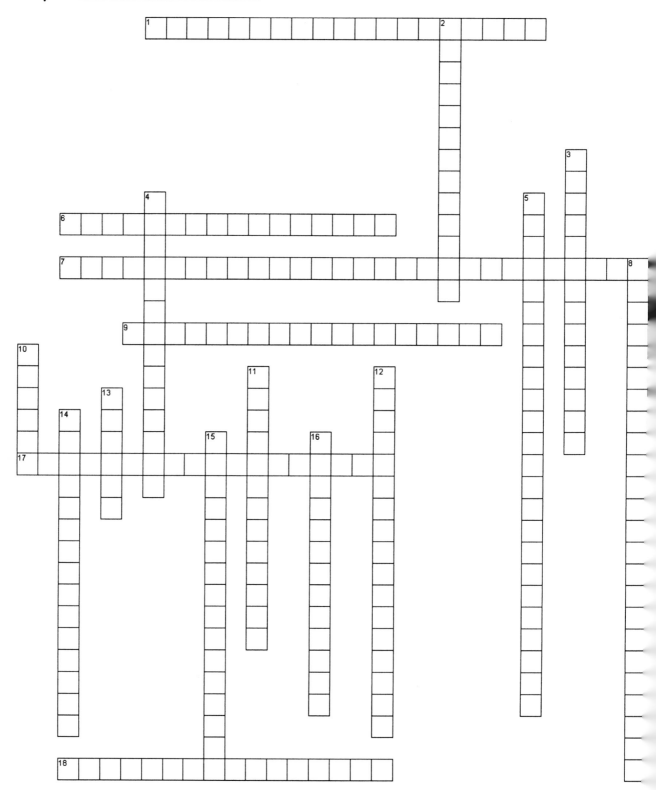

Across

1. Model that presumes that the governing principles vary from one domain of behavior to another
6. Form of exchange in which goods are divided according to a person's status in the group
7. Tendency to become friends with those who live or work nearby
9. Tendency to feel positively toward people, places, or things we have seen frequently
17. Model that attempts to explain a wide range of different behaviors according to a simple general rule
18. Form of exchange in which each person gets the same as the others

Down

2. Form of exchange in which everyone gets out in proportion to what they put in
3. Sharing of intimate information about oneself
4. Trading of benefits within relationships
5. Theory that we like people with whom we associate positive feelings and dislike those with whom we associate negative feelings
8. Observational technique in which subjects fill out frequent descriptions of who they are with and what is going on
10. Someone with whom we have an affectionate relationship
11. Assets that can be drawn from one's network of personal relationships
12. Desire to be near others and to have pleasant interactions with them
13. State of affairs in which one person's benefits and costs from a relationship are proportional to the benefits and costs incurred by his or her partner
14. Form of exchange in which members of a group share a pool of resources, taking when in need and giving when others are in need
15. Study of behavioral and psychological factors that affect illness
16. Emotional, material, or informational assistance provided by other people

Puzzle created with Puzzlemaker at DiscoverySchool.com

LOVE AND ROMANTIC RELATIONSHIPS

Before You Read...

This chapter discusses the multifaceted nature of love and how love can be reduced to three essential factors: passion, intimacy, and decision/commitment. You will learn how factor analysis uncovered the common factors underlying love. Then you will discover that the feelings associated with love combine differently depending on the type of relationship; loving relationships with family members are distinctly different from relationships with romantic partners. You will find that romantic relationships have three major goals, which include sexual satisfaction, forming family bonds, and gaining resources and social status. You will learn that sexual desire has been linked to testosterone, physical attractiveness, arousal, and cultural norms and that there are large gender differences in attitudes towards casual sex. Next, you will learn about the importance of attachment in establishing family bonds, how individuals differ in their styles of attachment, and how threats can affect a relationship. Finally, you will examine the differences between men and women with regard to a mate's status, wealth, and dominance. After exploring these three romantic relationship goals, you will look at the factors that affect relationship stability.

Chapter Learning Objectives

After reading this chapter, you should be able to:

- Describe Sternberg's (1986) three essential components of love

- Explain factor analysis and what it is used for

- Define passionate love and companionate love. Give examples of each.

- Outline the three major goals of love and romantic relationships

- Describe how testosterone affects sexual desire in men and in women

- Define sociosexual orientation. Explain the difference between restricted and unrestricted sexual orientations.

- Describe the physical characteristics associated with sexually attractive individuals

- Explain how men and women differ in their attitudes toward sex outside a committed relationship and whether these attitudes change when in a committed relationship

- Explain Berscheid and Walster's (1974) two-factor theory of love and discuss a limitation to this theory

- Describe the cultural differences regarding sexuality and how certain cultural practices may interfere with evolved mechanisms

- Explain why attachment is important. Describe the three categories of attachment style based on mother-infant relationships and how these early mother-infant experiences affect adult relationships.

- Explain how exchange versus communal orientation affects a relationship

- Explain how threat can affect a relationship.

- Define erotomania and describe the characteristics associated with the disorder

- Explain the jealousy differences between men and women

- Explain how gender affects our desire to seek status in a mate

- Give an example of how homosexuals can serve as a "control group" for the study of heterosexual mate choice

- Define monogamy and polygamy and describe the two types of polygamy

- Explain what happens to a woman's desire for status and resources in a mate when she herself achieves wealth, power, and status

- Explain how dominance affects mate selection

- Describe the factors that cause people to break up

- Explain how healthy communication can save relationships

As You Read...

KEY TERMS!

Listed below are the key terms from the chapter that are essential for your understanding of the material. Refer to the definitions from your textbook; they are located at the end of this chapter, within the text in boldface, and in the margins throughout this chapter. In order to enhance your recall ability for these terms, you may want to consider making flashcards which include a term on one side, and a definition on the other (with perhaps a brief example that makes sense to you).

Androgynous	Intimacy	Polygamy
Anxious/ambivalent attachment style	Monogamy	Polygyny
Avoidant attachment style	Need-based rule	Secure attachment style
Companionate love	Need to belong	Secure base
Decision/commitment	Passion	Sociosexual orientation
Equity rule	Passionate love	Three-stage pattern of separation distress
Erotomania	Polyandry	Two-factor theory of love
Factor analysis		

THE PUZZLING LOVE LIVES OF THE BRITISH MONARCHS

In the beginning of this chapter your authors introduced you to the love lives of British royalty. What individual and situational factors influenced Edward's decision to abdicate his throne for Wallis Simpson? Based on your understanding of the concepts discussed in this chapter, what factors contribute to the current public adoration of Prince William?

DEFINING LOVE AND ROMANTIC ATTRACTION

Love is a difficult word to define because it is multifaceted and there are different varieties of it. First, think of five different people for whom you have had different kinds of love. List their names below, describe their relationship to you, and describe the important characteristics that make up that type of loving relationship.

	Name of Person	Relationship	Important Characteristics for this Relationship
1.			
2.			
3.			
4.			
5.			

Now that you have had a chance to think about love, define what love means. Did your characteristics of love differ depending on the nature of the relationship?

THE DEFINING FEATURES OF LOVE

Robert Sternberg proposed that each love relationship contains three basic components that are present in varying degrees for different couples. Describe the three components of the theory and complete the figure that distinguishes between the different types of love.

Passion –

Intimacy –

Decision/Commitment –

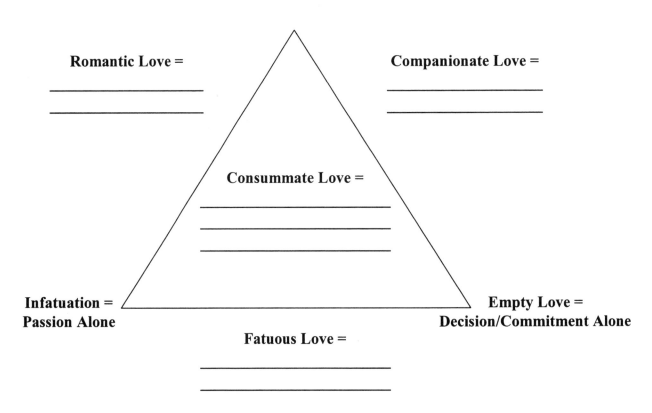

Liking = Intimacy Alone

Romantic Love =

_____

_____

Companionate Love =

_____

_____

Consummate Love =

_____

_____

_____

Infatuation =
Passion Alone

Empty Love =
Decision/Commitment Alone

Fatuous Love =

_____

_____

SUMMARY OF THE GOALS SERVED BY ROMANTIC RELATIONSHIPS

Complete the chart below to help you summarize the goals served by romantic relationships and the factors related to each goal. If you need assistance, see page 273 in your text (but be sure to use your own words in this exercise, rather than just copying).

The Goal	The Person	The Situation	Interactions
Obtaining Sexual Satisfaction	• • •	• •	• •
Establishing Family Bonds	• •	• • •	• • •
Gaining Resources and Social Status	• •	• • •	• •

MATCHING: KEY TERMS

Matching! Match each definition on the left side of the page with the concept on the right side of the page. Each concept on the right should be used only once.

___	1.	Factor on love scales - items tapping feelings of close bonding with another	A.	Androgynous
___	2.	Factor on love scales - items tapping decision that one is in love with and committed to another	B.	Anxious/ambivalent attachment style
___	3.	Individual differences in the tendency to prefer either unrestricted sex (without the necessity of love) or restricted sex (only in the context of a long-term, loving relationship)	C.	Avoidant attachment style
___	4.	Each person's benefits and costs in a social relationship should be matched to the benefits and costs of the other	D.	Companionate love
___	5.	Marital custom in which either one man marries more than one woman or one woman marries more than one man	E.	Decision/commitment
___	6.	Each person in a social relationship provides benefits as the other needs them, without keeping account of individual' costs and benefits	F.	Equity rule
___	7.	Marital custom in which one man marries one woman	G.	Erotomania
___	8.	State of intense longing for union with another	H.	Factor analysis
___	9.	Marital arrangement involving one man and more than one wife	I.	Intimacy
___	10.	Comfort provided by an attachment figure, which allows the person to venture forth more confidently to explore the environment	J.	Monogamy
___	11.	Affection/tenderness felt for those whose lives are entwined with our own	K.	Need-based rule
___	12.	Reaction sequence shown by infants or adults separated from those to whom they are intimately attached: (1) protest, (2) despair, and (3) detachment	L.	Need to belong
___	13.	Marital arrangement involving one woman and more than one husband	M.	Passion
___	14.	Attachments marked by trust that the other person will continue to provide love and support	N.	Passionate love
___	15.	Factor on love scales - items tapping romantic attraction and sexual desires	O.	Polyandry
___	16.	Theory that love consists of general arousal which is attributed to the presence of an attractive person (the cognitive label that the feeling is "love")	P.	Polygamy
___	17.	Human need to form and maintain strong, stable interpersonal relationships	Q.	Polygyny
___	18.	Attachments marked by defensive detachment from the other	R.	Secure attachment style
___	19.	Statistical technique for sorting test items or behaviors into conceptually similar groupings	S.	Secure base
___	20.	Attachments marked by fear of abandonment and the feeling that one's needs are not being met	T.	Sociosexual orientation
___	21.	Demonstrating a combination of masculine and feminine characteristics in one's behaviors	U.	Three-stage pattern of separation distress
___	22.	Disorder involving the fixed (but incorrect) belief that one is loved by another, which persists in the face of strong evidence to the contrary	V.	Two-factor theory of love

PUTTING IT ALL TOGETHER: THOUGHT QUESTIONS

Sociosexual orientation is described as an effect of the person on romantic relationships. Do you think that sociosexual orientation stays the same over the lifespan? What are some reasons it might change over the lifespan? What kinds of situations might cause a change in sociosexual orientation? How would you test your hypotheses experimentally?

Women in relationships with androgynous men report higher levels of happiness than do women in relationships with "traditionally male" partners. At the same time, women rate dominant, masculine men as more attractive. Based on what you have read in this chapter and Chapter 7: Affiliation and Friendship, discuss possible explanations for this apparent contradiction.

After You Read...Practice Tests

Practice Test 1

1. Sternberg (1986) proposed that love could be reduced to three essential components. What were these three components?
   a. companionate love, passionate love, commitment
   b. passion, intimacy, commitment
   c. arousal, labeling, attraction
   d. companionate love, intimacy, passionate love

2. If you describe your best friend as agreeable, you probably also describe her as warm, friendly, and nice. Which statistical technique would sort words like warm, friendly, and nice into a common category?
   a. content analysis
   b. multivariate analysis
   c. categorical analysis
   d. factor analysis

3. _____ is defined as "a state of intense longing for union with another."
   a. Consummate love
   b. Romantic love
   c. Passionate love
   d. Companionate love

4. Bill fantasizes often about having sex with women other than his partner Linda. Bill believes that sex without love is OK and is currently carrying on two additional relationships with Jasmine and Alexandria. Bill displays the characteristics of someone with
   a. an unrestricted sociosexual orientation.
   b. insecure attachment style.
   c. a restricted sociosexual orientation.
   d. erotomania.

5. Which of the following is true with regard to sexual attractiveness?
   a. Symmetrical men have sex later than do asymmetrical men.
   b. Women are considered attractive if they have small eyes.
   c. We prefer feedback that our partners see us as about as attractive as we see ourselves rather than far more or far less attractive than we see ourselves.
   d. Symmetrical men have more sexual partners than do asymmetrical men.

6. Clark and Hatfield (1989) had college students walk up to the opposite sex and ask them one of three questions: "Would you go out tonight?" or "Will you come over to my apartment?" or "Would you go to bed with me?" What did they find?
   a. Most women and all men readily agreed to each question.
   b. Almost all the women said no to each question and the men readily agreed to each question.
   c. Men were more willing to have sex than to go on a date.
   d. Half of the women agreed to go out on a date and five percent agreed to go to bed.

7. Which of the following is NOT a state in the three-stage pattern of separation distress?
   a. detachment
   b. despair
   c. avoidance
   d. protest

8. What is the defining feature of erotomania?
    a. discomfort with sexually explicit movies or reading material
    b. finding it difficult to trust romantic partners
    c. a reluctance to get as close as romantic partners desire
    d. a fixed, delusional belief that one is passionately loved by another

9. In a study by Townsend and Levy (1990), students rated the attractiveness of potential partners and found that
    a. physically attractive Burger King employees were preferred by both sexes.
    b. men prefer good-looking upper-class woman.
    c. women prefer good-looking men regardless of his apparent social class.
    d. women prefer a homely, well-dressed man to a handsome Burger King employee.

10. Women in long-term relationships with traditionally masculine men reported being
    a. completely satisfied with these relationships.
    b. less satisfied than women in relationships with more androgynous men.
    c. initially not attracted to their "macho" ways but grew to love them after being friends with them for a long time.
    d. less attracted to men who possessed nurturing or expressiveness characteristics.

Practice Test 2

1. _____ refers to feelings that promote a close bond while _____ is the romantic attraction and sexual desire for another.
    a. Passion; intimacy   b. Intimacy; decision/commitment
    c. Intimacy; passion   d. Decision/commitment; intimacy

2. What goal/s is served by being in a romantic relationship?
    a. obtaining sexual satisfaction   b. establishing family bonds
    c. gaining resources and social status   d. all of the above

3. Injections of what hormone increase sexual fantasies and sexual desire in both men and women?
    a. estrogen   b. testosterone
    c. epinephrine   d. progesterone

4. Margaret will only date someone she believes would be a good parent. She often tells her friends that the perfect mate for her is someone who is responsible, affectionate, stable, and faithful. Margaret is considered to have
    a. a restricted sociosexual orientation.   b. erotophobia.
    c. an unrestricted sociosexual orientation. d. erotomania.

5. Joe sees a woman walking in front of him on campus and says to his buddies, "She's a babe." According to your book, what is Joe likely to find attractive about this woman?
    a. her stylish shoes   b. her large jaw
    c. her small waist-to-hip ratio d. her small eyes

6. According to Berscheid and Walster's (1974) two-factor theory of love, why would standing on a narrow suspension bridge over a rocky canyon lead men to feel more attracted to an attractive woman?
   a. Mortality salience makes them think of love.
   b. Arousal caused by fear is misattributed to love.
   c. Fear of heights narrows his focus of attention on her attractiveness.
   d. Standing on high bridges makes people think about love.

7. Susan finds it relatively easy to get close to other people and is quite comfortable depending on them and having them depending on her. Susan also does not fear being abandoned by those she is close to. Which attachment style most closely fits Susan's relationship history?
   a. secure attachment style
   b. anxious/ambivalent attachment style
   c. avoidant attachment style
   d. none of the above

8. Studies of singles advertisements have found a relationship between gender and status seeking in relationships. Which of the following is not true of this relationship?
   a. Men are more likely to advertise status and wealth in singles ads.
   b. Women are more likely to answer ads in which men advertise their status and wealth.
   c. Men reading singles ads pay close attention to mention of a woman's status and wealth.
   d. In their ads, women are more likely to request status and wealth of men.

9. Norm Li and his colleagues (2002) asked a group of adults waiting in an airport to design an ideal mate. What did they find when participants were given more limited budgets with which to design their mate?
   a. Women and men prioritized attractiveness and gave up wealth.
   b. Women and men prioritized wealth and gave up attractiveness.
   c. Women prioritized social status and gave up good looks.
   d. Men prioritized social status and gave up good looks.

10. Simpson, Gangestad, and Lerma (1990) had participants' rate pictures of attractive members of the opposite sex. What did they find?
    a. People in relationships rated attractive persons lower than did people not in relationships.
    b. People in relationships were more attractive than those not in relationships.
    c. People in relationships rated everyone as more attractive than those not in relationships.
    d. People in relationships rated attractive members of the opposite sex as more attractive than did unattached, presumable available, individuals.

Practice Test 3
1. A statistical technique for sorting test items or behaviors into conceptually similar groupings is called
   a. factor analysis.
   b. multivariate analysis.
   c. categorical analysis.
   d. content analysis.

2.   Which of the following is NOT found to be a central component of love to most people (based on factor analyses)?
     a. passion
     b. commitment
     c. intimacy
     d. respect

3.   What type of love has been defined as the affection and tenderness we feel for those with whom our lives are entwined with our own?
     a. Consummate love
     b. Romantic love
     c. Passionate love
     d. Companionate love

4.   Mike and Lisa are considering whether or not to have sex. Lisa has been willing to have sex from the moment of their first encounter. Lisa is said to have
     a. an unrestricted sociosexual orientation.
     b. insecure attachment style.
     c. a restricted sociosexual orientation.
     d. erotomania.

5.   Unrelated children raised together in Israeli kibbutzim were not romantically attracted to each other later in life. What explanation does your book suggest for this?
     a. Children from the same kibbutz were forbidden to form romantic attachments with each other in adulthood.
     b. The children did not like each other even as friends, so they were unlikely to be romantically attracted to each other.
     c. People are simply usually not attracted to those that they live in close proximity to.
     d. The situation triggered an innate aversion to sexual relationships between people raised together.

6.   Which of the following statements is true regarding attachment?
     a. For 95 percent of mammals, adult males contribute little more than sperm to their offspring.
     b. Husbands mirror the hormonal changes of their expectant wives.
     c. A mother's presence reduces her child's stress and provides a secure base from which the child can safely explore the environment.
     d. All of the above are true.

7.   Karen has been in and out of relationships, and when she's in a relationship, she is constantly afraid that her partner doesn't love her. Which attachment most closely fits Karen's relationship history?
     a. passionate attachment style
     b. anxious/ambivalent attachment style
     c. avoidant attachment style
     d. none of the above

8.   According to Buunk and VanYperen (1991), an exchange-focused individual is someone who
     a. is likely to hold a grudge if they feel a loved one has not fulfilled an obligation in the relationship.
     b. will feel resentment if they believe they spent more on a friend's present than the friend spent on theirs.
     c. is generally more unhappy with their relationships.
     d. all the above

9. Of the 246 clinical erotomania cases reported between 1900 and 2000,
   a. the majority were men in their late 20s.
   b. the majority were single women in their mid-thirties who desired older, higher status men.
   c. the typical man afflicted with the disorder was attracted to older, higher status women.
   d. all of the men and women afflicted with the disorder harassed their intended object to the point that the law became involved.

10. _____ is defined as a marital arrangement involving one woman and more than one husband, while _____ is defined as a marital arrangement involving one man and more than one wife.
   a. Polygamy; polyandry
   b. Polyandry; polygyny
   c. Polygyny; polygamy
   d. Monogamy; polygamy

Comprehensive Test
(Note: Items 1-15 are multiple-choice questions, items 16-23 are true-false questions, and 24-25 are essay questions.)

1. Which of the following is NOT true about factor analytic studies of love?
   a. Most studies find more than one component of love.
   b. Feelings of intimacy are a central component of love for most people.
   c. The components of love don't overlap much at all.
   d. Feelings of intimacy often overlap with passion and commitment.

2. Sternberg's three-component theory of love used which type of analysis to derive the three core ingredients?
   a. multivariate analysis
   b. factor analysis
   c. categorical analysis
   d. content analysis

3. Ross is asked who he loves more, his mother or his fiancé. Ross, having just taken a social psychology course, explains that you can't compare the two, because while he feels _____ for his mother, he feels _____ for his fiancé.
   a. commitment; intimacy
   b. passionate love, companionate love
   c. companionate love; passionate love
   d. jealousy; passion

4. What key feature distinguishes romantic relationships from friendships?
   a. forgiveness
   b. sexual gratification
   c. commitment
   d. sharing of resources

5. How does testosterone affect sexual desire?
   a. It decreases sexual desire in women and increases sexual desire in men.
   b. It increases sexual desire in women and decreases sexual desire in men.
   c. It decreases sexual desire in both sexes.
   d. It increases sexual desire in both sexes.

6. Which of the following is true about sociosexual orientation?
    a. People with an unrestricted orientation tend to have more one-night stands than people who are restricted.
    b. People who are restricted have more positive attitudes about casual sex than people who are unrestricted.
    c. Sociosexual orientation is strongly related to the frequency of sex within a relationship.
    d. Restricted people have a lower sex drive and feel guilty when having sex.

7. In their study of the characteristics men and women look for in different types of relationships, what did Kenrick et al. (1990) find out about minimum standards for intelligence for a one-night stand versus a single date?
    a. Men had lower standards for a one-night stand than for a date.
    b. Women had lower standards for a one-night stand than for a date.
    c. Men had higher standards for a one-night stand than did women.
    d. Women had higher standards for a date than did men.

8. Which of the following might lead to increased attraction toward a potential partner?
    a. parental interference   b. fear of painful electric shock
    c. strenuous exercise   d. all of the above

9. According to Baumeister and Leary (1995) separated lovers go through the same three-stage pattern of separation distress shown by infants separated from their mothers. The _____ stage is characterized by crying and reluctance to be soothed, while _____ is characterized by passivity and sadness, and finally, _____ includes coolness toward the former lover when reunited.
    a. protest; despair; detachment   b. despair; detachment; protest
    c. detachment; protest; despair   d. protest; detachment; despair

10. Which of the following is NOT one of the attachment styles discussed in the text (research by Hazan and Shaver, 1987)?
    a. passionate   b. anxious/ambivalent
    c. avoidant   d. secure

11. Malcolm and Sandra have been dating for three years. According to your book's discussion of the effect of threat on relationships, which of these situations would most spark in Malcolm the need to be with Sandra?
    a. Sandra says she wants to make Malcolm a nice dinner.
    b. Sandra is frightened by a large insect.
    c. Sandra says she is considering a job offer in a distant city.
    d. Sandra finds $100 bill on the sidewalk.

12. According to Buss et al. (1992), the majority of men report being more distressed by _____ and the majority of women report being more distressed by _____.
    a. sexual infidelity; sexual infidelity   b. sexual infidelity; emotional attachment
    c. emotional attachment; sexual infidelity d. emotional attachment; emotional attachment

13. Women generally look for a mate with wealth and status. What pattern is true for women who themselves have high status and wealth?
    a. They seek young and attractive men.
    b. They are generally not concerned with their partner's wealth and status.
    c. They tend to be interested in men their same age.
    d. Like other women, they tend to be interested in relatively older high status men.

14. What would make a man more likely to take multiple wives?
    a. a steep social hierarchy
    b. a rich environment so one family can accumulate vast wealth
    c. occasional famines so the poor face occasional danger of starvation
    d. all of the above

15. Notarius and Markman (1993) videotaped couples discussing problems in their relationships and discovered that couples respond to conflict with "zingers." The researchers then developed a guide to help couples when they are thinking of throwing a zinger. Which of the following was NOT suggested when interacting with your partner?
    a. If you don't have anything nice to say, say nothing at all.
    b. When you have an opinion, say it rather than fishing around with questions to get your partner to guess what it is.
    c. It is OK to analyze your partner's behavior when you are trying to be helpful.
    d. Always speak for yourself, not your partner.

TRUE-FALSE
Indicate whether each statement is true or false by circling T or F. If you decide it is false, explain why. Correct answers appear at the end of the study guide in the ANSWERS section for Chapter 8.

T F 16. The component of love that involves feeling a close bond with another is the decision/commitment component.

T F 17. A person with a restricted sociosexual orientation feels comfortable having sex with someone he or she is not in love with.

T F 18. Testosterone increases sexual desire in men, but not in women.

T F 19. The most common marital arrangement in the world is polygamy.

T F 20. Individuals with an avoidant attachment style are fearful of intimacy and also more prone to jealousy.

T F 21. In Buss et al.'s (1992) study of jealousy, men were more upset by sexual infidelity, and women were more upset by emotional infidelity.

T F 22. In Notarius and Markman's (1993) study of married couples, they discovered that the most often cited relationship problem was disagreements about sex.

T F 23. Like heterosexual men, homosexual men show a strong attraction to romantic partners in their 20's, regardless of their own age.

ESSAY

24. Describe Robert Sternberg's three-component theory of love. Explain the statistical technique Sternberg used to develop and test his theory.

25. Researchers have discovered communication techniques that help de-escalate conflict for couples. Describe how Notarius and Markman (1993) came up with their guide to politeness for couples and give three examples of what a partner should do instead of throwing a "zinger."

When You Have Finished...

Now that you have had a chance to read this chapter and complete the activities associated with it, you may be interested in finding additional materials on this topic. The World Wide Web is a great and convenient resource for gathering additional information in a variety of areas. Listed below are web links and website descriptions that are relevant to this chapter.

Web Links and Website Descriptions
Be sure to visit Chapter 8 at the companion website: www.ablongman.com/knc3e
http://wps.ablongman.com/ab_baronbyrne_socialpsych_10/0,4608,185934-,00.html This is the companion website for the Baron and Byrne Social Psychology textbook. This website contains information relevant to close relationships and includes learning objectives, multiple choice questions, true-false questions, essay questions, activities, flashcards, and additional web links.
http://p034.psch.uic.edu/cgi-bin/crq.pl This website contains an Attachment Styles Questionnaire. You can submit your answers and find out your attachment style. This website also plots your two scores in the two-dimensional space defined by attachment-related anxiety and avoidance.
http://www.uwec.edu/counsel/pubs/qual.htm This website contains the Quality of Loving Relationships Assessment Scale to help you determine the quality of your loving relationship with a significant other.
http://www.yale.edu/rjsternberg/ This is the homepage of Robert Sternberg who proposed the three-component theory love. Here you will find information about Sternberg, his research interests, and additional information on love and hate.
http://www.indiana.edu/~kinsey/ This is the website for The Kinsey Institute which promotes interdisciplinary research and scholarship in the fields of human sexuality, gender, and reproduction.

Comprehensive Crossword Puzzle

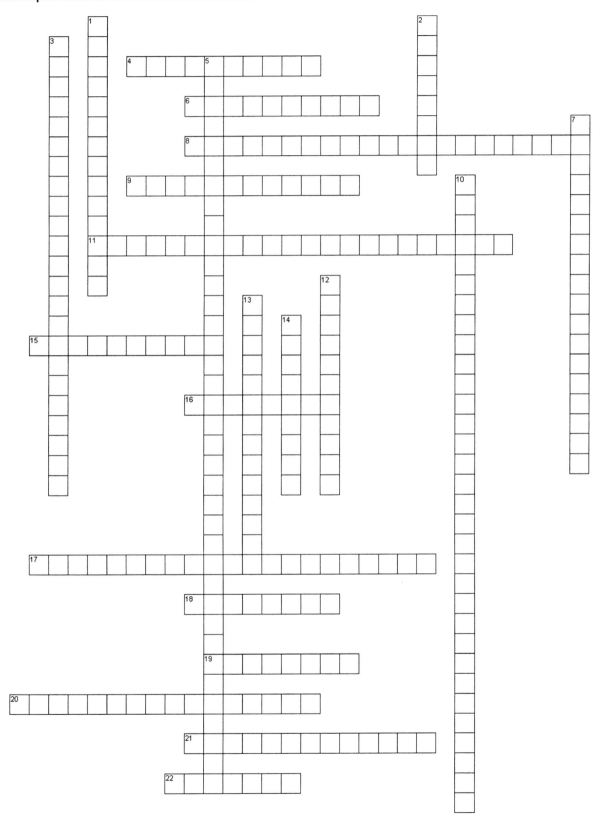

Across

4. Each person's benefits and costs in a social relationship should be matched to the benefits and costs of the other

6. Disorder involving the fixed (but incorrect) belief that one is loved by another, which persists in the face of strong evidence to the contrary

8. Attachments marked by trust that the other person will continue to provide love and support

9. Human need to form and maintain strong, stable interpersonal relationships

11. Individual differences in the tendency to prefer either unrestricted sex or restricted sex

15. Comfort provided by an attachment figure, which allows the person to venture forth more confidently to explore the environment

16. Marital custom in which one man marries one woman

17. Theory that love consists of general arousal which is attributed to the presence of an attractive person (the cognitive label that the feeling is "love")

18. Marital arrangement involving one man and more than one wife

19. Factor on love scales composed of items tapping feelings of close bonding with another

20. Affection and tenderness felt for those whose lives are entwined with our own

21. Each person in a social relationship provides benefits as the other needs them, without keeping account of individual costs and benefits

22. Factor on love scales composed of items tapping romantic attraction and sexual desires

Down

1. Statistical technique for sorting test items or behaviors into conceptually similar groupings

2. Marital custom in which either one man marries more than one woman or one woman marries more than one man

3. Attachments marked by defensive detachment from the other

5. Reaction sequence shown by infants or adults separated from those to whom they are intimately attached: (1) protest (2) despair, and (3) detachment

7. Factor on love scales composed of items tapping decision that one is in love with and committed to another

10. Attachments marked by fear of abandonment and the feeling that one's needs are not being met

12. Demonstrating a combination of masculine and feminine characteristics in one's behaviors

13. State of intense longing for union with another

14. Marital arrangement involving one woman and more than one husband

Puzzle created with Puzzlemaker at DiscoverySchool.com

PROSOCIAL BEHAVIOR

Before You Read...

Prosocial behavior is action intended to benefit another. In this chapter you will be given an overview of the four major goals of prosocial action and you will examine how each goal accounts for various types of helping. First, you will learn that people sometimes help to improve their own genetic welfare by assisting relatives and nonrelatives who are likely to help in return. Second, you will discover that helping is valued positively across human cultures and thus, helping may increase one's social standing and approval. Third, you will read about the fact that prosocial behaviors can affect how people view themselves and how people use prosocial behaviors to enhance and verify their self-definitions. Finally, you will learn that helping may occur because it is beneficial to the helper by removing the unpleasant state of arousal that comes from witnessing a victim's suffering or by enhancing the helper's mood state. After learning about these goals and factors that affect them, you will be introduced to a discussion regarding whether or not pure altruism exists.

Chapter Learning Objectives

After reading this chapter, you should be able to:

- Define prosocial behavior.

- Outline the four goals of prosocial action

- Explain Hamilton's concept of inclusive fitness and discuss how it relates to helping behavior

- Explain Trivers' concept of reciprocal aid and discuss how it helps explain prosocial behavior towards nonrelatives

- Describe how behavior geneticists use twins to study hereditary versus environmental effects on behavior

- Explain how the expanded sense of "we" impacts helping behavior

- Describe how similarity and familiarity increase helping

- Describe the practice of potlatching and explain why people engage in this practice

- Explain the social responsibility norm

- Explain diffusion of responsibility and pluralistic ignorance and discuss how they affect helping behavior

- Describe how the need for approval affects helping

- Explain the effect of helping models and population density on the tendency to help

- Outline the differences between males and females on helping

- List the two ways a personal norm differs from a social norm

- Describe the effect of self-focus on helping

- Describe the three circumstances in which an individual may reject help or minimize the value of that help

- Explain the arousal/cost-reward model and discuss when helping is most likely

- Explain the negative state relief model of helping

- Differentiate between perspective taking and empathic concern

- Explain the empathy-altruism sequence

- Explain the egoistic interpretation of Batson's studies of "pure altruism"

As You Read…

KEY TERMS!
Listed below are the key terms from the chapter that are essential for your understanding of the material. Refer to the definitions from your textbook; they are located at the end of this chapter, within the text in boldface, and in the margins throughout this chapter. In order to enhance your recall ability for these terms, you may want to consider making flashcards which include a term on one side, and a definition on the other (with perhaps a brief example that makes sense to you).

Arousal/cost-reward model	Mood management hypothesis	Pure (true) altruism
Diffusion of responsibility	Personal norms	Reciprocal aid
Empathic concern	Perspective taking	Social responsibility norm
Inclusive fitness	Prosocial behavior	

THE STRANGE CASE OF SEMPO SUGIHARA

In the beginning of this chapter your authors introduced a mystery regarding the strange case of Sempo Sugihara, Japan's Consul General in Lithuania during World War II. Please describe how Sugihara's puzzling prosocial behavior can be explained with regard to the four goals of helping that were discussed during the chapter.

DEFINING PROSOCIAL BEHAVIOR

Your textbook broadly defines prosocial behavior as an action intended to benefit another. However, there are also more restrictive types of prosocial behavior: benevolence and pure altruism. Benevolence can be defined as an action intended to benefit another without external reward or recognition to the helper. Pure altruism is defined as a selfless act intended to benefit another for no external or internal reward. For each of the following situations below, indicate whether the behavior is general prosocial behavior, benevolence, or pure altruism.

		Type of Behavior
1.	Laura tutors college students in organic chemistry three hours a week to improve her chances of going to medical school.	
2.	Alex, a Marine sergeant, throws himself on a live hand-grenade to save his comrades.	
3.	Tricia anonymously donates $500 each year to the Humane Society and feels good about it.	
4.	JoAnn sees a dog that has fallen into an icy lake and without thinking, risks her own life to save the dog.	
5.	Roger, a cancer survivor, feels it is important to donate half of his lottery winnings anonymously to fund cancer research.	
6.	Rick is very involved with Habitat for Humanity and makes a point of telling everyone about his involvement.	

THE GOAL: TO GAIN SOCIAL STATUS AND APPROVAL

Latané and Darley's explanation of the murder of New York City resident Catherine Genovese represents the beginning of this intriguing line of prosocial behavior research. Briefly describe the events of the murder and how Latané and Darley explained the witnesses' behavior.

THE GOAL: TO MANAGE SELF-IMAGE

Complete the following flow chart regarding self-focus and the decision to help. (p.299)

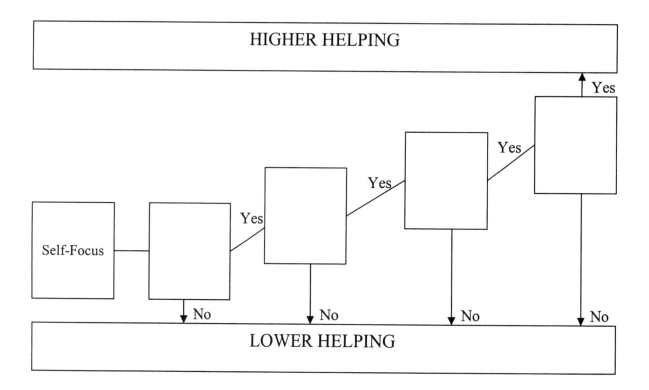

SUMMARY OF PROSOCIAL GOALS

Complete the chart below to help you summarize the four goals of prosocial behavior and the factors related to them. If you need assistance, see page 305 in your text (but be sure to use your own words in this exercise, rather than just copying).

The Goal	The Person	The Situation	Interactions
To Gain Genetic and Material Benefits	• •	• •	•
To Gain Social Status and Approval	•	• •	•
To Manage Self-Image	• • •	• •	• •
To Manage Our Moods and Emotions	•	• •	•

MATCHING: KEY TERMS

Matching! Match each definition on the left side of the page with the concept on the right side of the page. Each concept on the right should be used only once.

___ 1. Compassionate feelings caused by taking the perspective of a needy other

A. Arousal/cost-reward model

___ 2. Internalized beliefs and values that combine to form a person's inner standards for behavior

B. Benevolence

___ 3. Survival of one's genes in one's own offspring and in any relatives one helps

C. Diffusion of responsibility

___ 4. Action intended to benefit another but not to gain external reward

D. Empathic concern

___ 5. Process of mentally putting oneself in another's position

E. Inclusive fitness

___ 6. View that observers of a victim's suffering will want to help in order to relieve their own personal distress

F. Mood management hypothesis

___ 7. Action intended solely to benefit another and thus not to gain external or internal reward

G. Personal norms

___ 8. Societal rule that people should help those who need them to help

H. Perspective taking

___ 9. Helping that occurs in return for prior help

I. Prosocial behavior

___ 10. Idea that people use helping tactically to manage their moods

J. Pure (true) altruism

___ 11. Action intended to benefit another

K. Reciprocal aid

___ 12. Tendency for each group member to dilute personal responsibility for acting by spreading it among all other group members

L. Social responsibility norm

PUTTING IT ALL TOGETHER: THOUGHT QUESTIONS
FAILURE TO HELP:
HIT-RUN VICTIM LEFT TO DIE IN CAR'S WINDSHIELD

In October of 2001 a nurse's aide hit a homeless man with her car. The nurse's aide drove home with the victim stuck headfirst in her broken windshield. Ignoring his cries for help, he bled to death in her garage over the next three days. The accused told police that she had been drinking and using Ecstasy the night of the hit-and-run. According to police, if the victim had received immediate help, he would have lived since he suffered no internal injuries, and died only from a loss of blood. This disturbing story is indeed a mystery. Why would a nurse's aide, who is trained to help others, not help in this particular situation? Use the research findings in the chapter to help you explain the failure to help on the part of the nurse's aide.

After You Read...Practice Tests

Practice Test 1

1. _____ refers to any action intended to benefit another.
   a. Benevolence
   b. Prosocial Behavior
   c. Reciprocal aid
   d. Empathic concern

2. After leaving a friend's house, Amy drives past an auto accident and sees that her cousin was involved. She immediately pulls over and offers assistance to her cousin. What goal was primarily served by this prosocial action?
   a. gaining genetic and material benefits
   b. gaining social status and approval
   c. managing self-image
   d. managing our emotions and moods

3. According to your book, why are we more likely to help those who seem similar to us and who are familiar to us?
   a. We tend to feel better about ourselves when we help similar others.
   b. Similarity and familiarity are cues to genetic relatedness.
   c. We desire approval from those who are similar and familiar to us.
   d. all of the above

4. How can bystanders influence the action of the social responsibility norm and the decision to help?
   a. bystanders serve as sources of help
   b. bystanders serve as sources of information about whether helping is required
   c. bystanders serve as sources of approval or disapproval of helping action
   d. all of the above

5. When confronted by an emergency situation, bystanders will look to others to provide clues on how to react. Many times those clues can be misleading resulting in a failure to act when assistance is needed. This phenomenon is known as
   a. pluralistic ignorance.
   b. diffusion of responsibility.
   c. inclusive fitness.
   d. social responsibility norm.

6. During her five mile morning run, Susan stumbles to the ground gasping for air. What should Susan do to minimize bystander uncertainty and maximize helping behavior?
   a. Continue gasping for air and wait for someone to come forward and help.
   b. Yell loudly, "Help me!"
   c. Tell a passerby, "I need help! You, in the red jacket, please call an ambulance."
   d. Yell loudly, "I'm hurt, will someone help me?"

7. According to Robert Levine (2003), Rochester, Memphis, and Knoxville are more helpful than cities like New York and Los Angeles because
   a. Rochester, Memphis, and Knoxville had a higher ratio of women than men.
   b. Rochester, Memphis, and Knoxville were more densely populated.
   c. Rochester, Memphis, and Knoxville were less densely populated.
   d. Rochester, Memphis, and Knoxville were considered small in size.

8. Which of the following factors make an individual MORE likely to reject offers of needed help?
   a. being under the age of eight
   b. being female
   c. being over the age of 60
   d. all of the above

9. According to the arousal/cost-reward model of helping, in which of the following situations is helping most likely?
   a. when the person in need of help is someone we don't know
   b. when there is high cost for engaging in the helping behavior
   c. when the arousal caused by seeing someone in need of help is very strong
   d. when the rewards for engaging in helping behavior are small

10. Why are people in a positive mood more likely to be helpful?
    a. Elated people like others more than do neutral mood individuals.
    b. They feel more competent and optimistic about their future.
    c. Elated people recall the positive aspects of past helping situations and focus on the positive aspects of the present helping opportunity.
    d. all of the above

Practice Test 2

1. Linda drops a $20 bill into a Salvation Army kettle to impress a friend. This is an example of a/an _____ source of reward for helping.
   a. internal
   b. benevolent
   c. external
   d. altruistic

2. Which of the following is an example of reciprocal aid?
   a. When a company gives benefits to employees who work hard, and in return they work harder.
   b. When one prairie dog stands up tall to warn others in this family group of danger, and in the process makes himself more vulnerable.
   c. When female monkeys groom their sisters and get no grooming in return.
   d. When rescue workers help their family members first in an emergency.

3. How was Rabbi Kalisch able to convince the Japanese that the lives of the Jewish refugees in Shanghai should be spared?
   a. He offered to pay the Japanese for letting the refugees hide out in Shanghai.
   b. He asked the Japanese to take the perspective of the refugees.
   c. He labeled the Japanese as benevolent to convince them to actually be benevolent
   d. He convinced the Japanese that they and the Jews were similar by asserting that they were both of Asian origin.

4. How did Latané and Darley explain the complete failure to help on the part of New York City resident Catherine Genovese's neighbors the night of her murder?
    a. pluralistic ignorance
    b. diffusion of responsibility
    c. inclusive fitness
    d. social responsibility norm

5. Imagine you and two other students are filling out a questionnaire when smoke begins to billow into the room. It is difficult to ignore the smoke, but when you look at the other students, they do not appear alarmed. When you regain consciousness at the hospital, the other students tell you that they ignored the smoke because you did not look alarmed. This situation demonstrates the _____ phenomenon.
    a. pluralistic ignorance
    b. diffusion of responsibility
    c. inclusive fitness
    d. social responsibility norm

6. Dave lives in New York City, while John lives in Nashville, Tennessee. According to your book, who is more likely to offer help in an emergency and why?
    a. Dave because he has probably had more opportunities to help.
    b. Dave because he lives in a bigger city.
    c. John because he lives in the South.
    d. John because he lives in a city with a lower population density.

7. Even though women are rated as more compassionate and kinder than men, men are actually more likely to offer help in an emergency. What explanation does your book give for this?
    a. Men and women are both conforming to accepted gender roles.
    b. Men are trying to establish their status by helping.
    c. Women are simply not physically able to help in emergencies.
    d. Helping does not fit into a woman's personal norms.

8. Gibbons and Wicklund (1982) gave participants the opportunity to help after scoring poorly or scoring well on a test in the presence of a mirror. This research demonstrates that assistance is
    a. more frequent when self-focus is combined with the presence of a prominent, legitimate need for aid and when there is no absorbing personal problem.
    b. more frequent when self-focus is combined with the presence of a prominent, legitimate need for aid and when there is an absorbing personal problem.
    c. always undermined when a person is self-focused.
    d. increased when self-focus is combined with vague cues for aid.

9. The negative state relief model of helping in nonemergency situations states that we help to manage one particular mood. Which mood does helping allow us to manage?
    a. temporary guilt
    b. temporary sadness
    c. extreme arousal
    d. extreme fear

10. The compassionate feelings caused by taking the perspective of a needy other is known as _____.
    a. empathic concern
    b. benevolence
    c. perspective taking
    d. reciprocal aid

Practice Test 3

1. What is the concept that explains why we are more likely to help our children than our first cousins?
   a. pure altruism
   b. reciprocal aid
   c. inclusive fitness
   d. arousal/cost-reward

2. What does the fact that identical twins are more similar in their helping behaviors than are nonidentical twins suggest?
   a. Helping behavior is due solely to environmental factors.
   b. Identical twins are more likely to help each other than nonidentical twins.
   c. Helping behavior is partially due to genetic factors.
   d. A prosocial orientation cannot be learned.

3. In the late nineteenth century, potlatching was a thriving practice among Native American cultures of the Northwest coast. What was the goal of this type of prosocial behavior?
   a. to gain genetic and material benefits
   b. to gain social status and approval
   c. to manage self-image
   d. to manage moods and emotions

4. Responsibility for aid can become spread thin among a group of onlookers. No one person feels an obligation to act, so no one does. This process is known as
   a. pluralistic ignorance.
   b. diffusion of responsibility.
   c. inclusive fitness.
   d. social responsibility norm.

5. If you are completing a questionnaire in a laboratory, and smoke starts coming through the vent, you are most likely to report it if
   a. you are alone
   b. there are others in the room
   c. you are in a hurry to finish your task
   d. no one else seems willing to report it

6. In a study by Shotland and Straw (1976), participants were exposed to a staged fight between a man and a woman. Observers were least likely to help the woman when they believed she was shouting at
   a. a stranger.
   b. her husband.
   c. a friend.
   d. a homeless person.

7. According to Hodgkinson and Weitzman (1990), what were the two most frequently cited reasons that charitable individuals gave for helping others?
   a. personal values and religious beliefs
   b. religious beliefs and a prior personal or medical crisis
   c. parental example and having received help in the past
   d. having received help in the past and a prior personal or medical crisis

8. Which of the following would be MOST likely to ask for help?
   a. women
   b. males
   c. people with high self-esteem
   d. people over the age of 60

9. A study by Weyant (1976) explored whether students in a happy, neutral, or sad mood were likely to help in situations with either high or low costs and high or low benefits to themselves. Based on these costs and benefits, how did participant mood affect helping behavior?
   a. Happy people helped as long as the cost was low.
   b. Happy and neutral people all helped as long as the cost was low, regardless of the level of benefit.
   c. Sad people only helped when the benefits were high, regardless of the level of cost.
   d. Sad people were most likely to help when the cost was low and the benefit was high.

10. According to Batson (1991), what can change the basic motivation for helping from selfish to selfless?
   a. love
   b. anger
   c. empathy
   d. sadness

Comprehensive Test
(Note: Items 1-15 are multiple-choice questions, items 16-23 are true-false questions, and 24-25 are essay questions.)

1. According to Cunningham and colleagues (1995), individuals are more willing to help _____ in a wide variety of situations.
   a. attractive strangers
   b. first cousins
   c. grandparents
   d. parents, siblings, and children

2. Individuals whose parents regularly opened their homes to a wide range of people from diverse backgrounds are more likely to help. Which of the following is the likely reason these people are more likely to help?
   a. These people have an expanded sense of "we."
   b. These people have been taught to help.
   c. These people inherited the tendency to help from their parents.
   d. These people are less susceptible to diffusion of responsibility.

3. According to your textbook, what is the most likely reason for an individual to engage in potlatching – the giving away of enormous quantities of goods and property?
   a. Potlatches are intended to give individuals from distinct families and tribes the opportunity to strengthen social ties.
   b. Potlatches serve as a way to redistribute the wealth of society.
   c. Potlatches establish and validate the giver's rank and social status.
   d. Potlatches are an example of reciprocal aid because they create obligations that can be called upon in the future.

4. New York City college students heard another student having a seizure over an intercom system. Darley and Latané (1968) conducted this study to test their ideas about the effects of diffusion of responsibility on helping. What did they find?
   a. When participants thought they were the only one available to help, they left the experiment.
   b. When participants thought there were four fellow subjects who could help, very few of the participants offered assistance.
   c. If participants thought that one other person was also available to help, there was no effect on their helping behavior.
   d. All participants helped if they thought the situation was serious enough.

5. The pluralistic ignorance phenomenon is most powerful when the existence of an emergency is
   a. very straightforward.
   b. not clear.
   c. surrounded by bystanders who are confident.
   d. surrounded by bystanders who act alarmed.

6. Jessica is walking to class on a very crowded college campus when she is accosted by a man she does not know. He is holding on to her, preventing her from getting to class, and she is unable to get away from him. No one has stopped to help Jessica. What can she do to increase the possibility that someone will stop to help?
   a. Tell a passerby, "I need help! You, sir, with the green backpack, would you please get the campus police?"
   b. Yell loudly, "I don't know why I ever married you!"
   c. Yell loudly, "Will someone help me?"
   d. all of the above

7. Bryan and Test (1967) found that Los Angeles motorists were more likely to stop and help the driver of a disabled car if
   a. the driver was female.
   b. the driver was a teenager.
   c. they'd witnessed another motorist doing so a quarter mile before.
   d. they were in a good mood and the weather was beautiful.

8. The acquittal of the four officers responsible for the beating of Rodney King, a black man, ignited a 72-hour riot on the streets of South Central Los Angeles. During the riots, Reginald Denny, a white man, was pulled from his 18-wheel truck and beaten by a group of young black men. Lei Yuille, an African-American woman, saw the events on television and rushed to Denny's aid. What reason did Lei Yuille provide when asked why she helped "one of them?"
   a. prior medical crisis
   b. religious beliefs
   c. parental example
   d. having received help in the past

9. Tesser and Smith (1980) arranged for participants to perform poorly on a verbal skills task. Participants then had the opportunity to help a friend or a stranger on the same verbal skills task. What did they find?
   a. participants gave more clues to a friend than to a stranger when the task was described as a good indicator of "how well people can do in school"
   b. participants gave more clues to a friend than to a stranger when the task was described as just a game "that doesn't tell us anything about the person"
   c. participants gave more clues to a stranger than to a friend when the task was described as just a game "that doesn't tell us anything about the person"
   d. participants always helped their friend over a stranger

10. According to the arousal/cost-reward model of helping, when will assistance be maximized?
    a. when the arousal is strong
    b. when there is a "we" connection between the victim and the observer
    c. when the cost of helping is small while the rewards are large
    d. all of the above

11. Research has demonstrated that helping levels can jump significantly when people are asked to do all of the following EXCEPT
    a. reminisce about unhappy events.
    b. wait in a room with several aloof strangers.
    c. witness harm to another.
    d. read a series of depressing statements.

12. _____ is the process of mentally putting oneself in another's position.
    a. Benevolence   b. Empathic concern
    c. Perspective taking   d. Reciprocal aid

13. In the Batson et al. (1981) study, when were participants most likely to help Elaine, whom they thought was receiving painful electric shocks?
    a. when escape from the situation was difficult
    b. when they felt empathic concern for Elaine
    c. when they saw Elaine react badly to the shocks
    d. when escape from the situation was easy

14. What is an egoistic explanation for the effect of empathic concern on helping?
    a. It makes us feel good to help someone toward whom we feel empathy.
    b. Empathic concern makes us feel guilty if we don't help the person in need.
    c. Empathic concern suggests genetic relatedness.
    d. Empathic concern makes us more self-focused.

15. What evidence does your book give to explain why Sempo Sugihara, a member of Japanese society, helped Jewish refugees during World War II?
    a. an expanded sense of "we" flowing from exposure to diverse individuals in the home
    b. a prior attachment to the victim
    c. helping-relevant self-image
    d. all of the above

TRUE-FALSE

Indicate whether each statement is true or false by circling T or F. If you decide it is false, explain why. Correct answers appear at the end of the study guide in the ANSWERS section for Chapter 9.

T   F   16.   Helping directed toward relatives is intended to improve inclusive fitness.

T   F   17.   Behavior geneticists who conduct studies on twins have found that helping is primarily the result of environmental factors.

T   F   18.   The tendency of bystanders in an emergency to rely on what other bystanders do and say even though no one is sure about what is happening or what to do about it is called diffusion of responsibility.

T   F   19.   Bystanders can serve as both sources of approval and sources of disapproval of helping behavior.

T   F   20.   Densely populated cities have higher rates of helping behaviors.

T   F   21.   Personal values and religious beliefs are the most frequent reasons listed for decisions to help.

T   F   22.   According to the arousal/cost-reward model, the aversive arousal of seeing someone in trouble is decreased by providing help to that person.

T   F   23.   Help is often designed for personal gain, but when empathy enters the picture the basic motivation for providing help can shift from selfish to selfless.

ESSAY

24. After the terrible incident of Catherine Genovese's murder, Latané and Darley sought to explain the behavior of the witnesses. Describe the seizure study they used to explore when bystanders provided helping behaviors, and the conclusions they drew from these studies.

25. Some social psychologists have argued that pure altruism exists, while others have suggested that helping behavior that looks altruistic has another egoistic interpretation. Discuss Batson's work suggesting that altruism is motivated by the concern for other's welfare, and describe the empathy-altruism sequence. What is the egoistic interpretation of Batson's work?

When You Have Finished...

Now that you have had a chance to read this chapter and complete the activities associated with it, you may be interested in finding additional materials on this topic. The World Wide Web is a great and convenient resource for gathering additional information in a variety of areas. Listed below are web links and website descriptions that are relevant to this chapter.

Web Links and Website Descriptions
Be sure to visit Chapter 9 at the companion website: www.ablongman.com/knc3e
http://wps.ablongman.com/ab_baronbyrne_socialpsych_10/0,4608,186018-,00.html This is the companion website for the Baron and Byrne Social Psychology textbook. This website contains information relevant to the prosocial chapter in your book and includes learning objectives, multiple choice questions, true-false questions, essay questions, activities, flashcards, and additional web links.
http://www.crimelibrary.com/serial_killers/predators/kitty_genovese/ The Crime Library is a source for students researching current and historical subjects. This website provides a detailed account of the Kitty Genovese murder.
http://www.ushmm.org/research/library/bibliography/sugihara/right.htm This website provides information about Sempo Sugihara's life, rescue activities, and related works.
http://changingminds.org/explanations/theories/prosocial_behavior.htm On the Changing Minds website you will be able to get and in-depth description of prosocial behavior, examples, references, and links to related terms.
http://www.humboldt.edu/~altruism/home.html This website is home to The Altruistic Personality and Prosocial Behavior Institute founded by Dr. Samuel Oliner and Dr. Pearl Oliner at Humboldt State University. This website contains a definition of altruism, specific examples of heroic and conventional altruism, and publications on this topic.
http://bama.ua.edu/~sprentic/672%20prosocial%20theories.htm This website contains an overview of the major theories of prosocial behavior.

Comprehensive Crossword Puzzle

Across

1. View that observers of a victim's suffering will want to help in order to relieve their own personal distress
3. Internalized beliefs and values that combine to form a person's inner standards for behavior
5. Action intended to benefit another but not to gain external reward
10. Compassionate feelings caused by taking the perspective of a needy other
12. Process of mentally putting oneself in another's position

Down

2. Tendency for each group member to dilute personal responsibility for acting by spreading it among all other group members
4. Societal rule that people should help those who need them to help
6. Action intended to benefit another
7. Idea that people use helping tactically to manage their moods
8. Survival of one's genes in one's own offspring and in any relatives one helps
9. Action intended solely to benefit another and thus not to gain external or internal reward
11. Helping that occurs in return for prior help

Puzzle created with Puzzlemaker at DiscoverySchool.com

10 AGGRESSION

Before You Read...

Aggression is defined as behavior intended to injure another. In this chapter you will discover the social psychological motives that underlie aggressive acts. You will learn that social psychologists distinguish between different types of aggression. You will learn that gender differences in rates of aggression may be based more upon how you define and measure aggression than on actual differences. You will be given a framework for understanding the four functions that aggression serves: to cope with feelings of annoyance, to gain material and social rewards, to gain or maintain social status, and to protect oneself or the members of one's group. Your text will also provide theoretical support for each of the goals served by aggression.

First, you will be introduced to the *frustration-aggression hypothesis* and the *reformulated hypothesis* to help you understand that any event can lead to unpleasant feelings and may result in aggression. You will learn that general physiological arousal, irritability, and situational variables are related to annoyance, and that aggressive people often choose situations that make their lives more frustrating.

Next, you will be exposed to one of the most influential psychological theories of aggression, *social learning theory*. According to this theory, aggressive behavior is caused by material and social rewards for aggression.

Your text then discusses *sexual selection theory* and how female mating selectivity leads to increases in status-oriented aggressiveness in males. You will learn about the role testosterone plays in aggressiveness, how trivial insults to honor can lead to violence, and what happens when the pathways to success are blocked.

Finally, you will learn that self-defense is almost a universally accepted form of aggression across cultures. You will find that protection is influenced by attributional style, one's relative size and strength, and the way we perceive threats in the environment. This chapter concludes with suggestions of interventions to reduce violence and arguments for preventive approaches.

Chapter Learning Objectives

After reading this chapter, you should be able to:

- Define aggression and outline its three crucial components

- Distinguish between the four types of aggression discussed in the chapter

- Explain gender differences in aggression

- Compare and contrast Freud's "death instinct" with Lorenz's "aggressive instinct"

- Describe how displacement and catharsis relate to aggression

- Explain whether aggressive behavior is ever a goal in itself

- Outline the four goals served by aggression

- Describe the differences between the original frustration-aggression hypothesis and the reformulated frustration-aggression hypothesis

- Explain which two internal factors lead a person to act aggressively when they are annoyed

- Explain how unpleasant situations like pain, heat, and poverty influence aggression

- Explain why lynchings in the south between 1882 and 1930 were negatively related to cotton prices

- Explain the cognitive-neoassociation theory of aggression and discuss how the weapons effect is related to this theory

- Describe how some people create their own annoying situations

- Describe Bandura's social learning theory of aggression

- Describe how the violence of psychopaths is different from the violence of nonpsychopaths

- Explain how empathy and alcohol intoxication affect aggression

- Describe the research approaches that have been taken to examine the effects of multi-media violence

- Describe the statistical technique meta-analysis and discuss what meta-analyses have uncovered regarding the effects of violent media and aggression

- Describe the effects of violent video games and violent pornography on aggression

- Explain differential parental investment and sexual selection and how sexual selection may help explain aggressive tendencies in males

- Describe the evidence linking testosterone to aggression

- Explain how trivial altercations can elicit aggressive behavior

- Explain the differences in rates of homicide in the northern United States versus the southern United States and discuss whether Southerners are simply more violent

- Explain how status-driven aggression interacts with success and competition for mates

- Describe what is meant by defensive attributional style

- Explain the effect/danger ratio

- Outline the ways anti-violence programs seek to reduce violence. Explain Patterson's social learning perspective, Zillmann's theory of cognitive processes and aggressive feelings, and Novaco's cognitive approach to reducing aggression with self-statements.

- State the impact of legal punishment on violence

- Explain why our society should be trying to prevent violence before it happens

As You Read...

KEY TERMS!
Listed below are the key terms from the chapter that are essential for your understanding of the material. Refer to the definitions from your textbook; they are located at the end of this chapter, within the text in boldface, and in the margins throughout this chapter. In order to enhance your recall ability for these terms, you may want to consider making flashcards which include a term on one side, and a definition on the other (with perhaps a brief example that makes sense to you).

Aggression	Displacement	Meta-analysis
Assertiveness	Effect/danger ratio	Psychopath
Catharsis	Emotional aggression	Reformulated frustration-aggression hypothesis
Cognitive-neoassociation theory	Excitation-transfer theory	Sexual selection
Culture of honor	Frustration-aggression hypothesis (original)	Social learning theory
Defensive attributional style	Indirect aggression	Type A behavior pattern
Differential parental investment	Instrumental aggression	Weapons effect
Direct aggression		

A WAVE OF SENSELESS VIOLENCE

In the beginning of this chapter your authors introduced you to Patricia Krenwinkel, Charles Watson, Susan Atkins, and Linda Kasabian who were all members of the Manson Family. In August of 1969, these people participated in a senseless killing spree for two consecutive days. Describe the personal and situational factors that may have contributed to these murders for each of the Family members, including the role Charles Manson played.

THE FRUSTRATION-AGGRESSION HYPOTHESIS

Your text discusses John Dollard and his colleagues' frustration-aggression hypothesis that was originally proposed in 1939. Leonard Berkowitz later revised the frustration-aggression hypothesis. Describe the original and reformulated frustration-aggression hypotheses and discuss how they are different. Complete the figure below to help illustrate these differences. See page 320 if you need assistance.

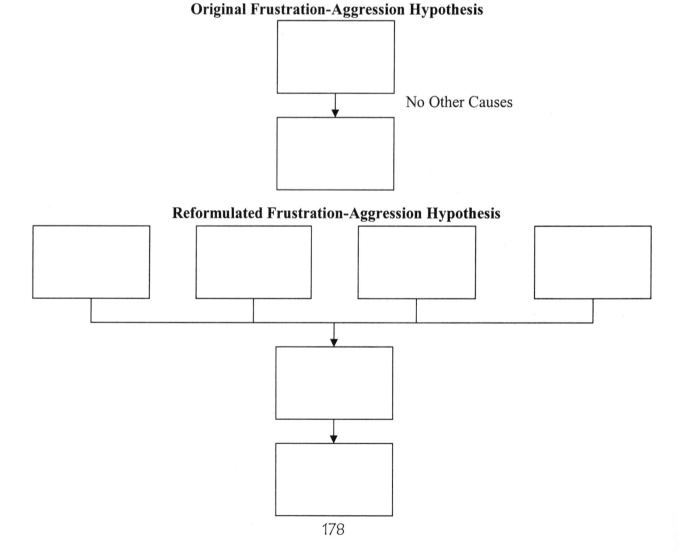

ANNOYANCE LEADS TO CHANGES IN PERCEPTION OF SITUATIONS

Beyond reformulating the frustration-aggression hypothesis, Berkowitz proposed a more elaborate theory on the relationship between unpleasant feelings and aggression, called the cognitive-neoassociation theory. Describe the theory and complete the figure to illustrate the process. See page 324 if you need assistance.

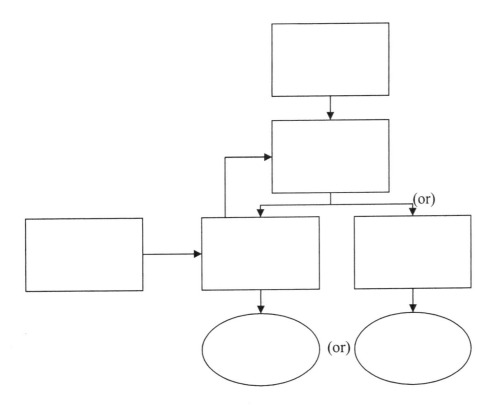

SOCIAL LEARNING THEORY AND MEDIA VIOLENCE

Describe Albert Bandura's social learning theory and how this model explains the occurrence of aggressive behavior. What were the findings and implications of the "Bobo Doll" study?

GLAMORIZED VIOLENCE IN THE MEDIA: RESEARCH APPROACHES

In order to study the effects of multi-media violence, researchers use a variety of approaches. Explain the differences between correlational studies and experimental studies. Provide an example of each to illustrate. Describe meta-analysis and explain how meta-analyses handle contradictory findings from correlational and experimental studies on violent media. How are meta-analyses able to reveal a clear conclusion regarding the "true" effect of media violence?

INSULTS AND OTHER "TRIVIAL ALTERCATIONS"

Your text discusses how trivial insults to honor can lead to violence. Describe the culture of honor and the historical findings that support the culture of honor. What laws are still in place that reflect that culture? Describe the findings of the Cohen, Nisbett, Bowdle, and Schwarz (1996) series of experiments that examined the differences between northern and southern aggression.

PROTECTING ONESELF OR OTHERS

What is the effect/danger ratio? What role does it play in an abusive relationship? Under what circumstances might a woman resort to murdering her partner?

SUMMARY OF THE GOALS SERVED BY AGGRESSION

Complete the chart below to help you summarize the goals served by aggression and the factors related to each goal. If you need assistance, see page 346 in your text (but be sure to use your own words in this exercise, rather than just copying).

The Goal	The Person	The Situation	Interactions
Coping with Feelings of Annoyance	• • •	• • •	• • •
Gaining Material and Social Rewards	• • •	• • •	•
Gaining or Maintaining Social Status	• •	• • •	• •
Protecting Oneself or Others	• •	• • •	• •

MATCHING: KEY TERMS

Matching! Match each definition on the left side of the page with the concept on the right side of the page. Each concept on the right should be used only once.

___ 1. Behavior intended to express dominance or confidence

___ 2. Theory that aggression is learned through direct reward or by watching others being rewarded for aggressiveness

___ 3. Tendency to notice threats and to interpret other people's behavior as intended to do one harm

___ 4. Theory that anger is physiologically similar to other emotional states, and that any form of emotional arousal can enhance aggressive responses

___ 5. Assessment of the likely beneficial effect of aggressiveness balanced against the likely dangers

___ 6. Theory that any unpleasant situation triggers a complex chain of internal events, including negative emotions and thoughts; depending on other cues in the situation (such as weapons), these negative feelings will be expressed as either aggression or flight

___ 7. Group of personality characteristics including time-urgency and competitiveness that is associated with higher risk for coronary disease

___ 8. Behavior intended to injure another

___ 9. Statistical combination of results from different studies of the same topic

___ 10. Tendency for weapons, such as guns, to enhance aggressive thoughts, feelings, and actions

___ 11. Behavior intended to hurt someone without face-to-face confrontation

___ 12. Principle that animals making higher investment in their offspring will be more careful in choosing mates

___ 13. Theory that any unpleasant stimulation will lead to emotional aggression to the extent that it generates unpleasant feelings

___ 14. Discharge of aggressive impulses

___ 15. Form of natural selection favoring characteristics that assist animals in attracting mates or in competing with members of their own sex

___ 16. Behavior intended to hurt someone to his or her face

___ 17. Set of societal norms whose central idea is that people (particularly men) should be ready to defend their honor with violent retaliation if necessary

___ 18. Indirect expression of an aggressive impulse away from the person or animal that elicited it

___ 19. Hurting another to accomplish some other (nonaggressive) goal

___ 20. Individual characterized by impulsivity, irresponsibility, low empathy, and lack of sensitivity to punishment; such individuals are inclined toward acting violently for personal gain

___ 21. Theory that aggression is an automatic response to any blocking of goal-directed behavior

___ 22. Hurtful behavior that stems from angry feelings

A. Aggression

B. Assertiveness

C. Catharsis

D. Cognitive-neoassociation theory

E. Culture of honor

F. Defensive attributional style

G. Differential parental investment

H. Direct aggression

I. Displacement

J. Effect/danger ratio

K. Emotional aggression

L. Excitation-transfer theory

M. Frustration-aggression hypothesis (original)

N. Indirect aggression

O. Instrumental aggression

P. Meta-analysis

Q. Psychopath

R. Reformulated frustration-aggression hypothesis

S. Sexual selection

T. Social learning theory

U. Type A behavior pattern

V. Weapons effect

PUTTING IT ALL TOGETHER: THOUGHT QUESTIONS

Two different treatments for reducing aggressive behavior were discussed in the chapter. One method was Novaco's (1975, 1995) cognitive approach, which focused on training people to modify their thoughts and feelings with "self-statements." The other method was Patterson's (1997) social learning theory approach. What are the conditions in which each of these methods would be more effective than the other? Design an experiment to test which of these methods was better at reducing aggression. What population would you use to test your hypothesis? What measures of aggression would you use?

After You Read…Practice Tests

Practice Test 1

1. Aggression can be defined as
   a. behavior that is hurtful.
   b. behavior that stems from angry feelings.
   c. behavior intended to injure another.
   d. behavior that is impulsive and destructive.

2. Amy wants to date Brian, but Brian is dating Sara. In order to convince Brian to stop dating Sara, Amy has her friend tell Brian a vicious rumor that Sara is cheating on him. Amy has engaged in _____, _____ aggression.
   a. indirect; emotional
   b. direct; emotional
   c. indirect; instrumental
   d. direct; instrumental

3. Some studies have shown that women are more physically violent in relationships, so why don't we consider them to be the more "aggressive" gender?
   a. The damage they do is less severe.
   b. In most other circumstances (i.e., outside of relationships), men are more violent.
   c. Women's violence in relationships is often motivated by self-defense.
   d. all of the above

4. Which of the following was an objection to the original frustration-aggression hypothesis?
   a. Frustration does not always lead to aggression.
   b. It couldn't explain emotional aggression.
   c. There wasn't enough research to support it.
   d. Frustration never leads to aggression.

5. According to Torestad (1990), the most anger-producing situations for Swedish teenagers were directly connected to
   a. pain.
   b. frustration and annoyance.
   c. sweltering heat.
   d. poverty.

6. In a study by Berkowitz (1993), students were assigned the role of supervisor and administered shocks and rewards to other students working under them. When the supervisors were made to feel uncomfortable by placing their hand in a tank of painfully cold ice water, they became
   a. less aggressive and recommended fewer shocks and more rewards for the students they were supervising.
   b. more aggressive and recommended more shocks and fewer rewards for the students they were supervising.
   c. aggressive and recommended more shocks and more rewards for the students they were supervising.
   d. irritated and stopped participating in the study due to the harsh unpleasant conditions.

7. Westra and Kuiper (1992) gave Canadian students the choice of working on the stock exchange as a trader or running a snowboarding shop. What did their findings suggest?
    a. People always chose the snowboarding shop due to its laid back nature.
    b. Type As more frequently chose the trader job that had unrealistic deadlines and time pressure thus creating the very circumstances that would set off their hostile tendencies.
    c. Type As more frequently chose the snowboarding job to avoid setting off their hostile tendencies.
    d. Type Bs more frequently chose the trader job to see how well they could function with unrealistic deadlines and time pressure.

8. Which of the following is true about psychopaths?
    a. Their violent acts are more likely to be the result of frustration or anger.
    b. They are very willing to take responsibility for their own acts of violence.
    c. They are often socially charming.
    d. Their violent acts are usually not motivated by social gain or material reward.

9. Which of the following statements is NOT true regarding alcohol intoxication and aggression?
    a. Wife abusers drink 13 times more alcohol than control subjects.
    b. Alcohol increases feelings of empathy for others.
    c. Alcohol leads to aggressiveness even in nonalcoholics.
    d. Fifty percent of assailants in violent crime cases are drunk at the time of the crime.

10. Anderson and Dill (2000) concluded that violent video games
    a. have no impact on aggressive behavior.
    b. increase aggressive thoughts but do not increase aggressive behaviors.
    c. can provide a forum in which young people learn and practice aggressive solutions to conflicts.
    d. increase verbal aggression only during game play.

Practice Test 2

1. Which of the following is NOT a crucial component of aggression?
    a. It is a behavior, not just a feeling.   b. It is the result of frustration or anger.
    c. It is purposeful.   d. It is intended to hurt another person.

2. _____ aggression is hurtful behavior that stems from angry feelings that get out of control.
    a. Direct   b. Emotional
    c. Indirect   d. Instrumental

3. Which of the following is true with regard to aggression and gender?
   a. Women are more likely to slap or hit their romantic partners.
   b. From kindergarten until the nursing home, males are more likely to hit, kick, knife, and shoot at one another.
   c. Men committed 90 percent of the homicides during the 1990s.
   d. all of the above are true

4. Which theory states that arousal generated by exercising or by watching an erotic film can enhance aggressive activity.
   a. excitation-transfer
   b. catharsis-aggression
   c. social learning
   d. cognitive-neoassociation

5. You're a boxing coach, and you want your fighter to be very aggressive in the ring. How can you manipulate the situation to make him more aggressive?
   a. Make the locker room slightly cold.
   b. Pinch him very hard before he goes into the ring.
   c. Give him a lot of money before the fight.
   d. Tell him that the economy is doing really well.

6. Reifman, Larrick, and Fein (1991) investigated the relationship between the number of times pitchers in major league baseball threw balls that hit batters and rising summer temperatures. What conclusion did they come to from these investigations?
   a. Pitchers became less accurate as the temperature went up.
   b. Heat was unrelated to pitching accuracy.
   c. Heat caused the pitchers to throw an excessive number of wild pitches resulting in hitting the batter.
   d. Pitchers took dead aim at batters the hotter it got.

7. Andrew Golden gunned down four students and a teacher at his school. Which of the following explanations best fits with the social learning theory of aggression?
   a. Andrew interpreted events in violent terms.
   b. Andrew had been encouraged to play with guns by his parents from the time he was a very small child.
   c. Andrew felt frustrated because he had recently failed a math test.
   d. Andrew had inherited an innate tendency both to act violently and to learn about social situations.

8. Using what you know about the connection between sexual selection and aggression, in which of the following species would you expect that males are the MOST aggressive?
   a. humans, where males invest emotional and financial resources in their offspring
   b. walruses, where males make very little investment in any particular offspring
   c. sea horses, where males invest their bodily resources in their offspring
   d. phalaropes, where males brood and rear the chicks

9. Which of the following is NOT true about the effects of testosterone on aggression?
    a. Testosterone can increase aggression in women.
    b. Military veterans with high levels of testosterone are more likely to have had trouble with the law and to have an unusually large number of sexual partners.
    c. Prison inmates with high testosterone levels commit more violent crimes on average.
    d. Testosterone only increases aggression in adults.

10. Rowe (1996) argues that aggression and violence are adopted by young men as feasible courses of action when other options are limited. Rowe stated that the combination of criminal violence and early sexual behavior is high amongst those having
    a. dropped out of school.
    b. a defensive attributional style.
    c. low testosterone.
    d. low intelligence.

Practice Test 3

1. _____ aggression involves an attempt to hurt another without obvious face-to-face conflict.
    a. Direct
    b. Emotional
    c. Indirect
    d. Instrumental

2. While Frank was robbing the bank, he shot the guard who tried to stop him. This is an example of what type of aggressive behavior?
    a. indirect; emotional
    b. direct; emotional
    c. indirect; instrumental
    d. direct; instrumental

3. The idea that aggressive impulses build up inside the individual and need to be released is a key component of the _____ theory.
    a. excitation-transfer
    b. catharsis
    c. social learning
    d. cognitive-neoassociation

4. Cantor, Zillmann, and Einseidel (1978) tested the excitation-transfer theory by showing women either an erotic film or a neutral film. They then gave both groups the opportunity to retaliate at a tormentor. What did they find?
    a. Women who were shown the erotic film were less aggressive later.
    b. Only women who were annoyed were aggressive later.
    c. Women who were shown the erotic film were more aggressive later.
    d. Only those women who labeled their arousal as anger were more aggressive later.

5. Which of the following is NOT a situational factor related to aggression and the goal of coping with feelings of annoyance?
    a. media violence
    b. pain
    c. heat
    d. poverty

6. Hepworth and West (1988) found that lynchings in the South were highest when a recession followed a period of rising economic well-being. The researchers described these findings according to
    a. excitation-transfer theory.
    b. the social learning theory of aggression.
    c. cognitive neo-association theory.
    d. relative deprivation.

7. _____ is a statistical combination of results from different studies of the same topic.
   a. Triangulation
   b. Meta-analysis
   c. Multi-dimensional scaling
   d. Structural equation modeling

8. Wood, Wong, and Chachere (1991) examined the data from 28 experimental studies that looked at children or adolescents who were observed after watching an aggressive film. What did they confidently conclude about media violence and aggressive behavior in children?
   a. Media violence enhances children's and adolescents' aggression in interaction with strangers, classmates, and friends.
   b. Media violence increases children's aggression, but the effect is so small, it is probably not worth worrying about.
   c. The third factor of poverty caused children to watch more TV and to be more violent.
   d. Non-aggressive children become extremely aggressive after watching violence on television.

9. You are a fourth grade teacher, and you notice that little David seems to be getting into fights quite a bit. David gets unreasonably upset when you ask him about his fighting, and says that it's always the other person who "starts it." You begin to suspect that David
   a. is a psychopath.
   b. has a defensive attributional style,
   c. is very frustrated, and this frustration is leading to aggressive behavior.
   d. is displacing his aggression.

10. Patterson's treatment for aggressive children, wherein the child wins points for appropriate behavior and loses points for aggressive behavior, is based on which theory or hypothesis of aggression?
    a. cognitive-neoassociation theory
    b. frustration-aggression hypothesis
    c. social learning theory
    d. excitation-transfer theory

Comprehensive Test
(Note: Items 1-15 are multiple-choice questions, items 16-23 are true-false questions, and 24-25 are essay questions.)

1. Physically striking, kicking, pushing, or shoving another person are examples of what type of aggression?
   a. Direct
   b. Emotional
   c. Indirect
   d. Instrumental

2. Late one night, Bob decided to deflate his landlord's tires because his landlord didn't respond immediately when the heat in Bob's apartment stopped working. This is an example of what type of aggressive behavior?
   a. indirect; emotional
   b. direct; emotional
   c. indirect; instrumental
   d. direct; instrumental

3. How does your text explain the contradictory evidence on sex differences in aggression?
   a. Sex-role stereotypes have changed since the 1960s which has resulted in a disappearance of traditional gender differences in aggression.
   b. Sex differences depend on how you define and measure aggression.
   c. Earlier studies on gender differences and aggression lacked experimental control.
   d. Non-representative samples were used in the 1940s and 1950s.

4. Freud held that aggression stems mainly from a/n _____ instinct, whereas some evolutionary theorists speculate that aggression stems mainly from a/n _____ instinct that could have evolved through natural selection.
   a. life, death
   b. death, life
   c. aggressive, death
   d. death, aggressive

5. Which of the following statements is true regarding the reformulated frustration-aggression hypothesis?
   a. Frustration is linked only to emotional aggression, not to instrumental aggression.
   b. Frustration leads to aggression only when it generates negative feelings.
   c. Any event that leads to unpleasant feelings, including pain, heat, or psychological discomfort, can lead to aggression.
   d. all of the above are true

6. Which of the following is NOT characteristic of the Type A behavior pattern?
   a. Type As feel a sense of time urgency and competitiveness.
   b. Type As are at higher risk for coronary disease.
   c. Type As are more accommodating in conflicts with their fellow workers.
   d. Type As tend to work harder and to rise higher in their profession.

7. In the cognitive neoassociation theory study conducted by Berkowitz and LePage (1967), in which condition did participants deliver the highest number of shocks to other subjects?
   a. when they were rewarded, and there were no weapons present
   b. when they were annoyed, and there were no weapons present
   c. when they were rewarded, and there were weapons present
   d. when they were annoyed, and there were weapons present

8. Bandura's "Bobo Doll" study examined the processes by which children came to imitate violent behavior. This study lends support to
   a. excitation-transfer theory.
   b. catharsis-aggression theory.
   c. social learning theory.
   d. cognitive-neoassociation theory.

9. Which of the following are the powerful evolutionary principles used (by researchers such as Daly and Wilson) to explain the relationship between aggression and status?
   a. differential parental investment and sexual selection.
   b. effect/danger ratio and sexual selection.
   c. differential parental investment and effect/danger ratio.
   d. defensive attributional style and assertiveness.

10. According to the text, why do innocuous events such as mild insults or trivial altercations cause some people (usually men) to be more aggressive?
    a. These events trigger the goal of being liked
    b. These events trigger low self-esteem, which in turn triggers a Freudian "death instinct."
    c. These events trigger the goal of avoiding a loss in status.
    d. These events trigger catharsis.

11. Cohen et al. (1996) conducted a series of experiments that showed that participants from the Southern and Western United States were much more likely than their counterparts in the North to react aggressively to a confederate who insulted them. To what did they attribute these findings?
    a. Participants from the South were not as intelligent as those from the North.
    b. Participants from the South were raised in a "culture of honor."
    c. Participants in the North were more likely to use indirect aggression.
    d. Participants in the North were more concerned about the effect/danger ratio.

12. Ramirez (1993) surveyed people in Spain, Finland, and Poland and found that _____ is at the top of the list of justified causes of aggression.
    a. coping with feelings of annoyance
    b. gaining material and social rewards
    c. gaining or maintaining social status
    d. protecting oneself or others

13. According to the effect/danger ratio, why are women more likely to kill an abusive boyfriend/spouse than to simply hurt him?
    a. Women reach a "breaking point" where they can no longer tolerate the abuse, and feel they must kill their abuser to protect themselves.
    b. The women perceive that it is actually safer to kill him than to hurt him, as hurting him may simply anger him and provoke more abuse.
    c. Women who are the victims of domestic abuse tend to be more aggressive than most women, and thus are more likely to kill an abuser.
    d. Women do not intend to kill their abuser, but typically lose control in a physical confrontation.

14. Novaco's (1975, 1995) cognitive approach focuses on training people to modify their own thoughts and feelings with rehearsed self-statements. Which of the following statements would be an effective way to deal with provocation?
    a. "I can manage this situation. I know how to regulate my anger."
    b. "It's really a shame that this person is acting the way he is."
    c. "Time to relax and slow things down."
    d. all of the above

15. According to the research cited in your book, what is the effect of legal punishment on reducing aggression?
    a. Legal punishment is effective at reducing violent crime, but not non-violent crime.
    b. Capital punishment has been found to be effective at reducing homicide rates.
    c. Arresting people is effective at reducing their rates of spousal abuse.
    d. There are no consistent effects of legal punishment on reducing aggression.

Indicate whether each statement is true or false by circling T or F. If you decide it is false, explain why. Correct answers appear at the end of the study guide in the ANSWERS section for Chapter 10.

T   F   16.   Throwing a vase at your spouse during a heated argument is an example of instrumental aggression.

T   F   17.   Catharsis is an indirect expression of aggression, as when a bird preens its feathers during a face-to-face conflict.

T   F   18.   In the reformulated frustration-aggression hypothesis, any unpleasant stimulation can lead to emotional aggression.

T   F   19.   Unpleasantly hot weather, in and of itself, can cause aggressive behavior.

T   F   20.   Since people don't have to be angry or upset to engage in reward-motivated aggressive behavior, social learning theory is particularly applicable to instrumental aggression.

T   F   21.   There is a weak relationship between spouse abuse and alcohol consumption.

T   F   22.   Wood's meta-analysis of media violence showed that media violence enhances aggression in children and adolescents.

T   F   23.   Only men tend to be involved in homicides that are the result of "trivial altercations."

ESSAY

24.   Define aggression. Distinguish between the different types of aggression: indirect and direct aggression and emotional and instrumental aggression. Provide an example of each type of aggression – indirect, direct, emotional, and instrumental.

25.   Describe Raymond Novaco's (1975, 1995) cognitive approach for reducing aggression.

When You Have Finished...

Now that you have had a chance to read this chapter and complete the activities associated with it, you may be interested in finding additional materials on this topic. The World Wide Web is a great and convenient resource for gathering additional information in a variety of areas. Listed below are web links and website descriptions that are relevant to this chapter.

Web Links and Website Descriptions
Be sure to visit Chapter 10 at the companion website: www.ablongman.com/knc3e
http://wps.ablongman.com/ab_baronbyrne_socialpsych_10/0,4608,186058-,00.html This is the companion website for the Baron and Byrne Social Psychology textbook. This website contains information relevant to the aggression chapter in your book and includes learning objectives, multiple choice questions, true-false questions, essay questions, activities, flashcards, and additional web links.
http://www.crimelibrary.com/manson/mansonmain.htm The Crime Library is a source for students researching current and historical subjects. This website provides a detailed account of the murders committed by the Manson Family.
http://www.crimelibrary.com/capone/caponemain.htm This Crime Library website provides a detailed account of the biography of Al Capone examining his youth and rise to power, the St. Valentine's Day Massacre, his imprisonment, and his death.
http://psychclassics.yorku.ca/FrustAgg/ This website contains papers that were read at the Symposium on Effects of Frustration at the meeting of the Eastern Psychological Association at Atlantic City, April 5, 1940.
http://www.oregoncounseling.org/HomicideSuicideInSchools.htm This website is sponsored by the Mentor Research Institute and provides information on preventing violence, homicide, and suicide in American schools.

Comprehensive Crossword Puzzle

Across

1. Behavior intended to hurt someone to his or her face
4. Tendency to notice threats and to interpret other people's behavior as intended to do one harm
9. Discharge of aggressive impulses
12. Hurtful behavior that stems from angry feelings
18. Form of natural selection favoring characteristics that assist animals in attracting mates or in competing with members of their own sex
19. Behavior intended to express dominance or confidence

Down

1. Principle that animals making higher investment in their offspring (female as compared to male mammals, for instance) will be more careful in choosing mates
2. Set of societal norms whose central idea is that people (particularly men) should be ready to defend their honor with violent retaliation if necessary
3. Individual characterized by impulsivity, irresponsibility, low empathy, and lack of sensitivity to punishment; such individuals are inclined toward acting violently for personal gain
5. Hurting another to accomplish some other (nonaggressive) goal
6. Indirect expression of an aggressive impulse away from the person or animal that elicited it
7. Assessment of the likely beneficial effect of aggressiveness balanced against the likely dangers
8. Theory that aggression is an automatic response to any blocking of goal-directed behavior
9. Theory that any unpleasant situation triggers a complex chain of internal events, including negative emotions and thoughts; depending on other cues in the situation (such as weapons),these negative feelings will be expressed as either aggression or flight
10. Theory that anger is physiologically similar to other emotional states, and that any form of emotional arousal can enhance aggressive responses
11. Group of personality characteristics including time-urgency and competitiveness that is associated with higher risk for coronary disease
13. Theory that aggression is learned through direct reward or by watching others being rewarded for aggressiveness
14. Behavior intended to hurt someone without face-to-face confrontation
15. Tendency for weapons, such as guns, to enhance aggressive thoughts, feelings, and actions
16. Statistical combination of results from different studies of the same topic
17. Behavior intended to injure another

Puzzle created with Puzzlemaker at DiscoverySchool.com

PREJUDICE, STEREOTYPING, AND DISCRIMINATION

Before You Read...

In this chapter, you will learn about the consequences of negative prejudices, stereotypes, and discrimination. You will find out why they exist, when they come into play, and what steps we can take to reduce them. You will be given an overview of the four goals served by prejudice, stereotyping, and discrimination: supporting and protecting one's group, gaining social approval, managing self-image, and seeking mental efficiency. You will then address the specific personal and situational factors related to each goal.

First, you will examine the large material and psychological burdens that the targets of negative stereotyping, prejudice, and discrimination often bear. Second, you will learn how people high in social dominance orientation are particularly likely to be prejudiced against low status groups, and how intergroup competition can bring about negative prejudices and spiral in intensity as it enhances groups' fears about one another. Third, you will discover how conformists, high self-monitors, and people with a peripheral group standing are more likely to adopt their group's prejudicial norms in order to be socially accepted. Furthermore, you will examine the role religion plays in contributing to prejudice. You will find that norms regarding prejudice and stereotypes change over time and affect how they are publicly expressed. Fourth, in order to view their self-images more favorably, people who are strongly identified with their group, who are high in authoritarianism, who are shaken by failure, and those who have threatened high self-esteem are especially likely to discriminate. Finally, you will see how stereotyping allows us to gain information about others without expending a great deal of cognitive effort, but often at a cost of inaccurately perceiving individual members of stereotyped groups. You will learn that people are more likely to use their stereotypes when they have a high need for structure, when their moods and emotions leave them unmotivated to think about things thoroughly, and when circumstances are cognitively taxing. Your text then discusses strategies for reducing prejudice, stereotyping, and discrimination; these strategies include goal-based approaches and intergroup contact.

Chapter Learning Objectives

After reading this chapter, you should be able to:

- Distinguish between old-fashioned versus modern expressions of racism and sexism

- Define prejudice, stereotype, and discrimination, provide an example illustrating each concept and differentiate between the three concepts

- Describe the material and psychological costs associated with being a target of negative prejudice

- Explain stereotype threat and describe how it leads people to perform below their potential and how it leads to disidentification

- Outline the four goals served by prejudice, stereotyping, and discrimination

- Describe the minimal intergroup paradigm

- Explain the possible evolutionary roots of ingroup bias

- Describe the characteristics of someone who is high in social dominance orientation

- Describe Sherif's "Robbers Cave" experiment and how it demonstrated the power of intergroup competition for creating prejudice

- Explain the self-fulfilling spiral of intergroup competition

- Describe how conformity seeking, self-monitoring, and perceived social standing influence prejudice

- Explain how changes over time have shifted people's expressions of stereotypes and prejudices

- Define the three types of religiosity – extrinsic, quest, and intrinsic – discussed in the chapter and describe how each relates to prejudice

- Describe how self-image is affected by scapegoating and social identity

- Describe the characteristics of an authoritarian personality and how it relates to stereotyping, prejudice, and discrimination

- Explain what happens when our self-image is shaken by failure

- Describe how self-esteem and self-esteem threat affect outgroup bias

- Describe the characteristics of efficient stereotypes

- Describe perceived outgroup homogeneity

- Explain how the semantic priming method automatically activates stereotypes

- Explain how the need for structure and moods and emotions affect stereotyping

- Explain the effects of overhearing an ethnic slur on racism

- Describe the ignorance hypothesis for prejudice and stereotyping

- Outline the four goal-based approaches for decreasing prejudice, stereotyping, and discrimination

- Provide an overview of the six principles under which contact with outgroups decreases prejudice, stereotyping, and discrimination

- Describe the jigsaw classroom

As You Read...

KEY TERMS!

Listed below are the key terms from the chapter that are essential for your understanding of the material. Refer to the definitions from your textbook; they are located at the end of this chapter, within the text in boldface, and in the margins throughout this chapter. In order to enhance your recall ability for these terms, you may want to consider making flashcards which include a term on one side, and a definition on the other (with perhaps a brief example that makes sense to you).

Authoritarianism	Minimal intergroup paradigm	Social dominance orientation
Discrimination	Perceived outgroup homogeneity	Social identity
Disidentify	Prejudice	Stereotype
Extrinsic religiosity	Quest religiosity	Stereotype threat
Ingroup bias	Realistic group conflict theory	Stereotyping
Intrinsic religiosity	Scapegoating	

THE UNLIKELY JOURNEY OF ANN ATWATER AND C. P. ELLIS

In the beginning of this chapter your authors introduced the caustic relationship between Ann Atwater and C. P. Ellis. Explain how the goals of prejudice outlined in this chapter served to fuel their hatred for each other. How do you explain their dramatic turnaround resulting in a true friendship?

THE SELF-FULFILLING SPIRAL OF INTERGROUP COMPETITION

Describe how the self-fulfilling prophecy amplifies intergroup competition. Complete the figure below to assist you with your answer. See page 365 if you need assistance.

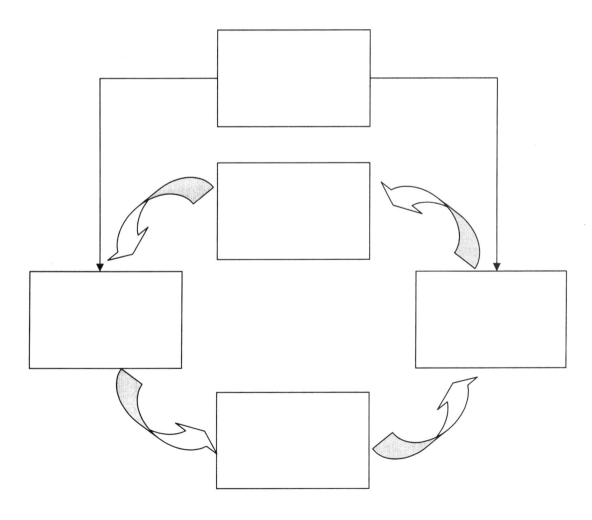

SUMMARY OF THE GOALS SERVED BY
PREJUDICE, STEREOTYPING, AND DISCRIMINATION

Complete the chart below to help you summarize the four goals of prejudice, stereotyping, and discrimination, and the factors related to them. If you need assistance, see page 381 in your text (but be sure to use your own words in this exercise, rather than just coping).

The Goal	The Person	The Situation	Interactions
Supporting and Protecting One's Group	•	•	•
Gaining Social Approval	• • •	•	• •
Managing Self-Image	• •	•	•
Seeking Mental Efficiency	• •	•	•

MATCHING: KEY TERMS

Matching! Match each definition on the left side of the page with the concept on the right side of the page. Each concept on the right should be used only once.

___	1.	Fear that one might confirm the negative stereotypes held by others about one's group	A.	Authoritarianism
___	2.	Extent to which a person desires that his or her own group dominate other groups and be socially and materially superior to them	B.	Discrimination
___	3.	Generalized attitude toward members of a social group	C.	Disidentify
___	4.	Process of blaming members of other groups for one's frustrations and failures	D.	Extrinsic religiosity
___	5.	Orientation to religion that sees it as a journey taken to understand complex spiritual and moral issues, usually accompanied by a belief that quick, simple answers are wrong	E.	Ingroup bias
___	6.	Beliefs and feelings we have toward the groups to which we see ourselves belonging	F.	Intrinsic religiosity
___	7.	Process of categorizing an individual as a member of a particular group and then inferring that he or she possesses characteristics generally held by members of that group	G.	Minimal intergroup paradigm
___	8.	Tendency to submit to those having greater authority and to denigrate those having less authority	H.	Perceived outgroup homogeneity
___	9.	Orientation to religion in which people attempt to internalize its teachings, seeing religiosity as an end in and of itself	I.	Prejudice
___	10.	Generalized belief about members of social groups	J.	Quest religiosity
___	11.	Behaviors directed toward people on the basis of their group membership	K.	Realistic group conflict theory
___	12.	Orientation toward religion that sees it as a means of gaining other things of value, such as friendships, status, or comfort	L.	Scapegoating
___	13.	Phenomenon of overestimating the extent to which members within other groups are similar to each other	M.	Social dominance orientation
___	14.	To reduce in one's mind the relevance of a particular domain (e.g., academic achievement) to one's self-esteem	N.	Social identity
___	15.	Tendency to benefit members of one's own groups over members of other groups	O.	Stereotype
___	16.	Proposal that intergroup conflict, and negative prejudices and stereotypes, emerge out of actual competition between groups for desired outcomes	P.	Stereotype threat
___	17.	Experimental procedure in which short-term, arbitrary, artificial groups are created to explore the foundations of prejudice, stereotyping, and discrimination	Q.	Stereotyping

GOAL BASED STRATEGIES FOR REDUCING NEGATIVE PREJUDICES, STEREOTYPING, AND DISCRIMINATION

Describe the four goal-based strategies for reducing negative prejudices, stereotyping, and discrimination. In the Figure below, provide a feature of the person and situation for one of the four goals served by prejudice, stereotyping, and discrimination. Then, include an intervention for each of the features.

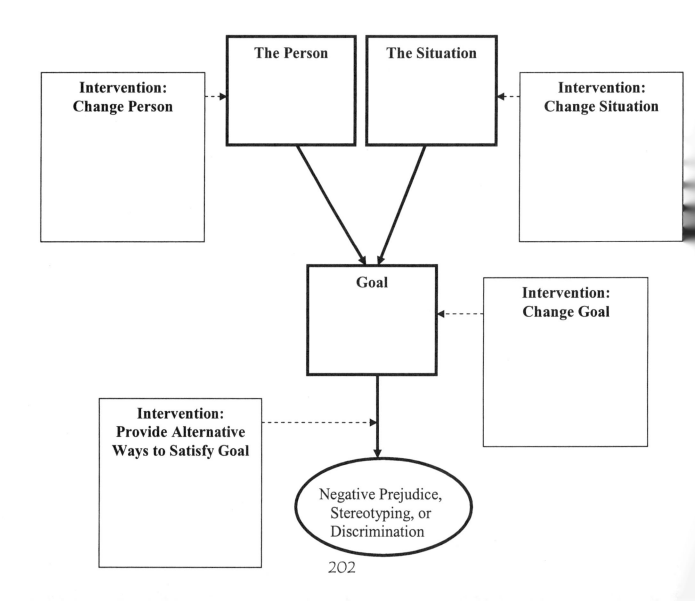

PUTTING IT ALL TOGETHER: THOUGHT QUESTIONS

When people argue for gay rights, they often preface their argument with, "I'm not gay, but. . ." Why do you think that is? What does this show about homophobia in our society? Is it acceptable to be homophobic?

Think about a situation that involves prejudice and conflict between groups that is in the news today. What goals are being served by the prejudices and conflict? In light of these goals, what might you do to reduce the conflict? Now, using the contact approach, design a second program to reduce conflict. How is your contact approach different from your goal based approach? How are they alike? What do these similarities and differences tell you about how these two approaches are related to one another?

After You Read...Practice Tests

Practice Test 1

1. _____ can be defined as a generalized attitude toward members of a social group.
   - a. Discrimination
   - b. Prejudice
   - c. Stereotypes
   - d. Ingroup bias

2. "It is more important to encourage boys than to encourage girls to participate in athletics."
   This comment is an example of
   - a. discrimination.
   - b. modern sexism.
   - c. old-fashioned sexism.
   - d. minimal intergroup relations.

3. In the Hebl et al. (2002) experiment, potential employers spoke less and came across as less helpful and less interested when job-seekers presented themselves as homosexual. This is an instance of
   - a. prejudice.
   - b. discrimination.
   - c. ingroup bias.
   - d. stereotyping.

4. Which factors lead to an increase in sexual harassment?
   - a. when men sees a strong connection between power and sex
   - b. when men is placed in settings where harassing opportunities are implicitly condoned
   - c. when both of the above conditions are met
   - d. when either of the above conditions are met

5. In the Tajfel et al. (1971) minimal intergroup paradigm experiment, how did participants respond when asked to allocate rewards and penalties?
   - a. They scapegoated for their group's failure.
   - b. They displayed ingroup bias in their allocation strategy.
   - c. They didn't seem to display any favoritism toward either group.
   - d. Only female participants were affected by group membership

6. Joyce is a Lutheran who believes that religion is a spiritual journey, and doesn't think that there are easy answers to most of her moral questions. What is Joyce's orientation towards religion?
   - a. quest religiosity
   - b. authoritarian religiosity
   - c. intrinsic religiosity
   - d. extrinsic religiosity

7. According to your book, how did C. P. Ellis create a positive social identity?
   - a. He exaggerated the KKK's favorable characteristics.
   - b. He labeled blacks with strong negative stereotypes.
   - c. He fought to block economic and educational gains by blacks.
   - d. all of the above

8.   The results from the Crocker et al. (1987) sorority study indicate which of the following groups is MOST likely to derogate outgroup members?
    a.   people with high self-regard in a low status group
    b.   people with high self-regard in a high status group
    c.   people with low self-regard in a low status group
    d.   people with low self-regard in a high status group

9.   According to the goal-based strategy, which of the following would be useful for reducing negative prejudices?
    a.   increase competition between groups
    b.   give people alternative ways to validate their self-worth
    c.   activate the goal to make judgments quickly
    d.   increase people's arousal level before they meet members of easily stereotyped groups

10.   What was the most important factor involved in the Rattlers and the Eagles finally coming to like each other in the "Robbers Cave" experiment?
    a.   They had contact with each other.
    b.   The camp leaders told them they had to stop fighting and be friends.
    c.   They worked together towards a common goal.
    d.   They were threatened with being sent home if they could not get along.

Practice Test 2

1.   "It's a bad idea for blacks and whites to marry one another." This comment is an example of
    a.   old-fashioned racism.   b.   modern racism.
    c.   ingroup bias.   d.   stereotyping.

2.   "Society has reached a point where women and men have equal opportunities for achievement." This comment is an example of
    a.   discrimination.   b.   modern sexism.
    c.   old-fashioned sexism.   d.   minimal intergroup relations.

3.   _____ refers to behaviors directed toward others because of their group membership.
    a.   Discrimination   b.   Prejudice
    c.   Stereotype   d.   Ingroup bias

4.   Goldin and Rouse (2000) examined the hiring records of eleven major orchestras. They found that females were more likely to advance to later rounds of auditions when
    a.   they dressed provocatively.   b.   judges were "blind" to their gender.
    c.   judges were in a good mood.   d.   judges held visible auditions.

5.   What has been found to reduce the damaging consequences of stereotype threat over both the short and long term?
    a.   deciding that the area is no longer relevant to self-concept or self-esteem
    b.   ignoring the stereotype
    c.   placing obstacles in the way of a successful performance
    d.   believing that one can improve one's abilities through additional hard work

6.   Which of the following is true of social dominance orientation?
      a.   Social dominance orientation is only found among Americans.
      b.   Individuals with high social dominance orientation tend to be more egalitarian.
      c.   Individuals with high social dominance orientation are more sexist.
      d.   Individuals with high social dominance orientation believe their group is equal to others
           and should be treated equally.

7.   Noel, Wann, and Branscombe (1995) demonstrated how the desire for _____
      influenced peripheral group members – such as the pledges of fraternities and sororities to
      become especially hostile toward outgroups (i.e., other fraternities and sororities).
      a.   mental efficiency   b.   social approval
      c.   managing self-image   d.   supporting and protecting one's group

8.   Why are people who are high in need for structure more likely to form simple stereotypes?
      a.   They seek easy, noncomplex ways of viewing the world.
      b.   They tend not to be as prejudiced and so they have less experience forming stereotypes.
      c.   They don't like to put people in categories.
      d.   They tend not to be very creative.

9.   Why was Lenell Geter, a black man, wrongfully identified as the perpetrator of armed
      robbery by a white witness?
      a.   prejudice   b.   ingroup bias
      c.   perceived outgroup homogeneity   d.   realistic group conflict

10.   According to the studies presented in your book, when are overheard ethnic slurs likely to
      lead to negative evaluations?
      a.   when there is stereotype disconfirming evidence available
      b.   when the characteristics of the individual being judged are inconsistent with the
           negative stereotype and slur
      c.   when a person already possesses negative prejudice toward the individual being judged
      d.   when a person is ambivalent toward the group to which the individual belongs

Practice Test 3
1.   "Discrimination against blacks is no longer a problem in the United States." This comment
      is an example of
      a.   old-fashioned racism.   b.   modern racism.
      c.   ingroup bias.   d.   stereotyping.

2.   Which of the following is true about stereotypes?
      a.   It is not possible for stereotypes to be positive.
      b.   Most stereotypes are based on completely false information about groups.
      c.   Stereotypes involve a generalized attitude toward a particular group.
      d.   It's possible to have a positive stereotype about a group against which you are
           negatively prejudiced.

3. Hebl and colleagues (2002) had student researchers apply for jobs in a shopping mall in Texas. The students wore either a baseball cap that had the words "Gay and Proud" or the words "Texan and Proud." What did they find?
    a. Potential employers were talkative and equally helpful regardless of what hat the students wore.
    b. Potential employers spoke less, came across as less helpful, and were less interested in both students because they were wearing baseball caps.
    c. Potential employers spoke less, came across as less helpful, and were less interested in students who were wearing baseball caps that had the words "Gay and Proud."
    d. The majority of potential employers refused to meet with students wearing baseball caps that had the words "Gay and Proud."

4. _____ harassment refers to attempts by the perpetrator to exchange something of value for sexual favors whereas _____ harassment refers to creating a professional setting that is sexually offensive, intimidating, or hostile.
    a. Quid pro quo; hostile environment   b. Modern sexual; Old-fashioned sexual
    c. Old-fashioned sexual; quid pro quo   d. Hostile environment; quid pro quo

5. Which of the following is true regarding the material costs associated with prejudice, stereotyping, and discrimination?
    a. Women and members of minority groups receive equal pay for the same work.
    b. An audit of the auto industry revealed that white men were offered better deals on cars than were white women, black women, and black men.
    c. Wages paid to heavyweight Hispanic women, black women, and heavyweight men are approximately the same.
    d. Well-to-do blacks and Hispanics are treated just as favorably as whites when being shown housing opportunities.

6. Hovland and Sears (1940) found that lynchings were most common during periods of poor economic conditions in the South. This relationship can best be explained by
    a. intergroup competition.   b. authoritarianism.
    c. one's perceived social standing.   d. cognitively taxing circumstances.

7. Which of the following is characteristic of people who have an authoritarian personality?
    a. They constantly question authority.
    b. They tend to be aggressive to their subordinates.
    c. They tend to see the world in complex terms.
    d. They are anticonformist and don't like obeying society's rules.

8. Amadou Diallo, a black man, was shot at 41 times by police officers who thought Diallo was carrying a gun. In actuality, he was carrying his wallet. This tragic mistake by police officers is an example of how the goal of _____ can affect behaviors when one uses stereotypes.
    a. social approval   b. supporting and protecting one's group
    c. managing self-image   d. mental efficiency

9.   Greenwald, Oakes, and Hoffman (2003) had college students play the role of police officers in a videogame. Students had to make split-second decisions on whether the individual who popped out from behind garbage dumpster was carrying a weapon or a harmless object. Researchers found that college students were
   a.   trigger happy and shot at anyone carrying anything.
   b.   more likely to shoot at men regardless of ethnicity.
   c.   less able to quickly distinguish between guns and harmless objects when held by a black individual and blacks were more likely to be shot at.
   d.   slower to react when casually dressed white citizens were carrying a gun.

10.   Which of the following is NOT effective at reducing prejudice?
   a.   empathize with the plight of others
   b.   make egalitarian values more salient
   c.   utilize jigsaw classrooms
   d.   simply increase contact among different groups

Comprehensive Test
(Note: Items 1-15 are multiple-choice questions, items 16-23 are true-false questions, and 24-25 are essay questions.)
1.   The fact that people are less likely to endorse stereotypical ideas now than they were 50 years ago probably means that
   a.   there is no longer any prejudice in society.
   b.   people are not as aware of stereotypes as they were 50 years ago.
   c.   because of societal norms, people are less willing to self-present as prejudiced.
   d.   the stereotypes no longer contain a kernel of truth.

2.   "Women should be cherished and protected by men." This comment is an example of
   a.   benevolent sexism.   b.   ingroup bias.
   c.   sexual harassment.   d.   hostile sexism.

3.   _____ refers to a generalized belief about members of social groups.
   a.   Discrimination   b.   Prejudice
   c.   Stereotype   d.   Ingroup bias

4.   Which of the following statements is NOT true regarding sexual harassment?
   a.   Eighty percent of high school students, girls and boys, report having been sexually harassed by their peers.
   b.   Fifty percent of American women have been sexually harassed during their academic or working lives.
   c.   In one year, the U.S. Army spent an estimated $250 million to deal with problems associated with sexual harassment.
   d.   Women and men are equally likely to see dating pressure and physical contact as harassing.

5. In the past, the United States has supported slavery laws and practices and laws discriminating against women. This illustrates what type of discrimination?
    a. hostile environment
    b. tokenism
    c. institutionalized
    d. social dominance

6. In the Steele and Aronson (1995) study of stereotype threat, why did black students perform below their abilities when race was made salient?
    a. They were concerned they might confirm the stereotype that blacks are less intelligent than whites.
    b. They were distracted by threats made by white confederates.
    c. They were attempting to disidentify academic achievement from their self-esteem.
    d. They didn't feel that scoring well was important.

7. In the Robber's Cave study, what caused the Eagles and the Rattlers to feel such animosity towards one another?
    a. There was racial tension between the two groups.
    b. The two groups were treated differently by the camp counselors, such that one group had higher perceived status.
    c. There was real intergroup competition for resources.
    d. The groups were composed of boys who were high in social dominance orientation.

8. People who possess a/an _____ tend to be the least prejudiced.
    a. quest religiosity
    b. nonreligious orientation
    c. intrinsic religiosity
    d. extrinsic religiosity

9. C. P. Ellis blamed his financial failures on blacks. He stated "I had to hate somebody. Hatin' America is hard to do because you can't see it to hate it. You gotta have something to look at to hate. The natural person for me to hate would be black people, because my father before me was a member of the Klan." This is an example of
    a. stereotyping.
    b. scapegoating.
    c. prejudice.
    d. discrimination.

10. Fein and Spencer (1997) found that participants who received negative feedback on an intelligence test
    a. rated the Jewish applicant less favorably than the Italian applicant, and subsequently showed increases in their self-esteem.
    b. did not rate the Jewish applicant less favorably than the Italian applicant, and subsequently showed increases in their self-esteem.
    c. rated the Jewish applicant less favorably than the Italian applicant, and subsequently showed further decreases in their self-esteem.
    d. did not rate the Jewish applicant less favorably than the Italian applicant, and subsequently showed further decreases in their self-esteem.

11. Researchers examining the automatic activation of stereotypes found that briefly flashing the word BLACK facilitated decisions about words related to negative black stereotypes. Which technique was utilized in this study?
    a. participant observation
    b. minimal intergroup paradigm
    c. meta-analysis
    d. semantic priming method

12. Ron likes movie directors, but dislikes Jewish people. Depending on Ron's mood when he meets him, how is he likely to view Jewish movie director Steven Spielberg?
    a. If he's in a good mood, he is less likely to rely on either stereotype.
    b. If he's in a bad mood, he is more likely to see Spielberg as a movie director.
    c. If he's in a good mood, he is more likely to see Spielberg as a movie director.
    d. none of the above, because mood doesn't affect stereotyping

13. The idea that prejudice and stereotypes exist because people simply don't know what members of other groups are really like is known as the
    a. ingroup bias effect.   b. ignorance hypothesis.
    c. realistic group conflict theory.   d. unfamiliarity hypothesis.

14. Which of the following is NOT a condition for the successful reduction of negative prejudice though the use of contact between groups?
    a. The contact should occur at the group level.
    b. Contact should be supported by local authorities and norms.
    c. Contact should be rewarding.
    d. Groups should work together toward common goals.

15. Which of the following is true about jigsaw classrooms?
    a. Students are accorded equal status in the classroom.
    b. Contact is at the individual level.
    c. Students work cooperatively with each other toward a common goal.
    d. all of the above are true

TRUE-FALSE
Indicate whether each statement is true or false by circling T or F. If you decide it is false, explain why. Correct answers appear at the end of the study guide in the ANSWERS section for Chapter 11.

T   F   16. Prejudice is a generalized attitude toward members of a social group whereas a stereotype is a generalized belief about members of social groups.

T   F   17. The Implicit Association Test is one technique researchers use to indirectly assess prejudice.

T   F   18. Individuals with high social dominance orientation are only found in western society.

T   F   19. Most stereotypes contain at least a kernel of truth.

T   F   20. The perceived outgroup homogeneity effect involves viewing members of other groups as lower in status than members of one's own group.

T   F   21. Individuals high in need for structure tend to form very complex stereotypes.

T   F   22. Contact and fact-based education are effective interventions for reducing prejudice.

T   F   23. Working together to achieve a common goal can reduce animosity between two individuals or groups.

ESSAY

24. Describe the three forms of spirituality discussed in your text. Explain the research findings on spirituality and prejudice. Are any forms of spirituality linked more with prejudice? If so, why?

25. <u>PART 1</u> One way to reduce intergroup conflict involves contact. Describe the six conditions under which contact is successful at reducing conflict.

<u>PART 2</u> Describe Sherif's "Robber's Cave" study and how it utilized the principles of effective contact.

When You Have Finished...

Now that you have had a chance to read this chapter and complete the activities associated with it, you may be interested in finding additional materials on this topic. The World Wide Web is a great and convenient resource for gathering additional information in a variety of areas. Listed below are web links and website descriptions that are relevant to this chapter.

Web Links and Website Descriptions
Be sure to visit Chapter 11 at the companion website: www.ablongman.com/knc3e
http://wps.ablongman.com/ab_baronbyrne_socialpsych_10/0,4608,185856-,00.html This is the companion website for the Baron and Byrne Social Psychology textbook. This website contains information relevant to the prejudice chapter in your book and includes learning objectives, multiple choice questions, true-false questions, essay questions, activities, flashcards, and additional web links.
http://www.civilrightsmuseum.org/ This is the website for the National Civil Rights Museum. It provides information on the Civil Rights Movement and its impact and influence on the human rights movement worldwide.
http://www.socialpsychology.org/social.htm#prejudice This is the website for the Social Psychology Network. It is the largest social psychology database on the Internet. Here you will find links related to prejudice, discrimination, and diversity.
http://www.jigsaw.org/ This is the official website for the jigsaw classroom. It provides an overview of the technique, history of the jigsaw classroom, how to implement a jigsaw classroom, and information about Elliot Aronson the creator of the technique.
http://www.tolerance.org/ Tolerance.org is a website for people interested in removing bigotry and creating diverse communities. It provides information from the news related to prejudice, tracks websites and music devoted to hate, tracks the location of hate groups in the U.S., gives suggestions for fighting hate, and helps you determine your hidden biases.
http://www.understandingprejudice.org/ This website is for those interested in the causes and consequences of prejudice. It contains more than 2,000 links to prejudice-related resources, searchable databases, teaching resources, and interactive exercises.

Comprehensive Crossword Puzzle

Across

1. Phenomenon of overestimating the extent to which members within other groups are similar to each other
5. Fear that one might confirm the negative stereotypes held by others about one's group
6. Orientation to religion that sees it as a journey taken to understand complex spiritual and moral issues, usually accompanied by a belief that quick, simple answers are wrong
10. Tendency to submit to those having greater authority and to denigrate those having less authority
12. Generalized attitude toward members of a social group
13. To reduce in one's mind the relevance of a particular domain (e.g., academic achievement) to one's self-esteem
14. Proposal that intergroup conflict, and negative prejudices and stereotypes, emerge out of actual competition between groups for desired outcomes
15. Beliefs and feelings we have toward the groups to which we see ourselves belonging
16. Extent to which a person desires that his or her own group dominate other groups and be socially and materially superior to them

Down

2. Behaviors directed toward people on the basis of their group membership
3. Process of categorizing an individual as a member of a particular group and then inferring that he or she possesses characteristics generally held by members of that group
4. Tendency to benefit members of one's own groups over members of other groups
5. Process of blaming members of other groups for one's frustrations and failures
7. Orientation to religion in which people attempt to internalize its teachings, seeing religiosity as an end in and of itself
8. Orientation toward religion that sees it as a means of gaining other things of value, such as friendships, status, or comfort
9. Experimental procedure in which short-term, arbitrary, artificial groups are created to explore the foundations of prejudice, stereotyping, and discrimination
11. Generalized belief about members of social groups

Puzzle created with Puzzlemaker at DiscoverySchool.com

GROUPS

Before You Read...

In this chapter you will examine the nature of groups. You will begin by looking at "groupings," mere collections of individuals. You will see how the presence of others affects performance on well-mastered tasks versus unmastered tasks, and how people can become deindividuated in crowds, resulting in behavior counter to their normal values. Although crowd behavior may appear chaotic, norms may emerge turning crowds into real groups where members are interdependent, share a common identity, and develop stable group structures. You will then focus on the three primary reasons individuals belong to groups: groups can help individuals get things done, they can help people make better decisions, and they can provide social and material benefits through leadership opportunities. You will discover what personal and situational characteristics contribute to group productivity and why individuals often decrease their efforts on group tasks. You will learn how transactive memory enables a group to make better decisions. You will see why information-hungry individuals and uncertain circumstances increase the likelihood an individual will join a group. Conversely, you will find that there are pitfalls to group decision making, such as group polarization and groupthink, which hinder the group's ability to make accurate decisions. In the remainder of the chapter, you will look at the benefits of gaining a position of leadership. Specifically, you will examine how leaders are chosen, what constitutes effective leadership, and what makes leaders fail. Finally, you will learn how certain leaders are able to transform the motivations, outlooks, and behaviors of their followers to enable the group to better reach its goals.

Chapter Learning Objectives

After reading this chapter, you should be able to:

- Define a group

- Define social facilitation and describe the conditions under which it is likely to occur

- Define deindividuation and describe the ways groups deindividuate their members

- Describe a dynamical system and how computer simulations can be useful for studying such systems

- Describe how "real" groups are different from minimal groups

- Define social loafing and describe when is it more or less likely to occur

- Explain how individual failure and goals affect an individual's decision to join a group

- Describe who is more likely to join multiple performance groups, members of collectivistic or individualistic societies and why

- Describe the characteristics that comprise a productive group

- Explain when cultural diversity is good for group performance and when it is not

- Define transactive memory and how it is relevant to making accurate decisions in groups

- Outline the characteristics of the person and the situation that affect the formation of groups for the purpose of making accurate decisions

- Describe group polarization and why it occurs

- Explain minority influence and describe when opinion minorities are most persuasive

- Define groupthink and explain how it can be avoided

- Describe the characteristics associated with those who want to lead

- Describe why men are more likely than women to become leaders

- Describe the "image" of a good leader

- Explain when leaders are effective

- Describe transformational leadership and the four key features of a transformational leader

- Explain under what conditions a man or a woman would make a more effective leader

As You Read...

KEY TERMS!

Listed below are the key terms from the chapter that are essential for your understanding of the material. Refer to the definitions from your textbook; they are located at the end of this chapter, within the text in boldface, and in the margins throughout this chapter. In order to enhance your recall ability for these terms, you may want to consider making flashcards which include a term on one side, and a definition on the other (with perhaps a brief example that makes sense to you).

Cohesiveness	Groupthink	Social loafing
Communication network	Group polarization	Status hierarchy
Deindividuation	Minority influence	Transactive memory
Dynamical system	Role	Transformational leadership
Group	Social facilitation	

BLOWING THE WHISTLE ON HIDDEN GROUP PATHOLOGIES

In the beginning of this chapter your authors introduced three women: Coleen Rowley, Sherron Watkins, and Cynthia Cooper. Coleen Rowley worked for the FBI in the Minneapolis field office. Sherron Watkins and Cynthia Cooper worked for two of the biggest American corporations of the 1990s: Enron and WorldCom. These three women uncovered the problems of their respective organizations and benefited the American public as a result. Discuss the goals, person factors, situation factors, and interactions which led these organizations to make poor decisions? Why was it difficult for Rowley, Watkins, and Cooper to have their voices heard within their organizations and receive fair hearings? How did the leadership of these organizations contribute to their own failures? What can we learn about leadership and decision-making from these failures?

THE MERE PRESENCE OF OTHERS AND SOCIAL FACILITATION

What is social facilitation? Under what conditions is it likely to occur? Complete the figure below to assist you in answering these questions.

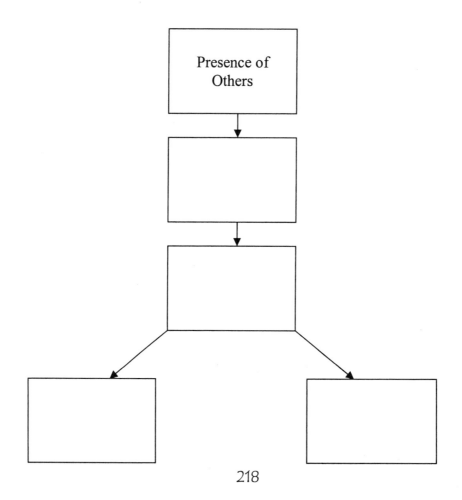

"REAL" GROUPS

Describe how "real" groups are different from minimal groups. Complete the figure to assist you in thinking about groups along a continuum.

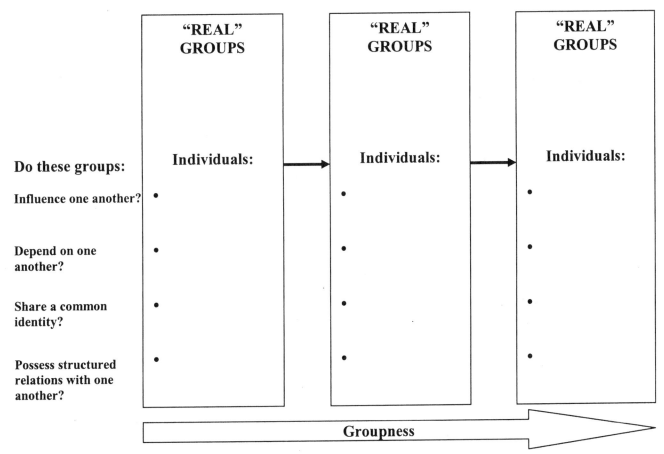

DISCUSSION AND DECISION MAKING

Define group polarization. Why does discussion exaggerate pre-discussion views?

What is minority influence?

How would someone with a minority opinion increase their persuasiveness to the majority?

Even when a minority opinion is persuasive, why would it still fail to change the majority view?

SUMMARY OF THE GOALS SERVED BY BELONGING TO GROUPS

Complete the chart below to help you summarize the three goals of groups and the factors related to them. If you need assistance, see page 422 in your text (but be sure to use your own words in this exercise, rather than just copying).

The Goal	The Person	The Situation	Interactions
Getting Things Done	•	• •	•
Making Accurate Decisions	•	•	• •
Gaining Positions of Leadership	• • •	• •	• •

MATCHING: KEY TERMS

Matching! Match each definition on the left side of the page with the concept on the right side of the page. Each concept on the right should be used only once.

___ 1. Style of group decision making characterized by a greater desire among members to get along and agree with one another than to generate and critically evaluate alternative viewpoints and positions

A. Cohesiveness

___ 2. Group memory system made up of (1) the knowledge held by individual group members and (2) a communication network for sharing this knowledge among the members

B. Communication network

___ 3. Minimally, two or more individuals who influence each other

C. Deindividuation

___ 4. When opinion minorities persuade others of their views

D. Dynamical system

___ 5. Patterns of information flow through a group

E. Group

___ 6. Ranking of group members by their power and influence over other members

F. Groupthink

___ 7. Expectation held by the group for how members in particular positions ought to behave

G. Group polarization

___ 8. Reducing one's personal efforts when in a group

H. Minority influence

___ 9. Strength of the bonds among group members

I. Role

___ 10. Leadership that changes the motivations, outlooks, and behaviors of followers, enabling the group to reach its goals better

J. Social facilitation

___ 11. When group discussion leads members to make decisions that are more extremely on the side of the issue that the group initially favored

K. Social loafing

___ 12. System (e.g., a group) made up of many interacting elements (e.g., people) that changes and evolves over time

L. Status hierarchy

___ 13. Process through which the presence of others increases the likelihood of dominant responses, leading to better performance on well-mastered tasks and worse performance on unmastered tasks

M. Transactive memory

___ 14. Process of losing one's sense of personal identity, which makes it easier to behave in ways inconsistent with one's normal values

N. Transformational leadership

PUTTING IT ALL TOGETHER: THOUGHT QUESTIONS

Make a list of all the different groups to which you belong. Based on the definition of groups in the chapter, which of these groups are "groupier"-that is, possess more of the characteristics of "real" groups? What is your goal in belonging to each of these groups? Pick one of these groups and describe a time where the group had to make a decision. How was the decision made? Did the group engage in any of the decision errors discussed in the book? Why or why not?

Go back to the list of groups you generated above. Who is the leader of each of those groups? What characteristics do they possess that made them especially likely to become leader? How was each leader chosen? Would you characterize any of these leaders as transformational leaders? Why or why not?

After You Read…Practice Tests

Practice Test 1

1. The process through which the presence of others increases the likelihood of dominant responses, leading to better performance on well-mastered tasks and worse performance on unmastered tasks is called _____.
   a. deindividuation
   b. amalgamation
   c. social facilitation
   d. social loafing

2. Deiner et al. (1976) found that trick-or-treaters arriving in groups stole extra candy or money compared to children arriving alone. As predicted, the anonymity provided by being in a group contributed to increased theft. This experiment illustrates the process of _____.
   a. deindividuation
   b. group polarization
   c. social facilitation
   d. social loafing

3. When the members of "real" groups need each other to reach their shared goals this is known as _____.
   a. group structure
   b. cohesiveness
   c. group identity
   d. interdependence

4. People belong to groups in order to
   a. accomplish tasks they can't effectively accomplish otherwise.
   b. acquire and share information.
   c. gain the material and social benefits of leadership.
   d. all of the above

5. Managers at the New England pickle factory hired additional employees to increase their overall productivity. However, this resulted in decreased productivity among individual pickle packers and countless pickle packing mistakes. This is an example of
   a. deindividuation.
   b. amalgamation.
   c. social facilitation.
   d. social loafing.

6. A well-functioning corporation has knowledge located within the minds of its individual members and ways to spread it through communication. This is known as
   a. a communication network.
   b. cohesiveness.
   c. a dynamical system.
   d. transactive memory.

7. _____ occurs when group discussion leads members to make decisions that are more extremely on the side of the issue that the group initially favored.
   a. Deindividuation
   b. Group polarization
   c. Social facilitation
   d. Social loafing

8. The prosecuting attorney finishes his closing statement and sits down, hoping the jury will reach a guilty verdict. He asks his jury consultant what she thinks. She says that 8 of the 12 jurors are probably in favor of a guilty verdict. Knowing that the decision must be unanimous, should the attorney be pleased or displeased? Why?
   a. displeased, because the jury's leniency bias will probably turn into a not-guilty verdict
   b. displeased, because opinion minorities frequently sway the opinions of most jurors
   c. pleased, because the influence power of majority jurors will likely convince the rest of the jury to vote guilty
   d. pleased, because the almost even split likely means the jury will end up deadlocked, giving the attorney another chance to convict

9. Which of the following factors can predispose a group to engage in groupthink?
   a. when decisions have to be made in a high pressure situation
   b. when group members have a lot of interaction with non-group members
   c. when a group is not very cohesive
   d. when the group has a leader who is not particularly charismatic

10. When are leadership opportunities more likely?
   a. when current leaders die or depart the group
   b. when groups grow larger
   c. when groups face a crisis
   d. all of the above

Practice Test 2

1. Social facilitation is
   a. the process through which the presence of others increases the likelihood of dominant responses.
   b. the process of losing one's sense of personal identity making it easier to behave in ways inconsistent with one's normal values.
   c. reducing one's personal efforts when in a group.
   d. a style of group decision making characterized by a greater desire among members to get along and agree with one another.

2. Computer simulations, such as the simulation of the Westgate housing complex, have indicated that dynamical systems obey which of the following rules?
   a. small changes in the initial arrangement of a group can lead to very different outcomes
   b. over time, chaos emerges from order
   c. chaotic groups tend to remain chaotic, whereas ordered groups tend to retain their initial order
   d. all of the above

3. Which of the following characteristics is a real group likely to possess?
   a. injunctive norms   b. cohesiveness
   c. communication network   d. all of the above

4. Why is group performance potentially more effective than individual performance?
   a. People in groups rarely make incorrect decisions.
   b. The competitive nature of groups causes the individual members to work harder than if they were alone.
   c. People in groups can share common burdens and divide their labor.
   d. Group performance is not potentially more effective than individual performance.

5. You are assigned to a group by your social psychology professor, and you will have to turn in a group project at the end of the semester. How can you decrease the probability that social loafing will occur?
   a. Have the group members contribute their work anonymously at the end of the semester, then put it all together in a single package to turn in.
   b. Tell the group members that the task is not such a big deal, and it will all get done somehow.
   c. Tell the group members that the task is very simple.
   d. Give each member of the group a specific task to complete.

6. Spencer doesn't have an opinion on same-sex marriage. After discussing same-sex marriage with his friends who hold strong Christian beliefs, he decides that homosexual marriages should not be allowed. This shift in opinion resulted from
   a. deindividuation.   b. group polarization.
   c. social facilitation.   d. groupthink.

7. Opinion minorities are most persuasive when
   a. they're willing to compromise a bit.
   b. they have at least some support from others.
   c. the audience wants to make an accurate decision.
   d. all of the above

8. Madeline is the very popular leader of her team at work. In order to get a bonus, her team has to come up with a better plan than all the other teams in the office. How can she prevent groupthink from occurring?
   a. She can refrain from presenting her ideas until her group members have presented theirs.
   b. She can appoint a man as leader.
   c. She can stress the importance of getting along together as a team.
   d. She can discourage group members from presenting alternative perspectives.

9. Ambition, energy, and male gender are all typical characteristics of
   a. people who fall victim to groupthink.
   b. people who will engage in social loafing.
   c. people who desire to be leaders.
   d. people who have transactive memory.

10. According to the meta-analysis conducted by Eagly et al. (1995), are men or women more effective leaders?
    a. Men tend to be better leaders for most tasks.
    b. Women tend to be better leaders for most tasks.
    c. Men are better leaders when the task requires a "hard-nosed" orientation, whereas women are better leaders when the task requires interpersonal sensitivities.
    d. There doesn't seem to be any difference between the effectiveness of men and women as leaders.

Practice Test 3

1. Michaels et al. (1982) found that the performance of good pool players improved when they were observed whereas the performance of less talented pool players worsened when they were observed. This study supports the theory of _____.
    a. deindividuation
    b. group polarization
    c. social facilitation
    d. social loafing

2. How do crowds deindividuate their members?
    a. by making them more accountable for their actions
    b. by making them less anonymous
    c. by distracting them away from their own personal values
    d. by focusing them on injunctive norms

3. Stable groups are often structured by _____.
    a. roles
    b. cohesiveness
    c. communication network
    d. all of the above

4. Vancouver and Ilgen (1989) had male and female university students choose whether they wanted to work alone or with another student on six different tasks. They found that
    a. males always worked alone on the tasks.
    b. females always chose to work with other females.
    c. students preferred to work alone on gender-consistent tasks and with others on gender-inconsistent tasks.
    d. students preferred to work alone on gender-inconsistent tasks and with others on gender-consistent tasks.

5. Michaelsen, Watson, and Black (1989) assigned students to small teams to work on various problems over the semester. These students took exams as individuals and as a group. The researchers found that the groups scored higher than their average individual members and higher than their best individual members. This illustrates the power of
    a. communication networks.
    b. cohesiveness.
    c . dynamical systems.
    d. transactive memory.

6. A group of investors in the Acme Paper Clip Company is meeting to discuss what the company should do with this year's profits. Most of the members arrive believing that the company should be cautious and invest the profit in low risk bonds. According to the group polarization phenomenon, what is the likely result of the meeting?
   a. The group will experience a risky shift, and decide to put the profits in the stock market.
   b. The group will be even more in favor of investing cautiously in bonds.
   c. The group will become more moderate in their views, and will probably decide to invest half the profit in bonds and half in the market.
   d. The group will decide that they should branch out and start making staples in addition to paper clips.

7. Which of the following characteristics will make minority influence LESS likely to be successful?
   a. The minority holds steady to their views.
   b. The minority originally held the majority position.
   c. The minority has at least some support from others.
   d. The minority refuses to compromise.

8. John F. Kennedy's decision to launch the Bay of Pigs attack on Cuba, Richard Nixon's decision to cover up the Watergate break-in, and the space shuttle Columbia disaster were all decisions characterized by _____.
   a. groupthink   b. group polarization
   c. social facilitation   d. deindividuation

9. Your book describes a fish species where small submissive males become larger, more colorful, and more competitive when the dominant male dies. These males have become motivated by _____ to seek leadership.
   a. social loafing   b. the void at the top
   c. response facilitation   d. the mere presence of others

10. Because Martin Luther King Jr. altered the motivations, outlooks, and behaviors of his followers, history remembers him as a
   a. transformational leader.   b. charismatic leader.
   c. dynamic system leader.   d. transactive leader.

Comprehensive Test
(Note: Items 1-15 are multiple-choice questions, items 16-23 are true-false questions, and 24-25 are essay questions.)

1. In which of the following situations is performance improvement LEAST likely to occur?
   a. when novice pool players are observed by others
   b. when running dogs are observed by other dogs as opposed to running without an audience
   c. when the task being observed is well-practiced and simple
   d. when people believe others are explicitly assessing their performance on a well-mastered task

2. According to your book, which of the following is common to "real" groups?
   a. structure
   b. interdependence
   c. group identity
   d. all of the above

3. The strength of the bonds among group members is known as
   a. interdependence.
   b. cohesiveness.
   c. groupthink.
   d. group polarization.

4. In a study by Shepperd (2001), groups of participants were asked to wrap pieces of bubblegum for 10 minutes. Participants wrapped less gum when they
   a. were told that the gum would be added to care packages sent to servicemen and service women stationed overseas.
   b. believed their performance couldn't be evaluated.
   c. believed their performance would be evaluated.
   d. wrapped gum with friends.

5. Workers have formed unions to gain increased control over their wages and working conditions because
   a. interpersonal or societal circumstances have become undesirable.
   b. of uncertain circumstances.
   c. they want to feel connected with other people.
   d. all of the above

6. Which of the following is true of culturally diverse groups?
   a. Diverse groups typically generate fewer solutions to any particular problem.
   b. Diverse groups often initially lack cohesion, which can harm performance.
   c. Diverse groups communicate much better than homogenous groups.
   d. Diverse groups tend to come up with less feasible solutions to problems.

7. In Schachter's (1959) shock experiment, participants were assigned either to the "quite painful" condition (high-fear) or to the "not in any way painful" condition (low-fear). They then had the choice of waiting alone or with others while the experimental equipment was being readied. Schachter found that
   a. high-fear participants preferred waiting with participants from either experimental condition.
   b. high-fear participants preferred waiting alone.
   c. high-fear participants preferred waiting with others who were in the same condition.
   d. high-fear participants refused to participate in the study.

8. How does group discussion exaggerate and enhance the group's pre-discussion views?
   a. through minority influence.
   b. through the social facilitation process.
   c. through the deindividuation process
   d. through the social comparison process.

9. Which of the following characteristics will make minority influence MORE likely to be successful?
   a. The minority holds steady to their views.
   b. The minority is willing to compromise a bit.
   c. The minority presents their views as compatible with the majority view but just a bit "ahead of the curve."
   d. all of the above would be successful

10. _____ is characterized by a greater desire among members to get along and agree with one another than to generate and critically evaluate alternative viewpoints and positions.
    a. Deindividuation
    b. Group polarization
    c. Social facilitation
    d. Groupthink

11. Meta-analytic review suggests that groups generally make lower quality decisions when communicating
    a. via computer.
    b. face-to-face.
    c. during social gatherings.
    d. during a business trip.

12. Which of the following is NOT a reason that there have been so few women national leaders throughout history?
    a. Men, in general, are more interested in becoming leaders.
    b. Women are less likely to be seen as having leadership skills.
    c. Women are not socialized to prefer leadership.
    d. Women do not make very good leaders.

13. Which of the following is a characteristic that fits the images and beliefs that people in the United States have about good leaders?
    a. They aren't particularly invested in the group.
    b. They are very self-confident.
    c. They are short.
    d. They have large eyes and a round face.

14. White and Lippitt (1960) conducted an experiment to determine whether particular leadership styles are more effective. They found that
    a. groups with autocratic leaders spent less time working than did groups having democratic leaders.
    b. groups with democratic leaders spent more time working than did groups having autocratic leaders.
    c. groups with autocratic leaders spent more time working than did groups having democratic leaders and worked harder when their leader was absent.
    d. groups with autocratic leaders spent more time working than groups with democratic leaders when their leader was present, but groups with democratic leaders spent more time working than groups with autocratic leaders when their leader was absent.

15. According to the Center for Leadership Studies, _____ leaders significantly alter the motivations, outlooks, and behaviors of their followers enabling the group to reach its goals better.
    a. transformational
    b. minority
    c. dynamic
    d. charismatic

TRUE-FALSE

Indicate whether each statement is true or false by circling T or F. If you decide it is false, explain why. Correct answers appear at the end of the study guide in the ANSWERS section for Chapter 12.

T   F   16. The performance of dominant responses by cockroaches is enhanced by the mere presence of other cockroaches.

T   F   17. An interacting crowd of strangers waiting at a bus stop is a minimal kind of group or "grouping."

T   F   18. Social loafing is less likely when each member of the group is doing the same job.

T   F   19. People facing uncertainty prefer to wait with people who are also uncertain, rather than people who have already faced the uncertainty.

T   F   20. Majority influence can often lead to group polarization after discussion of an issue.

T   F   21. Juries are often swayed by just one dissenting juror.

T   F   22. When President Kennedy expressed his opinion about the Bay of Pigs at the beginning of the discussion, he made it more likely that groupthink would occur.

T   F   23. History and social psychological research reveals that the old saying "it's not what you know, but who you know," is true in influencing who gains leadership.

ESSAY

24. What is social loafing? Why does social loafing occur and what steps can be taken to reduce its frequency? Describe how this problem affected the New England pickle factory.

25. What is groupthink? Explain why the space shuttle Columbia disaster may be another example of groupthink. How can groupthink be avoided?

When You Have Finished...

Now that you have had a chance to read this chapter and complete the activities associated with it, you may be interested in finding additional materials on this topic. The World Wide Web is a great and convenient resource for gathering additional information in a variety of areas. Listed below are web links and website descriptions that are relevant to this chapter.

Web Links and Website Descriptions
Be sure to visit Chapter 12 at the companion website: www.ablongman.com/knc3e
http://wps.ablongman.com/ab_baronbyrne_socialpsych_10/0,4608,186100-,00.html This is the companion website for the Baron and Byrne Social Psychology textbook. This website contains information relevant to the group chapter in your book and includes learning objectives, multiple choice questions, true-false questions, essay questions, activities, flashcards, and additional web links.
http://psychclassics.yorku.ca/Triplett/index.htm This site contains the classic article by Norman Triplett on bicycle racing and social facilitation (1897). Take time to read the article and see what social psychology looked like in the early years.
http://www.socialpsychology.org/social.htm#group The Social Psychology Network is the largest social psychology database on the Internet. Here you will find links related to group dynamics and leadership studies. This website is supported by the National Science Foundation.
http://www.abacon.com/commstudies/groups/groupthink.html This website discusses Groupthink and it examines the negative outcomes, symptoms, and solutions for groupthink. You can also complete an interactive exercise at the end of the discussion.

Comprehensive Crossword Puzzle

Across

8. Strength of the bonds among group members
10. When opinion minorities persuade others of their views
12. Expectation held by the group for how members in particular positions ought to behave
13. Ranking of group members by their power and influence over other members
14. Leadership that changes the motivations, outlooks, and behaviors of followers, enabling the group to reach its goals better

Down

1. Process of losing one's sense of personal identity, which makes it easier to behave in ways inconsistent with one's normal values
2. Patterns of information flow through a group
3. Process through which the presence of others increases the likelihood of dominant responses, leading to better performance on well-mastered tasks and worse performance on unmastered tasks
4. Group memory system made up of (1) the knowledge held by individual group members and (2) a communication network for sharing this knowledge among the members
5. Style of group decision making characterized by a greater desire among members to get along and agree with one another than to generate and critically evaluate alternative viewpoints and positions
6. Reducing one's personal efforts when in a group
7. System (e.g., a group) made up of many interacting elements (e.g., people) that changes and evolves over time
9. Minimally, two or more individuals who influence each other
11. When group discussion leads members to make decisions that are more extremely on the side of the issue that the group initially favored

Puzzle created with Puzzlemaker at DiscoverySchool.com

13 SOCIAL DILEMMAS: COOPERATION VERSUS CONFLICT

Before You Read...

In this chapter you will examine the complex interaction of the person and the environment. You will learn how global social dilemmas can result from the actions of single individuals that can combine into unexpected problems at the larger group level. You will begin with a definition of a social dilemma and discover what overpopulation, environmental destruction, and international conflict have in common. Then you will analyze in-depth the two goals that underlie these global dilemmas: the desire to gain immediate satisfaction and the desire to defend ourselves and valued others. For each goal, you will look at the factors in the person and the situation that affect each social dilemma. Finally, after outlining each of these factors, you will explore potential strategies on how they may be resolved.

Chapter Learning Objectives

After reading this chapter, you should be able to:

- Define a social dilemma

- Explain the tragedy of the commons and why it occurs

- Define and provide an example of a replenishing resource management dilemma

- Describe how a public goods dilemma is different from a replenishing resource management dilemma

- Outline the two goals affecting global social dilemmas

- Define social traps and discuss the three hidden components of social traps

- Define sliding reinforcers and discuss how they relate to social traps

- Describe the four value orientations presented in the text, explain the category into which most people fall, and explain the general orientations that the four value orientations can be grouped into

- Explain how prosocial versus egoistic orientations develop

- Describe the four strategies Platt (1973) suggested for drawing people out of social traps

- Describe how different types of norms can be used to affect social dilemmas

- Describe the three categories of environmental interventions, and how they tap into different motives

- Explain how outgroup bias leads to international conflict

- Outline the factors in the person and in the situation that contribute to international conflict by triggering the motivation to defend oneself or valued others

- Describe what is meant by a social dominance orientation and discuss whether there are gender differences in social dominance orientation

- Explain what distinguishes social dominance orientation from authoritarianism

- Explain the difference between the deterrence view and the conflict spiral view of international conflict

- Explain how group competition over resources escalates conflict and discuss the suggestions provided by the text for resolving intergroup competition

- Describe time-series analysis

- Explain how threats influence decisions in conflict situations and how integrative complexity is related to threat and decision-making

- Outline Kimmel's levels of cultural awareness

- Describe the three areas of research on the reciprocal dynamics of cooperation and conflict, and how research in this area can be used to increase international cooperation

- Describe the Graduated and Reciprocated Initiatives in Tension Reduction strategy (GRIT)

As You Read...

> **KEY TERMS!**
> Listed below are the key terms from the chapter that are essential for your understanding of the material. Refer to the definitions from your textbook; they are located at the end of this chapter, within the text in boldface, and in the margins throughout this chapter. In order to enhance your recall ability for these terms, you may want to consider making flashcards which include a term on one side, and a definition on the other (with perhaps a brief example that makes sense to you).

Altruist	Individualist	Social dilemma
Command-and-control policy	Integrative complexity	Social trap
Competitor	Market-based policy	Time-series analysis
Conflict spiral view	Perceptual dilemma	Tit-for-tat strategy
Cooperator	Public goods dilemma	Voluntarist policy
Deterrence view	Replenishing resource management dilemma	Xenophobia
GRIT (Graduated and Reciprocated Initiatives in Tension Reduction)	Sliding reinforcer	

CONTRASTING FUTURE WORLDS

In the beginning of this chapter, your authors discussed the population problems that faced Italy and Bangladesh in the early 1970s. Over the next three decades, Italy and Bangladesh went in completely different directions in response to this overpopulation problem. Describe how each country responded to this problem and the consequences associated with each response. What very simple solutions did your text provide to resolve the problems of overpopulation, environmental destruction, and international conflict?

CHANGING THE CONSEQUENCES OF SHORT-SIGHTED SELFISHNESS

Describe Platt's (1973) four suggestions for changing the consequences of short-sighted selfishness. Remember that these suggestions are based upon the timing of rewards and punishments. Provide an example for each suggestion.

①

②

③

④

Describe how the activation of descriptive and injunctive norms can be used to affect social dilemmas.

THREE TYPES OF ENVIRONMENTAL INTERVENTIONS

In the chart below, describe the three types of environmental interventions used to prevent the environmental damage caused by selfishness, explain the motive that is activated for the type of intervention, and provide three examples to illustrate the intervention strategy at work.

Description of Intervention	Motive Activated	Examples
Command-and-Control		1.) 2.) 3.)
Market-Based		1.) 2.) 3.)
Voluntarist		1.) 2.) 3.)

THE RECIPROCAL DYNAMICS OF COOPERATION AND CONFLICT

Describe the tit-for-tat strategy. How effective is this strategy in stabilizing conflict situations?

Describe the dollar game. What happens as the game progresses?

What is a perceptual dilemma? Describe the evidence suggesting that Soviet and American leaders were locked in a perceptual dilemma during the 1980s.

Describe the GRIT strategy. How does it increase intergroup cooperation? How did Mikhail Gorbachev use a variation of the GRIT strategy to end the Cold War?

| SUMMARY OF THE GOALS AFFECTING SOCIAL DILEMMAS |

Complete the chart below to help you summarize the goals served by social dilemmas and the factors related to them. If you need assistance, see page 455 in your text (but be sure to use your own words in this exercise, rather than just copying).

The Goal	The Person	The Situation	Interactions
Gaining Immediate Satisfaction	•	• •	• • •
Defending Ourselves and Valued Others	• • • • •	• • • • •	• • • •

MATCHING: KEY TERMS

Matching! Match each definition on the left side of the page with the concept on the right side of the page. Each concept on the right should be used only once.

___ 1.	Fear and distrust of foreigners	A. Altruist
___ 2.	Negotiating tactic in which the individual responds to competitiveness with competitiveness and to cooperation with cooperation	B. Command-and-control policy
___ 3.	Situation in which an individual profits from selfishness unless everyone chooses the selfish alternative, in which case the whole group loses	C. Competitor
___ 4.	Extent to which a person demonstrates simplified, "black and-white," categorical thinking as opposed to acknowledgement of all sides of an issue	D. Conflict spiral view
___ 5.	Method in which two or more recurring events are examined for linkages over time	E. Cooperator
___ 6.	Situation in which the whole group can benefit if some of the individuals give something for the common good but individuals profit from "free riding" if enough others contribute	F. Deterrence view
___ 7.	Situation in which members share a renewable resource that will continue to produce benefits if group members do not over-harvest it, but also whereby any single individual profits from harvesting as much as possible	G. GRIT (Graduated and Reciprocated Initiatives in Tension Reduction)
___ 8.	Someone oriented toward bringing the group benefits, even if they must personally sacrifice	H. Individualist
___ 9.	Someone oriented toward working together to maximize the joint benefits to the self and the group	I. Integrative complexity
___ 10.	Stimulus that brings rewards in small doses, which change to punishments when they occur in large doses	J. Market-based policy
___ 11.	Someone oriented to come out relatively better than other players, regardless of whether their personal winnings are high or low in an absolute sense	K. Perceptual dilemma
___ 12.	Someone oriented toward maximizing personal gains, without regard to the rest of the group	L. Public goods dilemma
___ 13.	Combination of social dilemma and outgroup bias - each side in a conflict believes it is best for both sides to cooperate, while simultaneously believing that the other side would prefer that "we" cooperated while "they" defected	M. Replenishing resource management dilemma
___ 14.	Prescriptive legal regulations that use police power to punish violators	N. Sliding reinforcer
___ 15.	Appeal to people's intrinsic sense of social responsibility	O. Social dilemma
___ 16.	Belief that signs of weakness will be exploited by the opponent and that leaders need to show their willingness to use military force	P. Social trap
___ 17.	Strategy for breaking conflict spirals by publicly challenging the opponent to match de-escalations	Q. Time-series analysis
___ 18.	Belief that escalations of international threat lead an opponent to feel more threatened and that leaders should thus demonstrate peaceful intentions to reduce the opponent's own defensive hostilities	R. Tit-for-tat strategy
___ 19.	Offer of rewards to those who reduce their socially harmful behaviors	S. Voluntarist policy
___ 20.	Situations in which individuals or groups are drawn toward immediate rewards that later prove to have unpleasant or lethal consequences	T. Xenophobia

PUTTING IT ALL TOGETHER: THOUGHT QUESTIONS

It is often politicians who make policies regarding behaviors that are harmful to or supportive of the environment. Based on what you've read in your textbook, what personality characteristics might politicians possess that may indicate whether they support or oppose environmental interventions? In your answer, you should consider the impact of being high or low in social dominance orientation, being egoistically oriented versus being more prosocially motivated, and being more or less authoritarian on the environmental stance of politicians.

PUTTING IT ALL TOGETHER: THOUGHT QUESTIONS CONTINUED

Watch the national news on television, or read the front page of the newspaper. Pick out several social dilemmas that are mentioned. Using the chart below, categorize the social dilemmas in terms of the dilemmas discussed in the chapter. For example, are they public goods dilemmas, perceptual dilemmas, replenishing resources dilemmas or some other type? For each dilemma, create an intervention that might help to solve the problem. What type of intervention or strategy did you use for each dilemma? Why? How would you go about actually implementing your intervention?

Social Dilemma from News	Type of Dilemma	Intervention or Strategy used? Why?	Implementation

After You Read...Practice Tests

Practice Test 1

1. A _____ is a situation in which an individual profits from selfishness unless everyone chooses the selfish alternative, in which case the whole group loses.
    a. public goods dilemma
    b. replenishing resource management dilemma
    c. social dilemma
    d. social trap

2. A situation in which group members share a renewable resource that will continue to produce benefits if group members do not overharvest it but also where by any single individual profits from harvesting as much as possible is called the
    a. social trap.
    b. social dilemma.
    c. public goods dilemma.
    d. replenishing resource management dilemma.

3. How are public goods dilemmas DIFFERENT from other social dilemmas?
    a. In public goods dilemmas, individuals are driven to be selfish.
    b. Public goods dilemmas involve individuals giving to the common good instead of taking from the common good.
    c. Public goods dilemmas involve hoping that someone else will do the socially responsible thing.
    d. all of the above

4. _____ value the group benefits, even if it means that they must make personal sacrifices. Whereas _____, try to maximize their own personal gains, without regard to the rest of the group.
    a. Competitors; altruists
    b. Individualists; cooperators
    c. Altruists; individualists
    d. Cooperators; competitors

5. Driving hybrid gas/electric or hydrogen cell vehicles, using solar power, and insulating one's home are all examples of
    a. using alternative technologies to change long-term negative consequences.
    b. moving the future negative consequences into the present.
    c. adding immediate punishments for undesirable behaviors.
    d. reinforcing more desirable environmental alternatives.

6. The Sierra Club's appeal to members to write to Congress in favor of a new wilderness area is an example of a(n)
    a. command-and-control policy.
    b. altruistic policy.
    c. market-based policy.
    d. voluntarist policy.

7. The belief that every escalation of international threat leads the opponent to feel more threatened, and that leaders need to demonstrate peaceful intentions in order to reduce the opponent's own defensive hostilities is called
    a. the deterrence view
    b. the conflict spiral view.
    c. GRIT.
    d. integrative complexity.

8. In the Deutsch (1986) study where participants were playing against a confederate for real money, the confederate sometimes responded with cooperation no matter how their opponent acted. This is known as a
    a. nonpunitive deterrent strategy.
    b. tit-for-tat strategy.
    c. punitive deterrent strategy.
    d. turn-the-other-cheek strategy.

9. Suedfeld, Wallace, and Thachuk (1993) analyzed over 1,200 statements made by national leaders before, during, and after the Persian Gulf crisis of 1991. The integrative complexity of public statements made by leaders such as President Bush and President Hussein indicated that as the stressfulness of the situation increased
    a. the leaders saw the conflict more in shades of gray rather than strictly "black-and-white."
    b. the leaders were more likely to acknowledge all sides of the issues in the conflict.
    c. the statements about the other side became more and more simple.
    d. the cultural chauvinism of the leaders decreased significantly.

10. What did the Rothbart and Hallmark (1988) study of perceptual dilemmas between the "Takonians" and the "Navalians" show?
    a. Perceptual dilemmas are often the result of cultural differences.
    b. Perceptual dilemmas are often the result of long-standing punitive anger between enemies.
    c. Perceptual dilemmas are related to cognitive tendencies toward ingroup favorability and outgroup bias.
    d. Perceptual dilemmas can be minimized by having students role-play cultural ministers who favor cooperation.

Practice Test 2

1. Social dilemmas have been researched through the use of a simple game called the _____. In the game you have the option to confess or not thus providing very different outcomes for yourself.
    a. dollar game
    b. nuts game
    c. prisoner's dilemma
    d. trucking game

2. Which of the following is another name for the tragedy of the commons?
    a. public goods dilemma
    b. perceptual dilemma
    c. sliding reinforcement dilemma
    d. replenishing resource management dilemma

3. Driving to work alone or adjusting your household thermostat to 75 degrees regardless of the outside temperature is immediately reinforcing. However, it may result in hidden costs such as polluted air or shrinking energy supplies. These are examples of
    a. social traps.
    b. command and control strategies.
    c. conflict spirals.
    d. social problems.

4. Jesse is in charge of designing a conservation program. He decides that he will institute a program in grade schools whereby the school that recycles the most newspaper each month will receive money for new computers. Jesse has designed
    a. a command-and-control policy.
    b. an altruistic policy.
    c. a market-based policy.
    d. a voluntarist policy.

5. Which of the following is NOT a reason that command-and-control policies are less effective than other environmental intervention policies?
    a. violators don't expect to get caught
    b. people are more likely to fear punishment than desire a reward
    c. the cost of punishment is outweighed by the benefits of noncompliance
    d. enforcement requires a great deal of policing effort

6. According to Sidanius et. al. (1994 & 2000) and Pratto (1996), what accounts for the cross-cultural gender difference in social dominance orientation?
    a. The difference is due to cultural factors that place importance on men's status.
    b. Men's social status is correlated with his reproductive success, and this correlation influences men's choice of occupations and political groups.
    c. Because men have higher levels of testosterone, they have more of a desire to attain status.
    d. Men are not as good at negotiating as women, and so they use social dominance to win conflicts.

7. The statistical research method that allows researchers to examine two or more recurring events for linkages is a
    a. dynamical systems analysis.
    b. meta-analysis.
    c. time-series analysis.
    d. retrospective analysis.

8. To what does integrative complexity refer?
    a. the belief that your opponents want to exploit you, when what they really want is to cooperate
    b. the extent to which a person views things that are biologically natural as "good"
    c. the belief that opponents have highly complicated, well-laid plans to defeat you in a conflict situation
    d. the extent to which a person demonstrates simplified and categorical thinking as opposed to acknowledgement of all sides of an issue

9. According to Kimmel's (1997) levels of cultural awareness, people who realize that one's own way of doing things is only one of many, and that others are not abnormal in any way would be classified as
    a. culturally chauvinistic.
    b. ethnocentric.
    c. tolerant.
    d. understanding.

10. Why would people playing the "dollar game" pay $20 to get a single dollar?
    a. The initial greed motivation due to competitive escalation which is then replaced with increasing fear of loss.
    b. They have a conflict spiral view, and believe they must win to prevent their opponent from taking advantage of them.
    c. They have failed to realize what they are doing because of a loss of integrative complexity.
    d. all of the above

Practice Test 3

1. Hardin (1968) described the overgrazing of common pastures in New England. When the pastures were public areas, sheepherders overgrazed the pasture and destroyed it. When the pastures were privately owned, herders only grazed as many animals as the land could support knowing that overgrazing would destroy the grass and the whole herd would starve. This is an example of a _____.
    a. public goods dilemma
    b. replenishing resource management dilemma
    c. sliding reinforcement dilemma
    d. social trap

2. When public broadcasting stations appeal for money, some minimum number of listeners need to contribute in order for the station to continue providing broadcasts for everyone to enjoy. This is an example of a _____.
    a. public goods dilemma
    b. perceptual dilemma
    c. sliding reinforcement dilemma
    d. replenishing resource management dilemma

3. In the Liebrand and VanRun (1985) study of value orientations, which of the following groups of participants continued to take more money than anyone else, even when the resources were nearly gone?
    a. individualists and cooperators
    b. cooperators and altruists
    c. competitors and altruists
    d. individualists and competitors

4. Which of the following is NOT an environmental intervention policy?
    a. command-and-control
    b. deterrence
    c. market-based
    d. voluntarist

5. _____ people tend to respect power, obey authority, and rigidly cohere to society's conventions. These people favor a strong military and are more hostile to foreigners.
    a. Authoritarian
    b. Democratic
    c. Individualistic
    d. Voluntarist

6. What was the view that led the U.S. and the U.S.S.R. to reach the point of "mutually assured destruction" during the Cold War?
    a. deterrence view
    b. conflict spiral view
    c. GRIT view
    d. the integrative complexity view

7. In Simonton's (1997) analysis of cultural achievements in Japan over time, he noted that when a country's well-being is threatened by an intrusion of outside influences on traditional values and norms, the result is often
   a. xenophobia.
   b. erotophobia.
   c. a perceptual dilemma.
   d. a social dilemma.

8. In the Deutsch (1986) study, when an accomplice responded to an attack with a defense and then otherwise cooperated, they were using the _____ strategy which turned out to be the most successful strategy.
   a. nonpunitive deterrent
   b. tit-for-tat
   c. punitive deterrent
   d. turn-the-other-cheek

9. According to Kimmel's (1997) levels of cultural awareness, people who are aware that there are religious, racial, and national differences, but nonetheless believe that their way is the "right" way would be classified as
   a. culturally chauvinistic.
   b. ethnocentric.
   c. tolerant.
   d. understanding.

10. Which strategy combines the "you scratch my back, I'll scratch yours" reciprocation with "an eye for an eye" retaliation?
    a. tit-for-tat strategy
    b. nonpunitive deterrent strategy
    c. punitive deterrent strategy
    d. turn-the-other-cheek strategy

Comprehensive Test
(Note: Items 1-15 are multiple-choice questions, items 16-23 are true-false questions, and 24-25 are essay questions.)

1. In the years between 1980 and 1984, the Alaska king crab harvest dropped 92 percent despite the increased number of boats and the increased use of sophisticated equipment to search for the crabs. These crab fisherman over harvested the population to maximize their yearly profits with devastating results. This example illustrates a _____.
   a. public goods dilemma
   b. replenishing resource management dilemma
   c. sliding reinforcement dilemma
   d. social trap

2. A situation in which the whole group can benefit if some of the individuals give something for the common good, but in which individuals profit from "free riding" if enough others contribute is called a
   a. public goods dilemma
   b. perceptual dilemma
   c. sliding reinforcement dilemma
   d. replenishing resource management dilemma

3. What explanation did your textbook provide for the villagers in Assam, India who went on a five-hour murder rampage that resulted in the massacre of 1,700 Bengali immigrants?
   a. overpopulation that lead to dwindling natural resources
   b. unusually hot temperatures the month prior to the murder rampage
   c. culturally biased communication
   d. the timing of positive and negative consequences for selfishness

4. Behavior with positive short-term consequences and negative long-term consequences, ignorance of long-term consequences, and sliding reinforcers can all lead to
   a. social traps.
   b. xenophobia.
   c. conflict spirals.
   d. social problems.

5. What influences people to seek immediate personal self-gratification over long-term benefits to the group?
   a. egotistic self-centeredness and competitiveness
   b. focus on immediate gratification not on long-haul benefits
   c. decreased feelings of social responsibility and interdependence
   d. all of the above

6. _____ are motivated to do relatively better than others, even if it increase their costs. Whereas _____, are motivated to maximize joint profits for themselves and group members.
   a. Competitors; cooperators
   b. Individualists; cooperators
   c. Altruists; individualists
   d. Cooperators; altruists

7. When an individual receives a fine for littering or when a company is penalized for pollution, these examples illustrate
   a. using alternative technologies to change long-term negative consequences.
   b. moving the future negative consequences into the present.
   c. adding immediate punishments for undesirable behaviors.
   d. reinforcing more desirable environmental alternatives.

8. _____ norms are what most people will do in a given situation. For example, in a social dilemma study students contributed more to the public good when a greater percentage of the rest of the group did so. Whereas, _____ norms are what people should do in a particular situation. For example, throwing litter in a trash receptacle rather than out the car window.
   a. Social; injunctive
   b. Injunctive; descriptive
   c. Descriptive; injunctive
   d. Descriptive; social

9. Historically, which of the following environmental intervention policies has been most commonly used and is also frequently used by the U.S. Environmental Protection Agency?
   a. command-and-control policies
   b. altruistic policies
   c. market-based policies
   d. voluntarist policies

10. The belief that signs of weakness will be exploited by the opponent and that leaders need to show their willingness to use military force is called
    a. the deterrence view
    b. the conflict spiral view.
    c. GRIT.
    d. integrative complexity.

11. Which of the following situational factors contributed to the Rattlers and the Eagles viewing each other more negatively in the "Robbers Cave" experiment?
    a. competition over scarce resources
    b. threats
    b. culturally biased communication
    d. all of the above

12. Kelman and his associates have brought together groups of influential Israelis and Palestinians for noncompetitive, interactive problem-solving workshops to resolve international conflict. Why does this solution work?
    a. Participants become familiar with the viewpoints of the other side.
    b. It allows participants to develop more complex images of the other side to help them overcome their prejudicial oversimplifications.
    c. It promotes new ideas for solutions.
    d. all of the above

13. Simonton (1997) used _____ to examine the cultural consequences of national xenophobia by Japan.
    a. dynamical systems analysis   b. meta-analysis
    c. time-series analysis   d. retrospective analysis

14. Which of the following strategies for intergroup cooperation did Gorbachev successfully use to help spin down the conflict spiral of nuclear weapons production between the U.S. and the U.S.S.R.?
    a. tit-for-tat strategy
    b. nonpunitive deterrent strategy
    c. deterrence strategy
    d. GRIT

15. Which of the following situational factors contributes to the primitive motivation to defend ourselves and valued others?
    a. competition over scarce resources   b. threats
    b. culturally biased communication   d. all of the above

TRUE-FALSE

Indicate whether each statement is true or false by circling T or F. If you decide it is false, explain why. Correct answers appear at the end of the study guide in the ANSWERS section for Chapter 13.

T   F   16.   A sliding reinforcer brings rewards when used in large doses, but brings punishment when used in small doses.

T   F   17.   Individuals with more siblings, and in particular more sisters, are likely to exhibit a more prosocial orientation than only children or those with only brothers.

T   F   18.   Payment for voluntary sterilization is an example of a voluntarist type of environmental intervention.

T   F   19.   Across most ethnic and cultural groups, women have lower social dominance orientation scores than men.

T   F   20.   Individuals playing against individuals tend to be more competitive than groups playing against groups.

T   F   21.   Xenophobia is a fear and distrust of foreigners.

T   F   22.   According to Kimmel's levels of cultural awareness, the highest level is tolerance.

T   F   23.   Soviet premier Gorbachev used a deterrence approach to break the conflict spiral between the U.S. and the U.S.S.R.

ESSAY

24. What is a replenishing resource management dilemma? Use the Alaska king crab harvest to illustrate this dilemma. Are there any solutions for this problem?

25. Describe the basic differences in the negotiation styles of the Americans and Iraqis in the 1991 Middle East conflict, and Kimmel's (1997) recommendations to improve negotiations?

When You Have Finished...

Now that you have had a chance to read this chapter and complete the activities associated with it, you may be interested in finding additional materials on this topic. The World Wide Web is a great and convenient resource for gathering additional information in a variety of areas. Listed below are web links and website descriptions that are relevant to this chapter.

Web Links and Website Descriptions
Be sure to visit Chapter 13 at the companion website: www.ablongman.com/knc3e
http://magnolia.net/~leonf/sd/sd-games.html This website discusses social dilemma games and puzzles and provides links to play the games. You can figure out whether it pays to cooperate or defect.
http://members.aol.com/trajcom/private/trajcom.htm This website provides a series of links to material on the tragedy of the commons.
http://www-personal.umich.edu/~rdeyoung/envtpsych.html This website provides a brief overview of environmental psychology.
http://web.uvic.ca/~apadiv34/ This is the American Psychological Association's Division 34 website for Population and Environmental Psychology. This website contains information relevant to population and environment issues and web links to additional sites.
http://www.greenpeace.org/international_en/ This is the home page of Greenpeace International. Greenpeace is an independent, campaigning organization that uses nonviolent confrontation to expose global environmental problems. Use this website to explore the possible consequences that social dilemmas pose.

Comprehensive Crossword Puzzle

Across

8. Belief that escalations of international threat lead an opponent to feel more threatened and that leaders should thus demonstrate peaceful intentions to reduce the opponent's own defensive hostilities

10. Strategy for breaking conflict spirals by publicly challenging the opponent to match de-escalations

12. Situation in which an individual profits from selfishness unless everyone chooses the selfish alternative, in which case the whole group loses

13. Someone oriented toward bringing the group benefits, even if they must personally sacrifice

14. Situations in which individuals or groups are drawn toward immediate rewards that later prove to have unpleasant or lethal consequences

15. Fear and distrust of foreigners

16. Someone oriented toward maximizing personal gains, without regard to the rest of the group

17. Stimulus that brings rewards in small doses, which change to punishments when they occur in large doses

18. Extent to which a person demonstrates simplified, "black and white," categorical thinking as opposed to acknowledgement of all sides of an issue

19. Appeal to people's intrinsic sense of social responsibility

Down

1. Offer of rewards to those who reduce their socially harmful behaviors

2. Negotiating tactic in which the individual responds to competitiveness with competitiveness and to cooperation with cooperation

3. Situation in which the whole group can benefit if some of the individuals give something for the common good but individuals profit from "free riding" if enough others contribute

4. Belief that signs of weakness will be exploited by the opponent and that leaders need to show their willingness to use military force

5. Someone oriented toward working together to maximize the joint benefits to the self and the group

6. Someone oriented to come out relatively better than other players, regardless of whether their personal winnings are high or low in an absolute sense

7. Prescriptive legal regulations that use police power to punish violators

9. Combination of social dilemma and outgroup bias-each side in a conflict believes it is best for both sides to cooperate, while simultaneously believing that the other side would prefer that "we" cooperated while "they" defected

11. Method in which two or more recurring events are examined for linkages over time

Puzzle created with Puzzlemaker at DiscoverySchool.com

INTEGRATING SOCIAL PSYCHOLOGY

Before You Read...

This chapter is the synthesis of all that you have learned while investigating the mysteries of social life. First, you will reconsider the four major theoretical perspectives in social psychology which include: the sociocultural perspective, the evolutionary perspective, the social learning perspective, and the social cognitive perspective. Then you will re-examine the two broad principles derived from the theoretical perspectives. Namely, social behavior is goal oriented and social behavior represents a continual interaction between the person and the situation. Specifically, you will look at the five broad motives that underlie social behavior and the six general principles in which the person and situation factors interact. You will then rediscover why research methodology is important for answering questions about social behavior. You will investigate how social psychology is closely connected to other subdisciplines of psychology, how it is connected to other basic sciences, and the important implications social psychological research has for applied fields. Finally, this chapter concludes by considering the future direction for the field of social psychology.

Chapter Learning Objectives

After reading this chapter, you should be able to:

- Define social psychology. Explain how individuals present themselves to fit together with their situation, interact with others, and the social processes involved at the group and global level.

- Explain how the major perspectives of social psychology can be placed on a continuum from proximate to ultimate levels of explanation for social behavior

- Describe the sociocultural perspective. What does your book describe as the "central legacy" of the sociocultural perspective?

- Describe the evolutionary perspective. How are evolutionary factors and sociocultural factors interdependent influences of social behavior?

- Describe the social learning perspective. What is the connection between the social learning and sociocultural perspectives?

- Describe the social cognitive perspective. Why is the social cognitive perspective the most influential perspective in modern social psychology?

- Explain the extent to which people accurately perceive sex differences and why. Why do people act in line with sex stereotypes?

- Outline the two broad principles that all five perspectives share

- List and describe the five broad goals that underlie social behavior

- Explain how does self-esteem function as a "sociometer"

- List the three component subgoals for which we evaluate ourselves and others

- Explain how the case of J. Edgar Hoover demonstrates the central lesson of the "Focus On Social Dysfunction" section in your textbook

- Describe the two other important points about goals that attracting and retaining mates demonstrates

- Describe the six general principles in which the person and situation factors interact

- Explain why we delve so deeply into the interactions between persons and situation

- Explain why it is important to use research methodology to answer questions about social behavior

- Describe the four general conclusions for consumers of social science information that were outlined in the Focus on Method section

- Explain what is meant by a "full-cycle" approach to social psychology

- Define meta-analysis and triangulation

- Explain how social psychology is related to other disciplines within psychology. What are some common questions shared with other subdisciplines of psychology?

- Explain how social psychology is related to the basic sciences. What are some common questions shared with other basic sciences?

- Explain social psychology's usefulness for business, medicine, and law. What are some common questions shared with these applied sciences?

As You Read...

KEY TERMS!
Listed below are the key terms from the chapter that are essential for your understanding of the material. Refer to the definitions from your textbook; they are located at the end of this chapter, within the text in boldface, and in the margins throughout this chapter. In order to enhance your recall ability for these terms, you may want to consider making flashcards which include a term on one side, and a definition on the other (with perhaps a brief example that makes sense to you).

Proximate explanation   Triangulation   Ultimate explanation

PUBLIC SPECTACLES, HIDDEN CONSPIRACIES, AND MULTIPLE MOTIVES

In the beginning of this chapter your authors discussed a dramatic shift in the course of race relations in the United States. This shift was marked by a speech that was given by the Reverend Martin Luther King on August 28, 1963. Please describe the highlights of this speech and why it is considered one of the greatest speeches of history. Explain why the Kennedys would try to split up the leadership in the civil rights movement when they were becoming more committed to solving race problems in this country. How is this mystery linked to FBI Director J. Edgar Hoover? Why would Hoover launch an attack on King? "And how could immense societal change arise out of all the self-focused personal motivations of everyone involved in this intrigue?"

MAJOR THEORETICAL PERSPECTIVES OF SOCIAL PSYCHOLOGY

The major theoretical perspectives fall along a continuum of proximate to ultimate levels of explanation. In the figure below, write in the names of the theoretical perspective (sociocultural, evolutionary, social cognitive, and social learning) according to this continuum.

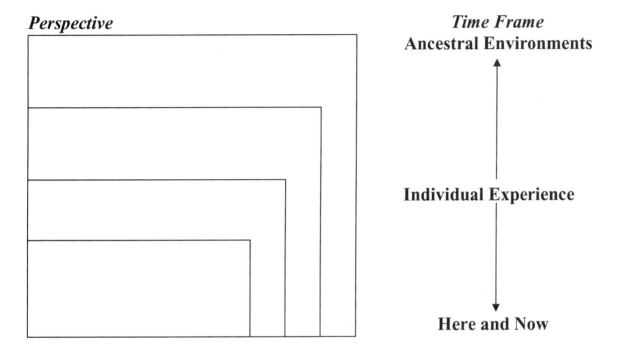

Perspective

Time Frame

Ancestral Environments

Individual Experience

Here and Now

What is a proximate explanation?

What is an ultimate explanation?

THE PERSON AND THE SITUATION INTERACT

According to Kurt Lewin (1951), the person and the situation work together to influence the way we think, feel, and behave. Your textbook reexamined the six ways in which the person and situation influence one another and interact to shape social life. The six ways are:

(1) different persons respond differently to the same situation
(2) situations choose the person
(3) persons choose their situations
(4) different situations prime different parts of the person
(5) persons change the situation
(6) situations change the person.

Below, indicate which one of the six person/situation interactions is operating in each of the following examples.

Person/Situation Interaction	Examples
1. _____	Hoover transformed the Federal Bureau of Investigation into a powerful and more paranoid organization.
2. _____	Many of us would stop a course of action if it involved threats to our lives. However, Martin Luther King Jr. fought even harder for civil rights surrounded by these threats.
3. _____	Hillary Rodham Clinton is happy when she speaks before women's organizations, she is upset when listening to republicans talk of removal of her husband from office, and is excited to see her daughter return from a business trip oversees.
4. _____	Many people dream of becoming famous, but only a select few will succeed.
5. _____	Charlie decided to go to the movies last Friday and watch the latest action-thriller.
6. _____	Angela was raised in a conservative home. After spending four years at a liberal arts college, Angela begins to find her political views to be more liberal.
7. _____	Margaret spends her Saturday nights with her church group instead of with her high school friends.
8. _____	Mike desperately wanted to play college football at Notre Dame but he wasn't selected to play there. Instead, Mike went to his second choice school.
9. _____	The events of September 11th forever changed Americans view on terrorism.
10. _____	When Cynthia arrived in Honolulu, she wanted her friends to entertain her while she was on vacation. Before Caleb arrived in Honolulu, he made plans to take in all the sites Hawaii had to offer by booking daily events with tourism companies.

MATCHING: KEY TERMS

Matching! Match each definition on the left side of the page with the concept on the right side of the page. Each concept on the right should only be used once.

___ 1. Statistical combination of results from different studies of the same topic

A. Confound

___ 2. Theoretical viewpoint that focuses on past learning experiences as determinants of a person's social behaviors

B. Evolutionary Perspective

___ 3. Focus on background or historical causes

C. Meta-analysis

___ 4. Theoretical viewpoint that searches for the causes of social behavior in influences from larger social groups

D. Proximate Explanation

___ 5. Examining the same problem using different research methods, each having different biases

E. Social Cognitive Perspective

___ 6. Theoretical viewpoint that searches for the causes of social behavior in the physical and psychological dispositions that helped our ancestors survive and reproduce

F. Social Learning Perspective

___ 7. Focus on relatively immediate causes

G. Sociocultural Perspective

___ 8. Variable that systematically changes along with the independent variable, potentially leading to a mistaken conclusion about the effect of the independent variable

H. Triangulation

___ 9. Theoretical viewpoint that focuses on the mental processes involved in paying attention to, interpreting, judging, and remembering social experiences

I. Ultimate Explanation

PUTTING IT ALL TOGETHER: THOUGHT QUESTIONS

In the Thought Questions of Chapter 1, you were asked what was meant by Kurt Lewin's statement "There is nothing so practical as a good theory." Now that you have read the textbook, has your answer to this question changed? Do you agree with the statement? Why or why not?

The book concludes by stating that there is still much to learn about human social behavior. Think back about one of the major topics covered (e.g., aggression, attraction, persuasion, prosocial behavior). Formulate a new question about a specific behavior within that major topic. What goals drive that behavior? Are there any existing theories that would explain the behavior? What is your theory of why that behavior occurs? Design an experiment to test your theory.

After You Read...Practice Tests

Practice Test 1

1. _____ explanations focus on immediate causes in the here and now.
   - a. Central
   - b. Primary
   - c. Proximate
   - d. Ultimate

2. Which of the following theoretical perspectives adopts the LEAST proximate time frame?
   - a. Sociocultural
   - b. Social Learning.
   - c. Social Cognitive.
   - d. Evolutionary.

3. Compared to her working-class Polish grandmother, a modern-day university professor has different attitudes about premarital sex and women's roles in the workplace. This example can be explained best by which theoretical perspective?
   - a. Sociocultural
   - b. Evolutionary
   - c. Social Learning
   - d. Social Cognitive

4. The idea that social problems stem from motivations that were once adaptive in promoting the survival and reproduction of our ancestors and their kin, but that are not designed for the modern world, is most consistent with which theory?
   - a. Evolutionary
   - b. Social learning
   - c. Sociocultural
   - d. Social cognitive.

5. How does self-esteem function as a sociometer?
   - a. People with high self-esteem are more successful in their social environments than those with low self-esteem.
   - b. We feel lowered self-esteem when we are excluded by others, and increased self-esteem when we are included by others.
   - c. People don't like individuals who have very high self-esteem.
   - d. We base our self-esteem on the situation and the goal of that situation.

6. The fact that geese raised by humans try to mate with the wrong species, or that ants will attack a human being with a can of bug spray illustrates what about the goals of social behavior?
   - a. Animals, including humans, are always conscious of the goals of their behavior.
   - b. The goals of behavior change depending on the situation.
   - c. The goals of animals are not as finely tuned as the goals of humans.
   - d. Goals involve imperfectly tuned mechanisms.

7. J. Edgar Hoover was appointed to direct the FBI; Martin Luther King, Jr. was drafted by his peers to lead the Montgomery bus boycott; and John F. Kennedy was elected president of the United States in 1960. These events can best be explained by which of the following principles regarding the interaction between the person and the situation?
   - a. Different persons respond differently to the same situation.
   - b. Situations choose the person.
   - c. Persons choose their situations.
   - d. Different situations prime different parts of the person.

8. A social psychologist has been studying attraction for many years. Her findings are the same when she does laboratory experiments, naturalistic observations, archival research and a meta-analysis. By comparing the results across very different methods, what process has she used?
    a. meta-analysis
    b. a focus on proximate causes of behavior
    c. triangulation
    d. confounded methods

9. Which were discussed in the text as broad trends for the future of social psychology?
    a. Increasing specialization of social psychology, becoming more distinct from fields of sociology and clinical psychology.
    b. Increasing focus on underlying biochemistry and less emphasis on vaguely defined "cognitive" factors.
    c. Increasing development of rigorous methods, and de-emphasis of theoretical speculation.
    d. Increasing integration with broad theories of evolution, cognitive science, and dynamical systems.

10. Social psychology is closely connected with many other areas of psychology. Which question below overlaps with one of those areas?
    a. How is paranoia connected to normal group defensiveness?
    b. Are there universal patterns to human marriage?
    c. How do group processes affect policy decisions in international conflict situations?
    d. Do the mating rituals of peacocks shed any light on human courtship?

Practice Test 2

1. _____ explanations focus on background or historical causes.
    a. Central
    b. Primary
    c. Proximate
    d. Ultimate

2. Which of the following theoretical perspectives adopts the most "proximate" time frame?
    a. Sociocultural
    b. Social learning.
    c. Social cognitive.
    d. Evolutionary.

3. During the 1950s, most American men had short hair. During the 1960s long hair became a fad. This is most consistent with which theoretical perspective?
    a. Sociocultural.
    b. Evolutionary.
    c. Social Cognitive.
    d. Phenomenological.

4. Which perspective was strongly influenced by Charles Darwin?
    a. Sociocultural
    b. Evolutionary
    c. Social learning
    d. Social cognitive

5. A researcher suggests that prejudice often stems from limited attentional capacities that lead us to think heuristically rather than systematically about ethnic groups. That researcher's statement is most consistent with which perspective?
    a. Sociocultural.
    b. Social learning.
    c. Social cognitive.
    d. Phenomenological.

6. You are busy figuring out why your friend decided to take you out to dinner and you are wondering if it's because your friend knows that you have two tickets to the upcoming concert or if they are being genuinely nice. This example illustrates which of the following motives (goals) underlying social behavior?
    a. to establish social ties
    b. to understand ourselves or others
    c. to gain and maintain status
    d. to attract and retain mates

7. Which of the following is NOT a central lesson about social behavior demonstrated by the story of J. Edgar Hoover?
    a. Understanding normal psychological mechanisms can help us understand the function of apparently disordered behavior.
    b. At some level, there is usually a rational explanation for social dysfunction.
    c. The use of cognitive biases is often related to an underlying personality disorder.
    d. Disordered social behaviors are usually normal psychological mechanisms that have been magnified.

8. Violent-prone people are more likely to watch a violent film; delinquent teens are more likely to hang out with other ruffians; and intellectuals tend to join the science club. These scenarios can best be explained by which of the following principles regarding the interaction between the person and the situation?
    a. Different persons respond differently to the same situation.
    b. Situations choose the person.
    c. Persons choose their situations.
    d. Different situations prime different parts of the person.

9. The use of field studies, laboratory experiments, and surveys allows a researcher to draw more confident conclusions when investigating the relationship between children and aggression. This is an example of _____.
    a. triangulation
    b. a focus on proximate causes of behavior
    c. meta-analysis
    d. confounded methods

10. Your textbook notes that social psychology has had a positive influence on which of the following disciplines?
    a. law
    b. medicine and health sciences
    c. business
    d. all of the above

Practice Test 3

1. _____ explanations examine causes of behavior in the immediate present, whereas, _____ explanations examine background or historical causes of behavior.
    a. Proximate; ultimate
    b. Primary; central
    c. Ultimate; proximate
    d. Central; primary

2. A theorist who talks about prejudice against different ethnic groups in terms of fads or conformity to the rules of one's social class grouping would be adopting which perspective?
    a. Sociocultural.
    b. Evolutionary.
    c. Social cognitive.
    d. Phenomenological.

3.   What is the evolutionary perspective on the vast array of cross-cultural differences between societies?
a.   The differences are anomalies.
b.   The differences are the result of different evolutionary pressures on people from different societies.
c.   The differences exist because societies have very different goals and concerns.
d.   Under the surface of differences, there is usually a core of similarity.

4.   A researcher says that leaders are not born, but are trained and shaped by successful parents, who model leadership for them. That researcher is adopting which theoretical perspective?
a.   Evolutionary   b.   Social learning
c.   Sociocultural   d.   Social cognitive.

5.   When boys are punished for playing with dolls and girls are rewarded for playing house, the _____ perspective helps us understand some of the differences found between the sexes.
a.   evolutionary   b.   social learning
c.   sociocultural   d.   social cognitive.

6.   J. Edgar Hoover's antagonism toward King and the civil rights movement was linked to the exaggerated goal of
a.   establishing social ties.   b.   understanding ourselves or others.
c.   gaining and maintaining status.   d.   defending ourselves and those we value.

7.   Hillary Rodham Clinton is happy when she is about to speak before women's organizations, she is upset when listening to republicans speak on environmental policy, and excited to see her daughter return from a business trip oversees. These events can best be explained by which of the following principles regarding the interaction between the person and the situation?
a.   Different persons respond differently to the same situation.
b.   Situations choose the person.
c.   Persons choose their situations.
d.   Different situations prime different parts of the person.

8.   What is meant by a "full-cycle" approach to social psychology?
a.   Researchers should use many different types of laboratory experiments to study the same phenomenon.
b.   Researchers should move between experimental research to determine causes of behavior and field work to make sure they are studying real-world phenomena.
c.   Researchers should study only those behaviors that can also be studied by other disciplines of psychology.
d.   Researchers should do meta-analyses of all their previous studies to look for overall trends in the causes of behavior.

9. The text discusses triangulation as related to which general conclusion about consuming social science information (from the methods sections)?
   a. Look for good descriptions to accompany explanations.
   b. Don't trust everything people say.
   c. Beware of confounds.
   d. Ask for converging evidence.

10. Social psychology is closely connected with many other areas of psychology and other basic sciences. Which of the following questions is connected to social psychology and to another area/s of psychology? (516d)
   a. What individual differences predict aggressive behavior?
   b. What social conditions lead people to recycle?
   c. How does the limited human attention span affect stereotypes?
   d. all of the above

Comprehensive Test
(Note: Items 1-15 are multiple-choice questions, items 16-23 are true-false questions, and 24-25 are essay questions.)

1. Which of the following is the correct order of the four major perspectives in social psychology from the proximate to the ultimate level of explanation?
   a. evolutionary, sociocultural, social learning, social cognition
   b. evolutionary, social cognition, social learning, sociocultural
   c. social cognition, social learning, sociocultural, evolutionary
   d. sociocultural, social learning, social cognition, evolutionary

2. What is a central legacy of the sociocultural perspective?
   a. a focus on learning
   b. a focus on norms
   c. a focus on the commonalities between people
   d. a focus on the subjective reality of the person

3. Which of the following is true about the link between the sociocultural perspective and the evolutionary perspective?
   a. Human predispositions influence which cultural norms are likely to be adopted.
   b. Social norms influence the success of different survival and reproduction strategies.
   c. Human culture is shaped by human nature.
   d. all of the above

4. To say that ethnocentrism often stems from classical and instrumental conditioning experiences would be to adopt which perspective?
   a. Sociocultural   b. Social learning
   c. Social cognitive   d. Phenomenological

5. You decide to run for class president because you feel that it would be personally rewarding and you think could win the office. What perspective best explains your decision to run for class president?
   a. Sociocultural   b. Evolutionary
   c. Social learning   d. Social cognitive

INTEGRATING SOCIAL PSYCHOLOGY

6. Why is the social cognitive perspective considered the most influential perspective in modern social psychology?
    a. All of the other perspectives rely on the mental processes of noticing, interpreting, and remembering our social world.
    b. The social cognitive perspective is the most proximate explanation for social behavior.
    c. The social cognitive perspective is the newest, and is thus the most popular.
    d. The social cognitive perspective provided the definitive explanation of sex differences.

7. According to Eagly (1995) why do people end up with a fairly good idea about the size of gender differences (such as physical violence)?
    a. because news reports frequently focus on gender differences
    b. because our common sense is very helpful when it comes to gender
    c. because gender is a salient cognitive category
    d. none of the above

8. When a person remembers a woman's behavior in line with a stereotype including "nurturance" and a man's behavior in line with a stereotype including "aggressiveness," the _____ perspective helps us understand this difference found between the sexes.
    a. evolutionary   b. social learning
    c. sociocultural   d. social cognitive.

9. Which of the following are broad principles shared by the major perspectives in social psychology?
    a. Social behavior is the result of learning.
    b. Social behavior is goal-oriented.
    c. Social behavior represents an interaction between the person and the situation.
    d. b and c

10. On the TV show "Survivor," participants are placed on an island with one of two groups of strangers where they compete for food, shelter, and other essentials. Those who have won the game are those who have been able to
    a. establish social ties.   b. understand themselves and others.
    c. gain and maintain status.   d. defend themselves.

11. The text discussed J.Edgar Hoover's paranoid tendencies to demonstrate:
    a. how disordered behavior often reveals the operation of normal psychological mechanisms.
    b. why motives are often more important than cognitions.
    c. why cognitions are often more important than motives.
    d. the importance of cross-cultural awareness.

12. Carol was raised in a very liberal home by strongly democratic parents. She goes to college at a military institution and gradually her views become much more conservative. This is an example of the way in which
    a. situations choose people.
    b. people choose their situations.
    c. situations change people.
    d. different situations activate different parts of the self.

13. _____ are like invisible variables that make it difficult to know what caused the subject's behavior.
    a. Confounds
    b. Demand characteristics
    c. Observer biases
    d. Environmental characteristics

14. The text discusses meta-analysis as related to which general conclusion about consuming social science information (from the methods sections)?
    a. Look for good descriptions to accompany explanations.
    b. Don't trust everything people say.
    c. Beware of confounds.
    d. Ask for converging evidence.

15. To what other disciplines can the findings of social psychology be applied?
    a. medicine
    b. business
    c. law
    d. all of the above

TRUE-FALSE

Indicate whether each statement is true or false by circling T or F. If you decide it is false, explain why. Correct answers appear at the end of the study guide in the ANSWERS section for Chapter 14.

T   F   16. The social cognitive perspective is considered a proximate level of explanation for social behavior.

T   F   17. Some societies are polygamous, indicating that monogamy is not a cultural universal.

T   F   18. According to your book, the field of social psychology has concluded that gender differences are the result of cultural learning experiences.

T   F   19. The goal to protect oneself and others always leads to hostility.

T   F   20. Social situations change whether the same stimulus is viewed as a reward or a punishment.

T   F   21. The way that people respond to persuasive arguments, orders from authority, and attractive members of the opposite sex, varies as a function of their personalities.

T   F   22. When people admit to things like masturbation or homicidal fantasies, it is safe to assume that they are overestimating.

T   F   23. Social psychology has implications for both basic sciences like anthropology and biology as well as applied sciences like education and engineering.

ESSAY

24. Gender represents a vivid social category. Explain whether gender differences are real or all in our minds. Explain how gender differences are perpetuated through our cultural learning experiences and our genes.

25. Why is it important for psychologists to use research methods to explain social behavior? Describe the four general conclusions for consumers of social science information that were outlined in the Focus on Method section. Why would a researcher use meta-analysis and triangulation?

When You Have Finished...

Now that you have had a chance to read this chapter and complete the activities associated with it, you may be interested in finding additional materials on this topic. The World Wide Web is a great and convenient resource for gathering additional information in a variety of areas. Listed below are web links and website descriptions that are relevant to this chapter.

Web Links and Website Descriptions
Be sure to visit Chapter 14 at the companion website: www.ablongman.com/knc3e
http://www.scirus.com/ Scirus is a comprehensive science-specific search engine on the Internet. Scirus searches over 150 million science-specific web pages, enabling you to quickly pinpoint scientific data, peer-reviewed articles and journals, and locate university sites and scientists' home pages.
http://www.spsp.org/ Society for Personality and Social Psychology website generates and disseminates research in personality and social psychology.
http://www.apa.org/students/ American Psychological Association's student website will help you with careers in psychology, undergraduate resources, getting into graduate school, post-doctoral information funding opportunities, and best-selling books.
http://www.psycline.org/journals/psycline.html *PSYCLINE* started in 1995 under its former name *Links to Psychological Journals* and has a high reputation as a comprehensive and up-to-date index of psychology and social science journals on the web.

Comprehensive Crossword Puzzle

Across

3. Theoretical perspective that searches for the causes of social behavior in influences from larger social groups
4. Theoretical perspective that searches for the causes of social behavior in the physical and psychological dispositions that helped our ancestors survive and reproduce
5. Theoretical perspective that focuses on past learning experiences as determinants of a person's social behaviors
6. Focus on background or historical causes
8. Variable that systematically changes along with the independent variable, potentially leading to a mistaken conclusion about the effect of the independent variable
9. Statistical combination of results from different studies of the same topic

Down

1. Focus on relatively immediate causes
2. Examining the same problem using different research methods, each having different biases
7. Theoretical perspective that focuses on the mental processes involved in paying attention to, interpreting, judging, and remembering social experiences

Puzzle created with Puzzlemaker at DiscoverySchool.com

CHAPTER ANSWERS: "AFTER YOU READ" PRACTICE TESTS AND SHORT ANSWER/ESSAY QUESTIONS

Chapter 1 – Introduction to Social Psychology

Item Number	Practice Test 1	Practice Test 2	Practice Test 3	Comprehensive Test
1	C (p. 3)	A (p. 4)	C (p. 3)	D (p. 3)
2	B (p. 3)	B (p. 5)	B (p. 4)	C (pp. 4-5)
3	A (pp. 4-5)	B (p. 5)	A (pp. 5-6)	A (p. 4)
4	B (p. 5)	C (p. 7)	C (p. 6)	D (p. 4)
5	B (p. 6)	D (p. 7)	B (pp. 7-8)	B (p. 5)
6	A (p. 7)	B (p. 13)	A (p. 8)	D (p. 7)
7	D (p. 8)	A (p. 3)	C (p. 11)	B (p. 7)
8	D (p. 13)	A (p. 15)	C (p. 12)	D (p. 10)
9	B (p. 18)	A (p. 16)	A (pp. 18-19)	D (pp. 10-11)
10	A (p. 20)	D (p. 18)	B (p. 20)	B (p. 14)
11				B (p. 16)
12				A (p. 17)
13				B (p. 17)
14		Correct Responses to Multiple Choice Questions		C (pp. 18-20)
15				D (p. 18)
16				F (p. 4)
17				T (p. 5)
18				T (pp. 7-8)
19				T (p. 10)
20				F (p. 10)
21				F (p. 13)
22				T (p. 17)
23				F (p. 18)

Major Theoretical Perspectives Matching

1. C
2. B
3. D
4. A

Matching

1. G	6. D	11. M
2. O	7. I	12. B
3. E	8. A	13. J
4. F	9. H	14. C
5. N	10. L	15. K

Summary of Research Methods

Descriptive Correlational Methods	Strengths	Weaknesses
Naturalistic Observation	2, 5	14, 15, 17, 25
Case Studies	1, 6	20, 24, 26
Archives	7	21
Surveys	9	16, 18
Psychological tests	3	12, 22
Experimental Methods		
Laboratory Experiment	4, 8	23
Field Experiment	10, 11	13, 19

Comprehensive Crossword Puzzle

ACROSS

1. Culture
3. Social norm
4. Correlation
6. Sociocultural perspective
7. Naturalistic observation
8. Case study
9. Survey method
12. Hypothesis
13. Reliability
14. Independent variable
15. Experiment
16. External validity
17. Dependent variable
18. Theory
19. Social cognitive perspective
20. Internal validity

DOWN

2. Random assignment
5. Archival method
9. Social psychology
10. Validity
11. Debriefing

Chapter 2 – The Person and the Situation

Item Number	Practice Test 1	Practice Test 2	Practice Test 3	Comprehensive Test
1	A (p. 33)	C (p. 32)	D (p. 33)	D (p. 32)
2	A (p. 34)	B (p. 33)	C (p. 34)	C (p. 33)
3	B (p. 35)	D (p. 35)	D (p. 33)	D (p. 36)
4	A (p. 37)	B (p. 37)	D (p. 38)	B (p. 37)
5	C (p. 38)	A (p. 38)	A (p. 38)	D (p. 38)
6	A (p. 44)	D (p. 39)	B (p. 39)	C (p. 39)
7	C (pp. 41-42)	C (p. 42)	D (p. 43)	D (pp. 39-40)
8	A (p. 45)	C (p. 45)	A (p. 45)	B (p. 40)
9	B (p. 45)	D (pp. 46-47)	B (p. 49)	D (p. 45)
10	B (p. 52)	C (p. 58)	C (pp. 54-55)	C (p. 45)
11				A (p. 47)
12				D (pp. 50 & 52)
13				C (pp. 51-52)
14		Correct Responses to		A (p. 53)
15		Multiple Choice Questions		D (p. 60)
16				T (p. 33)
17				F (p. 62)
18				T (p. 35)
19				T (p. 39)
20				F (p. 42)
21				F (p. 45)
22				F (p. 49)
23				T (p. 60)

The Person and the Situation Interact

1. 2	6. 6
2. 5	7. 4
3. 6	8. 2
4. 3	9. 5
5. 1	10. 3

Matching

1. C	6. J	11. O
2. G	7. L	12. F
3. I	8. N	13. B
4. H	9. D	14. K
5. A	10. M	15. E

Word Scramble

1. Self-esteem 2. Socialization 3. Exemplar 4. Priming 5. Attitude
   Bonus Word - Schema

Comprehensive Crossword Puzzle

ACROSS
2. Mood
4. Automaticity
5. Individualistic culture
6. Social comparison
7. Affordance
8. Counterfactual thinking
9. Goal

ACROSS CONTINUED
10. Self-esteem
11. Emotion
12. Motivation
13. Schema
14. Willpower
15. Attention

DOWN
1. Exemplar
3. Descriptive norm
8. Collectivistic culture

Chapter 3 – Social Cognition: Understanding Ourselves and Others

Item Number	Practice Test 1	Practice Test 2	Practice Test 3	Comprehensive Test
1	C (pp. 71-72)	A (p. 71)	B (p. 71)	D (p. 71)
2	B (p. 72)	A (p. 71-72)	D (p. 73)	D (p. 73)
3	D (p. 73)	A (p. 75)	D (p. 74)	A (p. 75)
4	A (p. 76)	C (p. 76)	A (p. 78)	C (pp. 77-78)
5	B (p. 78)	A (p. 79)	C (p. 79)	A (p. 79)
6	C (p. 80)	B (p. 81)	A (p. 81)	B (p. 80)
7	C (p. 83)	D (pp. 82-85)	B (p. 83)	D (p. 80-81)
8	D (p. 84)	C (p. 88)	C (p. 84)	A (p. 83)
9	C (p. 86)	C (pp. 90-92)	B (p. 92)	A (p. 85)
10	A (p. 92)	A (p. 92)	C (p. 93)	B (p. 89)
11				D (pp. 88-89)
12				B (p. 92)
13				A (pp. 92-93)
14		*Correct Responses to Multiple Choice Questions*		D (pp. 92-93)
15				B (pp. 95-97)
16				T (p. 74)
17				T (p. 75)
18				F (p. 78)
19				T (p. 76)
20				F (p. 82)
21				T (p. 89)
22				F (p. 92)
23				T (p. 95)

Errors in Social Cognition

1. 2
2. 5
3. 1
4. 3
5. 4
6. 2
7. 3

Matching

1. D
2. J
3. H
4. E
5. I
6. M
7. A
8. K
9. G
10. B
11. L
12. F
13. N
14. O
15. C

Comprehensive Crossword Puzzle

ACROSS
1. Fundamental attribution error
3. Availability heuristic
13. Dispositional inference

DOWN
2. Actor-observer difference
4. Downward social comparison
5. Upward social comparison
6. Social cognition
7. Cognitive heuristic
8. Representativeness heuristic
9. Discounting principle
10. False consensus effect
11. Self-serving bias
12. Covariation model
14. Self-fulfilling prophecy

Chapter 4 – Presenting the Self

Item Number	Practice Test 1	Practice Test 2	Practice Test 3	Comprehensive Test
1	A (p. 105)	C (p. 107)	A (p. 105)	D (p. 105)
2	D (p. 106)	A (p. 107)	C (pp. 106-107)	D (pp. 107-108)
3	D (p. 107)	D (pp. 109-110)	C (p. 110)	B (p. 109)
4	D (p. 108)	D (p. 113)	C (pp. 111-112)	A (p. 111)
5	A (p. 114)	C (p. 114)	B (p. 115)	C (p. 111)
6	C (p. 118)	A (p. 116)	D (p. 119)	D (p. 113)
7	B (p. 119)	A (p. 120-121)	B (p. 121)	D (pp. 114-115)
8	C (p. 120-122)	D (p. 123)	B (pp. 123-124)	A (p. 116)
9	D (p. 121)	A (p. 127)	A (p. 127)	A (p. 117)
10	B (p. 128)	B (pp. 120-121)	D (p. 127)	B (p. 121)
11				B (p. 125)
12				B (p. 127)
13				D (p. 128)
14		Correct Responses to Multiple Choice Questions		C (p. 131)
15				D (pp. 130-131)
16				T (p. 107)
17				T (pp. 109-110)
18				T (pp. 111-113)
19				F (p. 113)
20				T (p. 120)
21				F (p. 123-124)
22				F (p. 129-130)
23				T (p. 130)

Matching

1. D
2. H
3. G
4. J
5. A
6. C
7. K
8. B
9. L
10. N
11. M
12. F
13. I
14. E

Comprehensive Crossword Puzzle

ACROSS
4. Self monitoring
11. Competence motivation
13. Self promotion
14. Public self consciousness

DOWN
1. Basking in reflected glory
2. Cutting off reflected failure
3. Self presentation
5. Self handicapping
6. Multiple audience dilemma
7. Dramaturgical perspective
8. Shyness
9. Social anxiety
10. Body language
12. Ingratiation

Chapter 5 – Attitudes and Persuasion

Item Number	Practice Test 1	Practice Test 2	Practice Test 3	Comprehensive Test
1	B (p. 141)	A (p. 141)	B (p. 141)	D (p. 141)
2	D (pp. 141-142)	B (p. 142)	C (p. 141)	A (p. 141)
3	B (p. 144)	A (p. 145)	D (pp. 143-144)	D (p. 145)
4	A (p. 145)	B (p. 146)	A (p. 147)	C (p. 145)
5	A (p. 146)	D (p. 148)	B (p. 149)	B (pp. 146-147)
6	A (pp. 150-151)	D (p. 151)	D (pp. 151-152)	C (pp. 148-149)
7	C (p. 156)	B (p. 156)	B (p. 156)	C (pp. 152-153)
8	B (pp. 161-162)	A (p. 158)	D (pp. 160-161)	D (p. 155)
9	C (p. 164)	C (p. 162)	D (p. 163)	C (p. 158)
10	B (p. 170)	D (pp. 170-171)	C (p. 165)	C (p. 163)
11				A (p. 164)
12				C (p. 167)
13				A (p. 169)
14		*Correct Responses to*		C (p. 170)
15				B (p. 173)
16		*Multiple Choice Questions*		F (p. 142)
17				T (p. 148)
18				T (p. 150)
19				T (p. 152)
20				F (p. 156)
21				T (p. 158)
22				F (p. 161)
23				F (p. 170)

Matching

1. D
2. N
3. I
4. O
5. C
6. H
7. L
8. J
9. F
10. A
11. M
12. K
13. G
14. E
15. B

Comprehensive Crossword Puzzle

ACROSS

1. Consistency principle
9. Operant
11. Observational
12. Need for cognition
13. Classical
14. Persuasion
15. Cognitive response model

DOWN

2. Nonreactive measurement
3. Dual process model of persuasion
4. Balance theory
5. Elaboration likelihood model
6. Postdecisional dissonance
7. Counterattitudinal action
8. Counterargument
10. Impression motivation

Chapter 6 – Social Influence: Conformity, Compliance, and Obedience

Item Number	Practice Test 1	Practice Test 2	Practice Test 3	Comprehensive Test
1	B (p. 179)	C (p. 179)	B (p. 179)	A (p. 179)
2	C (p. 179)	C (p. 179)	D (p. 179)	D (p. 179)
3	D (pp. 180-181)	A (p. 180)	A (p. 182)	C (p. 180)
4	B (pp. 182-183)	D (p. 182)	D (p. 183)	A (p. 183)
5	C (p. 184)	D (p. 185)	C (p. 186)	C (p. 185)
6	B (p. 187)	B (p. 190)	A (p. 192)	B (p. 190)
7	B (p. 189)	A (p. 195)	B (p. 193)	B (p. 189)
8	A (p. 194)	D (p. 197)	C (p. 195)	A (p. 193)
9	B (p. 196)	A (pp. 199-200)	C (p. 200)	C (p. 195)
10	D (p. 197)	C (pp. 204-205)	C (p. 204)	B (p. 195)
11				B (pp. 196-197)
12				D (p. 197)
13				B (pp. 201-202)
14		Correct Responses to Multiple Choice Questions		B (p. 205)
15				D (p. 207)
16				F (p. 182)
17				T (p. 183)
18				F (p. 192)
19				T (p. 195)
20				T (p. 196)
21				F (p. 198)
22				T (p. 199)
23				T (p. 207)

Compliance Techniques

1. 5
2. 6
3. 1
4. 3
5. 2
6. 4

Matching

1. F
2. J
3. L
4. A
5. M
6. B
7. E
8. G
9. P
10. C
11. N
12. I
13. O
14. Q
15. H
16. K
17. D

Comprehensive Crossword Puzzle

ACROSS

1. Personal commitment
7. Norm of reciprocity
9. Expert power
12. Social influence
13. Compliance
15. Bait and switch technique
16. Door in the face technique

DOWN

2. That's not all technique
3. Social validation
4. Participant observation
5. Labeling technique
6. Foot in the door technique
8. Obedience
10. Conformity
11. Low ball technique
14. Reactance theory

Chapter 7 – Affiliation and Friendship

Item Number	Practice Test 1	Practice Test 2	Practice Test 3	Comprehensive Test
1	C (p. 216)	B (p. 216)	D (p. 216)	D (p. 216)
2	C (p. 217)	A (p. 217)	D (p. 218)	B (pp. 217-218)
3	B (p. 219)	B (p. 219)	C (p. 218)	B (p. 219)
4	A (p. 221)	C (p. 221)	A (p. 219)	A (p. 220)
5	B (pp. 222-223)	B (p. 222)	B (p. 219)	D (p. 222)
6	A (pp. 224-225)	D (p. 224)	A (pp. 223-224)	B (p. 223)
7	B (p. 229)	A (p. 228)	C (p. 225)	A (p. 223)
8	C (pp. 230-231)	A (p. 233)	C (p. 232)	D (pp. 225-226)
9	B (p. 233)	A (p. 234)	C (pp. 219-220)	C (p. 229)
10	D (p. 237)	A (p. 239)	D (p. 236)	D (p. 231)
11				C (p. 233)
12				D (pp. 234-235)
13				B (p. 236)
14		*Correct Responses to*		A (p. 237)
15		*Multiple Choice Questions*		D (p. 239)
16				T (p. 216)
17				T (p. 230)
18				F (pp. 232-233)
19				T (p. 233)
20				T (p. 238)
21				F (p. 236)
22				T (p. 237)
23				F (p. 239)

Matching

1. F
2. E
3. K
4. N
5. C
6. M
7. J
8. D
9. R
10. B
11. P
12. I
13. H
14. L
15. Q
16. A
17. O
18. G

Word Scramble

1. Affiliation motive
2. Self-disclosure
3. Social support
4. Equity
5. Experience Sampling Method

Bonus Word - Friend

Comprehensive Crossword Puzzle

ACROSS

1. Domain specific model
6. Authority ranking
7. Proximity attraction principle
9. Mere exposure effect
17. Domain general model
18. Equality matching

DOWN

2. Market pricing
3. Self disclosure
4. Social exchange
5. Reinforcement affect model
8. Experience sampling method
10. Friend
11. Social capital
12. Affiliation motive
13. Equity
14. Communal sharing
15. Health psychology
16. Social support

Chapter 8 – Love and Romantic Relationships

Item Number	Practice Test 1	Practice Test 2	Practice Test 3	Comprehensive Test
1	B (p. 247)	C (p. 247)	A (p. 248)	C (p. 248)
2	D (p. 248)	D (pp. 249-250)	D (p. 248)	B (p. 248)
3	C (p. 249)	B (p. 250)	D (p. 249)	C (p. 249)
4	A (p. 251)	A (p. 251)	A (p. 251)	B (p. 249)
5	D (p. 252)	C (p. 252)	D (pp. 256-257)	D (p. 250)
6	C (p. 253)	B (p. 255)	D (p. 258)	A (p. 251)
7	C (p. 258)	A (pp. 258-259)	B (p. 259)	A (p. 253)
8	D (p. 261)	C (p. 264)	D (p. 259)	D (pp. 254-255)
9	D (p. 264)	C (p. 266)	B (p. 261)	A (p. 258)
10	B (p. 269)	A (p. 271)	B (p. 267)	A (pp. 258-259)
11				C (pp. 260-261)
12				B (p. 262)
13				D (p. 266)
14		Correct Responses to		D (pp. 266-268)
15		Multiple Choice Questions		C (pp. 272-273)
16				F (p. 247)
17				F (p. 251)
18				F (p. 250)
19				F (p. 267)
20				T (p. 259)
21				T (p. 262)
22				F (p. 272)
23				T (p. 265)

Matching

1.	I	4.	F	7.	J	10.	S	13.	O	16.	V	19. H	22. G
2.	E	5.	P	8.	N	11.	D	14.	R	17.	L	20. B
3.	T	6.	K	9.	Q	12.	U	15.	M	18.	C	21. A

Comprehensive Crossword Puzzle

ACROSS

4. Equity rule
6. Erotomania
8. Secure attachment style
9. Need to belong
11. Sociosexual orientation
15. Secure base
16. Monogamy
17. Two factor theory of love
18. Polygyny
19. Intimacy
20. Companionate love
21. Need based rule
22. Passion

DOWN

1. Factor analysis
2. Polygamy
3. Avoidant attachment style
5. Three stage pattern of separation distress
7. Decision commitment
10. Anxious ambivalent attachment style
12. Androgynous
13. Passionate love
14. Polyandry

Chapter 9 – Prosocial Behavior

Item Number	Practice Test 1	Practice Test 2	Practice Test 3	Comprehensive Test
1	B (p. 281)	C (p.281)	C (pp. 282-283)	D (pp. 282-283)
2	A (p. 282)	A (p. 283)	C (pp. 283-284)	A (p. 285)
3	B (pp. 286-288)	D (p. 287)	B (p. 289)	C (p. 289)
4	D (pp. 289-292)	B (p. 290)	B (p. 290)	B (p. 290)
5	A (p. 291)	A (p. 291)	A (p. 291)	B (p. 291)
6	C (p. 292)	D (p. 293)	B (p. 292)	A (p. 292)
7	C (p. 293)	A (pp. 293-294)	A (p. 295)	C (p. 293)
8	C (pp. 299-300)	A (p. 298)	A (p. 300)	B (pp. 296-297)
9	C (pp. 301-302)	B (p. 302)	D (p. 303)	B (pp. 298-299)
10	D (pp. 304-305)	A (p. 306)	C (p. 306)	D (p. 301)
11				B (p. 303)
12				C (p. 306)
13				B (p. 307)
14		*Correct Responses to*		A (pp. 307-308)
15		*Multiple Choice Questions*		D (p. 309)
16				T (pp. 282-283)
17				F (pp. 283-284)
18				F (p. 291)
19				T (p. 291)
20				F (p. 293)
21				T (p. 295)
22				T (p. 301)
23				T (p. 306)

Defining Prosocial Behavior

1. Prosocial
2. Pure altruism
3. Benevolence
4. Pure altruism
5. Benevolence
6. Prosocial

Matching

1. D
2. G
3. E
4. B
5. H
6. A
7. J
8. L
9. K
10. F
11. I
12. C

Comprehensive Crossword Puzzle

ACROSS

1. Arousal cost reward model
3. Personal norms
5. Benevolence
10. Empathic concern
12. Perspective taking

DOWN

2. Diffusion of responsibility
4. Social responsibility norm
6. Prosocial behavior
7. Mood management hypothesis
8. Inclusive fitness
9. Pure altruism
11. Reciprocal aid

Chapter 10 – Aggression

Item Number	Practice Test 1	Practice Test 2	Practice Test 3	Comprehensive Test
1	C (p. 315)	B (p. 315)	C (p. 315)	A (p. 315)
2	C (pp. 315-316)	B (p. 315)	D (p. 316)	A (pp. 315-316)
3	D (pp. 315-316, 341)	D (p. 316)	B (p. 318)	B (pp. 315-317)
4	A (p. 319)	A (p. 320)	C (p. 320)	D (p. 317)
5	B (p. 321)	B (pp. 321-323)	A (pp. 321-323)	D (p. 319)
6	B (p. 321)	D (pp. 321-322)	D (p. 323)	C (p. 321)
7	B (p. 325)	B (p. 327)	B (p. 330)	D (pp. 323-325)
8	C (p. 328)	B (pp. 334-336)	A (p. 331)	C (p. 327)
9	B (pp. 328-329)	D (p. 336)	B (p. 341)	A (p. 334)
10	C (p. 332)	D (p. 339)	C (p. 343)	C (p. 337)
11		Correct Responses to Multiple Choice Questions			B (pp. 337-338)
12					D (p. 340)
13					B (pp. 341-342)
14					D (p. 344)
15					D (p. 345)
16					F (p. 315)
17					F (p. 318)
18					T (p. 319)
19					T (pp. 321-322)
20					T (p. 327)
21					F (pp. 328-329)
22					T (p. 331)
23					T (p. 337)

Matching

1. B	4. L	7. U	10. V	13. R	16. H	19. O	22. K
2. T	5. J	8. A	11. N	14. C	17. E	20. Q
3. F	6. D	9. P	12. G	15. S	18. I	21. M

Comprehensive Crossword Puzzle

ACROSS

1. Direct aggression
4. Defensive attributional style
9. Catharsis
12. Emotional aggression
18. Sexual selection
19. Assertiveness

DOWN

1. Differential parental investment
2. Culture of honor
3. Psychopath

DOWN CONTINUED

5. Instrumental aggression
6. Displacement
7. Effect danger ratio
8. Frustration aggression hypothesis
9. Cognitive neoassociation theory
10. Excitation transfer theory
11. Type A behavior pattern
13. Social learning theory
14. Indirect aggression
15. Weapons effect
16. Meta analysis
17. Aggression

Chapter 11 – Prejudice, Stereotyping, and Discrimination

Item Number	Practice Test 1	Practice Test 2	Practice Test 3	Comprehensive Test
1	B (p. 356)	A (p. 356)	B (p. 356)	C (p. 355)
2	C (p. 356)	B (p. 356)	D (p. 356)	A (p. 355)
3	B (p. 357)	A (p. 357)	C (p. 357)	C (p. 356)
4	C (p. 358)	B (pp. 358-359)	A (p. 357)	D (p. 357)
5	B (p. 362)	D (p. 361)	B (p. 359)	C (p. 358)
6	A (p. 367)	C (p. 363)	A (p. 364)	A (p. 360)
7	D (pp. 369-370)	B (p. 366)	B (p. 370)	C (p. 364)
8	A (pp. 372-373)	A (p. 377)	D (p. 373)	A (p. 367)
9	B (pp. 381-382)	C (pp. 375-376)	C (pp. 373-374)	B (p. 369)
10	C (pp. 384-385)	C (pp. 379-380)	D (pp. 382-386)	A (p. 372)
11				D (pp. 376-377)
12				C (p. 378)
13				B (p. 380)
14		Correct Responses to		A (p. 384)
15		Multiple Choice Questions		D (pp. 385-386)
16				T (p. 356)
17				T (p. 357)
18				F (p. 363)
19				T (p. 375)
20				F (p. 375)
21				F (p. 377)
22				F (p. 380)
23				T (p. 384)

Matching

1. P
2. M
3. I
4. L
5. J
6. N
7. Q
8. A
9. F
10. O
11. B
12. D
13. H
14. C
15. E
16. K
17. G

Comprehensive Crossword Puzzle

ACROSS
1. Perceived outgroup homogeneity
5. Stereotype threat
6. Quest religiosity
10. Authoritarianism
12. Prejudice
13. Disidentify
14. Realistic group conflict theory
15. Social identity
16. Social dominance orientation

DOWN
2. Discrimination
3. Stereotyping
4. Ingroup bias
5. Scapegoating
7. Intrinsic religiosity
8. Extrinsic religiosity
9. Minimal intergroup paradigm
11. Stereotype

Chapter 12 – Groups

Item Number	Practice Test 1	Practice Test 2	Practice Test 3	Comprehensive Test
1	C (p. 394)	A (p. 394)	C (p. 394)	A (p. 394)
2	A (pp. 395-396)	A (pp. 397-399)	C (p. 396)	D (p. 399)
3	D (p. 399)	D (pp. 399-400)	D (pp. 399-400)	B (p. 400)
4	D (p. 401)	C (p. 402)	C (p. 404)	B (p. 403)
5	D (pp. 402-403)	D (p. 403)	D (p. 408)	A (p. 405)
6	D (p. 408)	B (p. 410)	B (p. 410)	B (p. 407)
7	B (p. 410)	D (pp. 411-412)	D (pp. 411-412)	C (p. 409)
8	C (pp. 412-413)	A (pp. 414-415)	A (pp. 413-415)	D (p. 411)
9	A (pp. 413-414)	C (pp. 417-418)	B (p. 418)	D (pp. 411-412)
10	D (p. 418)	C (p. 421)	A (p. 420)	D (p. 413)
11				A (p. 415)
12				D (pp. 418-422)
13				B (p. 419)
14		Correct Responses to		D (p. 420)
15		Multiple Choice Questions		A (p. 420)
16				T (p. 395)
17				T (p. 393)
18				F (pp. 402-404)
19				F (pp. 409-410)
20				T (p. 410)
21				F (pp. 412-413)
22				T (p. 413)
23				T (p. 418)

Matching

1. F
2. M
3. E
4. H
5. B
6. L
7. I
8. K
9. A
10. N
11. G
12. D
13. J
14. C

Comprehensive Crossword Puzzle

ACROSS

8. Cohesiveness
10. Minority influence
12. Role
13. Status hierarchy
14. Transformational leadership

DOWN

1. Deindividuation
2. Communication network
3. Social facilitation
4. Transactive memory
5. Groupthink
6. Social loafing
7. Dynamical system
9. Group
11. Group polarization

Chapter 13 – Social Dilemmas: Cooperation versus Conflict

Item Number	Practice Test 1	Practice Test 2	Practice Test 3	Comprehensive Test
1	C (p. 431)	C (p. 431)	B (p. 432)	B (p. 432)
2	D (p. 432)	D (p. 432)	A (p. 433)	A (p. 433)
3	B (p. 433)	A (p. 435)	D (p. 437)	A (p. 433)
4	C (p. 436)	C (pp. 440-441)	B (p. 440)	A (pp. 435-436)
5	A (p. 438)	B (p. 441)	A (p. 444)	D (p. 436)
6	D (p. 441)	B (pp. 443-444)	A (p. 445)	A (p. 436)
7	B (p. 445)	C (p. 447)	A (p. 448)	C (pp. 438-439)
8	D (p. 449)	D (p. 449)	A (p. 449)	C (p. 439)
9	C (pp. 449-450)	D (p. 451)	B (p. 451)	A (p. 440)
10	C (pp. 452-453)	A (p. 452)	A (p. 452)	A (p. 445)
11				A (p. 446)
12				D (p. 447)
13				C (p. 448)
14		Correct Responses to Multiple Choice Questions		D (p. 455)
15				D (p. 455)
16				F (p. 435)
17				T (p. 437)
18				F (p. 440)
19				T (p. 443)
20				F (pp. 446-447)
21				T (p. 448)
22				F (p. 451)
23				F (p. 455)

Matching

1. T	4. I	7. M	10. N	13. K	16. F	19. J
2. R	5. Q	8. A	11. C	14. B	17. G	20. P
3. O	6. L	9. E	12. H	15. S	18. D	

Comprehensive Crossword Puzzle

ACROSS

8. Conflict spiral view
10. GRIT
12. Social dilemma
13. Altruist
14. Social trap
15. Xenophobia
16. Individualist
17. Sliding reinforcer
18. Integrative complexity
19. Voluntarist policy

DOWN

1. Market based policy
2. Tit for tat strategy
3. Public goods dilemma
4. Deterrence view
5. Cooperator
6. Competitor
7. Command and control policy
9. Perceptual dilemma
11. Time series analysis

Chapter 14 – Integrating Social Psychology

Item Number	Practice Test 1	Practice Test 2	Practice Test 3	Comprehensive Test
1	C (p. 464)	D (p. 464)	A (p. 464)	C (p. 465)
2	D (p. 465)	C (p. 465)	A (p. 465)	B (p. 465)
3	A (p. 465)	A (p. 465)	D (p. 466)	D (p. 468)
4	A (p. 466)	B (p. 466)	B (p. 469)	B (p. 469)
5	B (p. 473)	C (p. 469)	B (p. 469)	D (p. 469)
6	D (p. 477)	B (p. 474)	D (pp. 474-475)	A (p. 469)
7	B (p. 479)	C (pp. 475-476)	D (p. 479)	C (p. 471)
8	C (p. 482)	C (p. 479)	B (p. 481)	D (p. 471)
9	D (pp. 485-486)	A (p. 482)	D (p. 482)	D (pp. 472 & 478)
10	A (pp. 483-484)	D (pp. 484-485)	D (pp. 481-483)	A (p. 473)
11				A (pp. 475-476)
12				C (p. 480)
13				A (p. 482)
14		*Correct Responses to*		D (p. 482)
15		*Multiple Choice Questions*		D (pp. 484-485)
16				T (p. 465)
17				F (p. 467)
18				F (pp. 470-471)
19				F (pp. 474-475)
20				T (p. 478)
21				T (pp. 478-479)
22				F (p. 482)
23				T (pp. 484-485)

The Person and the Situation Interact

1. 5   6. 6
2. 1   7. 3
3. 4   8. 2
4. 2   9. 6
5. 3   10. 1

Matching

1. D   6. A
2. E   7. B
3. G
4. F
5. C

Comprehensive Crossword Puzzle

ACROSS

3. Sociocultural
4. Evolutionary
5. Social learning
6. Ultimate explanation
8. Confound
9. Meta-analysis

DOWN

1. Proximate explanation
2. Triangulation
7. Social cognitive

NOTES

NOTES

NOTES

NOTES

NOTES

NOTES

NOTES

NOTES